The Best Day Hikes of the
CALIFORNIA NORTHWEST

By Art Bernstein

Published by Mountain N'Air Books

This is a Mountain N'Air Book
Copyright 1991 by Art Bernstein ©

First Edition, 1991

Published in the United States of America by
Mountain N'Air Books, P.O.Box 12540, La Crescenta CA 91224

Library of Congress Cataloging-in-Publication Data

Bernstein, Art.
The Best Day Hikes of the California Northwest : From Marin to Crescent City, to Mt. Shasta / by Art Bernstein -- 1st Edition.
    p. cm.
Rev. ed. of: Northwest California's Best Day Hikes. 1989
1. Hiking--California, Northern--Guide-books.
2. Trails--California, Northern--Guidebooks.
3. California, Northern--Description and travel--Guide-books.
I Bernstein, Art. Northwest California's Best Day-Hikes.
II. Title. GV199.42.N684B47 1991   917.94'1--DC20 91-36007CIP

Printed in the United States of America.
Cover Photo by Art Bernstein. © (see Chapter 62)

ISBN: 1-879415-02-X

Twenty-five years ago, when I was on the fast-track to nowhere in an office in downtown Detroit, Michigan, I stumbled across a book at the public library which changed my life forever.

The book was John Muir's MOUNTAINS OF CALIFORNIA. I've been living in and exploring his mountains ever since.

To John Muir and his glorious mountains, this book is gratefully dedicated.— Art Bernstein

Paradise Lake and Kings Castle-Marble Mt.Wilderness (Ch.54)

The Best Hikes...

INTRODUCTION

Northwest California.

Few would disagree that California is by far the most scenically varied and magnificent of the 50 states. Its vast northwest triangle—from Marin to Crescent City to Mt.Shasta — greatly contributes to this splendor. While some of the region is well known—Mount Shasta, the redwoods and the Trinity Alps, which have inspired countless imaginations—all too much of it lays hidden among the Golden State's secrets.

Researching this book, in fact, yielded many surprises, even though I've spent years exploring the Northern California backcountry. I was astonished, for example, to discover that Kings Peak, on the Humboldt Coast, rises 4000 feet from the ocean in 3 miles. Also unexpected was the Snow Mountain Wilderness, in which a 7000 foot summit soars abruptly from the Sacramento Valley's flat expanse.

This book includes 94 trails in 6 National Forests, 9 federal Wilderness Areas, 4 National Park Service components, 19 California State Parks, a 'BLM' unit and a county park. To add depth and up-to-date information, I spoke with dozens of rangers and administrators, all but one of whom were enthusiastically cooperative.

What is a day-hike?

As addicted as I am to Northern California's secret peaks, lost coastlines, alpine lakes and majestic wilderness forests, fulfillment of my craving is hampered by lack of time and minor back problems. Both render long hikes, heavy packs and nights sleeping on boulder beds, very difficult.

My back country excursions, however, remain uncurtailed. Every trail in this book (except the Mt. Shasta climb and the Caribou Lakes Trail), may be done on the spur of the moment. Some require an early start, and a night at a nearby campground or motel may be advisable, especially if you live in San Francisco and selected a trail at the end of a Siskiyou Wilderness logging road.

The paths presented are ideal for auto or motor home vacationers who make day trips from a central location.

Day-hiking ranks among the least environmentally damaging back country uses. The pristine quality of some of the Trinity Alps, for example, has been damaged by competition for campsites and horse pasture. Even the purest looking spring water there may be unfit to drink.

Not enough visitors realize that one may comfortably hike many spectacular Trinity Alps trails with nothing more than a cold lunch, and be back for dinner.

What this book includes.

With a few exceptions, every path herein is at least one mile and less than five miles long, one way. While three or four paths exceed this, all are routes I couldn't bring myself to omit. One or two may be slightly shorter than a mile but are likewise too interesting to pass up.

While reasonably thorough, this book is far from comprehensive. The 25,000 square mile area covered is simply too vast. Aside from length criteria, the decision on what to include was based on my particular taste and a desire to present a balanced cross section.

All trails presented are nature oriented. While several visit old mines, homesteads and military emplacements, that is not their focus. Drop by the local Chamber of Commerce or Historical Society for information on things like walking tours of historic buildings.

Also, it makes no sense to me to hike somewhere to which one can drive, or to walk a trail paralleling a road, unless country significantly different from that seen from the car is revealed. A trail should offer wonders unattainable by other means.

I like my trails scenic and varied. They should lead to a well defined objective such as a mountain summit, lake basin, the ocean, an alpine meadow, a waterfall or a botanical or geological feature.

I have, nevertheless, included a few paths which simply follow creeks or beaches. And I realize that to many, just strolling through the woods can be rejuvenating and even spiritual. For the most part, however, this book emphasizes the region's highlights.

My selection criteria led to a few notable omissions. Sadly, nothing in Redwood National Park's Tall Trees Area qualified. Nor did most trails at the beautiful Humboldt Redwoods. The paths of the Shasta-Trinity-Whiskeytown National Recreation Area also rank among the missing. While trails in these places are worthwhile, all were either too long, too short or too near roads.

Many routes herein follow either combinations of trails or segments of longer trails. Hiking only the best chunks of longer trails should heighten the experience. The Pacific Crest Trail, for instance, sometimes goes 20 miles between highlights. While the PCT is omitted, 14 of this book's paths either include portions of it or intersect it.

How to use this book.

Describing every rock, tree and bend in the path makes very dull reading. I've tried instead, to capture the essence of each place. Ideally, even if you never hike the trail, you'll know what it feels like. This is enhanced by notes and observations on natural history and enough information to get you there and back without major mishapes.

A. Maps. Readers should reach most objectives using the maps and descriptions in this book. The maps include the trail itself and the last connecting road or two. All maps are oriented with north up (with a couple exceptions, noted on the maps in question). The scale varies with the trail length. Contour lines are omitted to avoid clutter and enhance readability.

Supplemental material can be helpful. National Forest maps and other privately produced maps, based on United States Geological Survey topographic maps, cost a few dollars and are available at most bookstores and outdoors shops.

The California State Parks put out excellent map/brochures for most parks. Most include contour lines and cost around 50 cents. They may be difficult to obtain in winter, however. *Write to the California Department of Parks and Recreation, P O box 942896, Sacramento, California 94296-0838* or phone (916)445-6647.

National Park Service brochures are also of high caliber, although most omit contour lines. All are free. *Write the National Park Service, Western Regional Information Office, Fort Mason, Building 201, San Francisco, California 94123, or phone (415) 556-0560.*

The fact that I borrowed liberally from these agencies' maps, plus the amazingly detailed *DeLorme Northern California Atlas*, is herewith gratefully acknowledged.

B. Trail length. Each chapter heading gives length as distance from the trailhead to the farthest objective or turn around point. For loop trails, both the distance to the farthest point and the loop distance is given. Distances are rounded to the nearest ¼ mile.

Hiking time, being highly variable, is not given. A mile takes me 20 to 30 minutes. While I leave many people in the dust, however, others leave me in the dust.

C. Access. Since life doesn't begin when you step out of the car, the drive to the trailhead is treated as part of the experience. In some instances, automobile reconnaissance is crucial to understanding the trail's natural history. A brief description of the access road in the chapter heading is backed up, when necessary, by comments in the text.

In most cases, only a rough road mileage estimate is provided, or no mileage at all, unless an exact figure is crucial to locating the trailhead.

D. Difficulty. In general, an "easy" rating means the path is nearly level or rises at a grade of less than 5% (5 feet vertical per 100 feet horizontal). The "difficult" ratings begin at about 15%. Everything in between is "moderate." This is sometimes modified by the trail's length and whether upgrades are concentrated or spread out.

E. Water. If a trail is less than 2 or 3 miles, if it's below 70 degrees out or the path is rated "easy," you probably needn't worry about water. Consider leaving a canteen or cooler in the car, however.

As for drinking from creeks, my personal rule is not to if there are human dwellings, cattle or heavy horse use between me and the stream source. Also, if I can't cross a creek in a step or two, or the water is stagnant, I won't drink from it. Icy springs in the deep woods of a Wilderness Area are probably safe.

I tend to be a little reckless, however. Any water can make you sick and the means through which disease is spread are numerous. So except in an emergency, it's never wise to drink unpurified water.

F. Season. Since northwest California weather varies greatly, the seasons indicated are based largely on elevation and should be considered extremely general. If it snowed down to 1000 feet a few days earlier, you should inquire before setting out on a 3000 foot high trail. Look for mud and high water in the wet season. A couple low elevation trails are closed in winter when floating bridges are removed.

California winters can be marvelous, with clear, sunny days and temperatures which keep you cool yet invigorated. I climbed 6000 foot Devil's Peak in January and encountered only a few small snow banks. Two weeks later, 15 feet of snow inundated the spot.

G. Elevation. Elevations are given in feet and most are rounded to the nearest 100. When two numbers are present, they represent the trail's highest and lowest points. A single number means the elevation change is insignificant.

H. Use. While this book is hiker oriented, some other permitted uses are noted. My experience with such uses is limited, however. Horses would be incompatible with my tendency to plan outings the night before or the same day.

The use designations address only motorized vehicles, horses and foot traffic. While mountain bikes, cross-country skiing and other uses are fast gaining popularity, regulations and restrictions on their use are in constant flux. To be safe, I suggest telephoning ahead before undertaking any activity other than hiking or if you plan to bring a dog.

The text generally indicates if there's room at the trailhead to park and turn around.

I. Ownership. The proprietary agencies have devoted much time, money and expertise designing, building and maintaining the routes under their jurisdiction. They are justifiably proud of their efforts and I am pleased to acknowledge them.

J. Phone. The number given is for the nearest agency office, meaning you'll reach a Forest Service ranger station rather than a main headquarters. In a few state parks where the phone may go unanswered in winter, I threw in a district number.

Campground reservations for any California State Park may be made by phoning 1-800-444-PARK.

A free permit is required for some federal Wilderness Areas. Phone or write the appropriate forest for information.

About hiking.

Before getting to my list of day-hike do's and don'ts, I'd like to offer a few unscientific observations on conditioning.

Since hiking offers a means of getting in shape, lack of previous conditioning shouldn't dissuade you. Start on easy or moderately easy paths and take your time. If you have a heart condition or other limitation, consult your physician first.

In my experience, weight control (and avoiding cigarettes) contributes more to negotiating a steep trail than does leg conditioning. I say this having hiked in all possible combinations of obesity, slimness, in shape-ness and out of shape-ness.

A consistent upper body program, combined with diet and a little jogging or pace walking, should keep the average person in shape for most trails herein, presuming no heavy pack is carried. You'd be amazed at the effect of upper body strength on lung capacity.

Physical stress is not confined to uphill tracks. The overweight or out of shape person is likely to notice upgrades more because they stress the cardiovascular system. Steep downgrades, on the other hand, stress the knees, ankles and feet. That's when most blisters occur, which can ruin a trip far more quickly than huffing and puffing. With a touch of arthritis in one hip, downgrades bother me more than upgrades.

No hiking book is complete without a sanctimonious list of Boy Scout aphorisms: Never hike alone. Always bring matches. Inform someone of your destination. Never leave home without a map, canteen and whistle. Never drink unpurified water. Get a doctor's OK. Carry toilet paper, etc.

I've rarely observed the above. Usually, I hike alone and rarely tell my wife my destination. Half the time I forget map, camera, canteen, lunch and gas money. I've gotten sick, lost, injured and stuck on my excursions but somehow always made it home. It's part of the adventure.

I've only been lost twice, fortunately. Once I spent the night at 8000 feet with no food, jacket, water or matches. After that, I vowed never to leave home without a basic survival kit. I haven't forgotten my lunch since.

The once popular heavy hiking boots with non-skid, Vibram soles are somewhat out of vogue, by the way. They're considered environmentally damaging and should be worn only when rock climbing, in snow, or off the trail in wet weather. I find a soft soled sneaker much more comfortable and less tiring, although I jab an ankle in them occasionally.

Finally, the Forest Service offers a list of camping guidelines far more important than mine. As part of "no trace" camping, they ask the following:

1. Pack out all litter.

2. For human waste, select a spot at least 200 feet from open water and dig a hole six to eight inches deep. Cover it with dirt when done.

3. If a fire is absolutely necessary, build it in a safe, previously used spot. Wood collection can be environmentally damaging and portable stoves are recommended. I suggest cold meals on day-hikes.

4. Pitch tents so no drainage ditch is required and replace rocks and other material removed from sleeping areas. Camp sites should be at least 100 feet from open water and animals should be pastured at least 200 feet from open water.

About the land.

The descriptions of the land include the local natural history. Since several trails may penetrate the same area, and since each description is written to stand on its own, some repetition was unavoidable. Five chapters, for instance, describe the King Range and six discuss Point Reyes geology. Each, however, contains material not in other chapters.

While natural history is often described in detail, listing the identifying traits of every rock type, tree species and flower at each mention, would take far too much space.

The following concepts, for the most part, failed to find their way into the chapters or are spread thinly among many:

A. Geology. Three distinct geological provinces are represented in this book. Most spectacular are the Cascade Mountains, capped by 14,161 foot Mt. Shasta, Northern California's highest peak.

While the Cascades stretch from California's Mt. Lassen to British Columbia's Mt. Garibaldi, this book only nicks a corner of them. The range is characterized by extremely young volcanic peaks. Outpourings of lava and ash cover the landscape. Lassen National Park and Lava Beds National Monument superbly interpret the range's California portion.

The Klamath Mountains rank as northern California's oldest, remotest and most rugged. They consist of an immense granite intrusion, formed in the age of dinosaurs, probably as part of the Sierra. Other important Klamath rocks include an ancient, metamorphosed lava known as greenstone, plus various schists and marbles.

The Klamaths' jumbled cluster of jagged peaks, topping out at over 9000 feet, are dotted with hundreds of exquisite alpine lakes. Renowned for their beauty, the Klamaths include such ranges as the Trinity Alps, Marble Mountains, Siskiyous and North Yolla Bollys. They do not include the South Yolla Bollys.

Technically, the system does not quite extend to the coast. Detached segments, however, floating atop the younger Coast Ranges, bump the coast between Coos Bay, Oregon and Eureka.

Northwest California's dominant system is the Coast Range, also called the Mendocino Mountains. Geologically, it is known as the Franciscan Formation, a region of steeply folded and faulted sandstone and other marine rocks. Extending from San Francisco Bay to Eureka, the range attains 8000 feet elevation at South Yolla Bolly and 7000 feet at Snow Mountain. Few summits exceed 4000 feet, however.

Unlike the Klamaths, the Coast Range forms a series of lineal ridges, cut by deep river valleys, parallel to the coast. The highest peaks line up along the system's eastern edge, rising sharply above the Sacramento Valley.

A couple of small, isolated volcanic regions, unrelated to the Cascades or Coast Range, are tucked inside the Franciscan Formation between Clear Lake and Napa. This book does not address Northern California's Great Valley or Modoc Plateau geological provinces.

Serpentine is a granitic rock lacking in calcium and rich in heavy metals. The Klamaths and the Coast Ranges contain more of this rock than any other section of the United States.

Both serpentine, and the closely related peridotite, are the basement rock of the ocean floor. On land, they appear as elongated dikes and sills parallel to the coast. Such formations are believed bulldozed from the sea by the advancing continental plate.

Douglas-fir, ponderosa pine, madrone and other common species won't grow on serpentine or are stunted by it. Other species will, however, including Jeffrey pine, knobcone pine, western white pine, incense cedar, Baker cypress and Brewer spruce. Numerous endangered shrubs and wildflowers grow nowhere else.

Many northwest California peaks over 5000 feet elevation have experienced glaciation. Glaciers form when annual snowfall exceeds melt and ice starts oozing down the mountain. The only glaciers these days are on Shasta, plus a few tiny ones in the Trinity Alps. Gouged out scars from former glaciers abound, however.

Glaciers not only carve out round-bottomed valleys as they move downward, they also chisel sharply backward into the peak. This headward cutting creates cirque basins with steep, amphitheater headwalls rising above a bowl. Almost all the Klamath Mountains' hundreds of alpine lakes decorate glacial cirques.

B. Botany. Different plant species growing in similar kinds of places are called "associations." Associations range from the broadly geographic to the highly site specific.

Several major geographic associations cross northwest California, including the Pacific Northwest forest region, the Sierra Nevada forest region, the Northern Coastal forest region and the California Coastal forest region. The area also boasts several unique species, including Brewer spruce, a couple of rare cypresses and Shasta red fir. Coastal redwood, Bishop pine, knobcone pine, tanoak and California torreya don't extend far outside the region.

Look also for riverbank associations, serpentine associations, upland associations, bog associations, north slope associations (shady), south slope associations (sunny), elevational associations, etc. Component species are elaborated upon in the individual chapters.

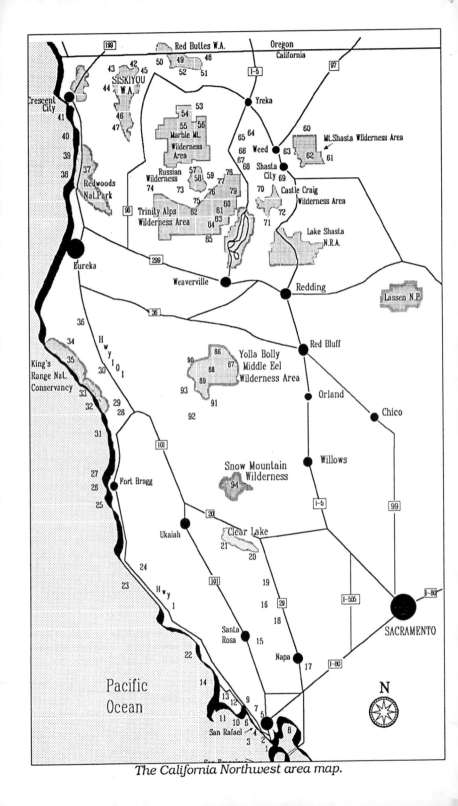

The California Northwest area map.

1. HILL 88/COASTAL TRAIL
(Golden Gate National Rec. Area)

Length: 1½ miles (3 miles to Wolf Ridge)
Water: None, or very little
Access: Good, paved roads
Season: All
Difficulty: Moderately difficult
Elevation: 10 to 882 feet
Use: Hikers only
Ownership: Golden Gate NRA
Phone: (415) 331-1540

Directions: From Hwy 101, take the first exit north of the Golden Gate Bridge (Alexander Road). Heading south, take the first exit after the tunnel, labelled only "Sausalito." Follow the brown signs to the Marin Headlands area of Golden Gate National Recreation Area.

Look for the road west of the freeway (Conzelman Road), taking off up the bluff tops. For the trailhead, turn off Conzelman onto McCullough Road at the saddle, then left on Bunker Road at the bottom of the hill, to Rodeo Beach. The trail follows the gated road at the far end of the beach parking lot. Parking is ample, although the area can be mobbed in summer. Bus service is available.

For an even more scenic trailhead route, continue on Conzelman Road to the one-way area and proceed past Point Bonita to the Rodeo Beach junction. Turn left for Rodeo Beach. The tunnel with the six minute red light, which used to access Rodeo Beach, has been closed since the 1989 earthquake.

Like all others herein, this is a nature oriented trail. However, it also happens to be the trail closest to San Francisco. The Marin Headlands' beauty and solitude contrasts sharply with a colorful history and a chaotic cityscape not far away.

Much of this history is military. Bunkers and gun emplacements along the trail underscore the area's significance in that regard. San Francisco's beautiful blue ocean, so deeply entwined with the city's essence, has several times become an object of threat and paranoia.

The Golden Gate channel, entrance to one of the world's great harbors, is of utmost strategic importance. The fortifications on the Presidio and Marin Headlands once constituted a first line defense of the San Francisco area. Although most are now relics, the area is still militarily significant.

The drive from the bridge's north end, along the bluffs above the Golden Gate, is one of the country's great scenic experiences. Although it gets crowded on summer weekends these days, the route is just starting to become known. Rodeo Beach used to have its own one lane-tunnel under Hwy 101, leading to a secluded, peaceful valley while masses of autos scrambled overhead. The tunnel, damaged in the 1989 earthquake, is now closed.

By all means, spend a few minutes at Point Bonita on your way to the trailhead, if the road uphill from the saddle where Conzelman and McCullough Roads meet is open, which it often isn't. The drive is spectacular, especially beyond Battery 129, where Point Bonita first comes into view and the road becomes one way and starts downhill.

At Point Bonita, a spectacular, ¾ mile trail leads from the parking area, along a rocky spit, to the lighthouse guarding the Golden Gate's actual entrance. Lighthouse tours are offered on weekends in summer and at other times as posted at the visitor center. Between tours, the path is blocked ⅔'s of the way along by a massive gate at the entrance to a tunnel.

Because of the road routing, it's much easier to visit Point Bonita on the way into Rodeo Beach than on the way out. This is unfortunate because Point Bonita and the headlands are often foggy in the morning. A late afternoon, "apres-hike" visit offers the best vistas and most dramatic lighting.

The Rodeo Beach Visitor Center is housed in a deceptively plain looking Army building. I found the Rangers there particularly pleasant, knowledgeable and down to earth. They contributed significantly to this book.

The Coastal Trail to Hill 88 and Wolf Ridge begins at the end of the parking lot. To avoid confusion, hike up the closed-off road. The stairs immediately left of the road lead to a maze of pathways exploring the bluffs above the ocean. They're very pretty but don't all connect with the Hill 88 Trail.

This is a fairly steep route which climbs at a steady rate with few level spots. Fortunately, since it faces the ocean, there are usually plenty of cool breezes. There are also occasional typhoons.

After the route winds around a little basin and comes out atop a point, a sign directs hikers off the paved road onto an actual trail. Most of the lower paths along the bluffs converge here. The road above is washed out. The cut-across trail, however, soon rejoins the road above the washout and continues uphill.

Eventually the path hits the ridgetop. At a well marked junction, one can continue to the top of the hill or turn onto the Wolf Ridge Trail. It's another 1½ miles to the 1029 foot summit of Wolf Ridge. From there, it's two miles to the Tennessee Valley Trail.

The Wolf Ridge Trail, following the lee side of Hill 88, deserves exploration. This moist, sheltered area is excellent for spring wildflowers. It also offers an outstanding view of Tennessee Valley, particularly the little ranch halfway down the Tennessee Valley Trail.

Wolf Ridge, like Hill 88 and all other slopes hereabouts, is virtually devoid of vegetation except grass. The extremely occasional cypresses and pines, near structures and along the road, were planted by the military. Aside from grass, the major vegetation consists of coyote brush, found throughout the Bay area coastal hills, and coastal sage. The latter's leaves are extremely aromatic when crushed.

This trail's dramatic highlight is the unfolding San Francisco skyline. Not visible at the trailhead, the Golden Gate Bridge towers appear first, then the towers atop Mt. Davidson. Finally, the entire city emerges, rising out of the ocean and nestled in a patchy blanket of fog.

While the trail up explores Battery Townsley and other gun emplacements, Hill 88's fenced summit is decorated with a myriad of abandoned buildings, blockhouses and towers. It's a little junky but offers excellent vantage points and unmatched views of the city.

Rodeo Beach and Wolf Ridge, seen from McCullough Road.

2. TENNESSEE VALLEY TRAIL
(Golden Gate Nat. Rec. Area)

See map, chapter 1
Length: 2 miles
Water: No
Access: Excellent paved road
Season: All
Difficulty: Easy
Elevation: 100 ft. to sea level
Use: Non-motorized
Ownership: Golden Gate Nat. Rec. Area
Phone: (415) 331-1540

Directions: Take Hwy 101 to the Hwy 1/Mill Valley Exit, just north of Sausalito. Head west on Hwy 1. Tennessee Valley Road is the first left after leaving the freeway, just before Tamalpais Junction. Follow Tennessee Valley Road to the end. Parking is ample.

This gentle trail, minutes from downtown San Francisco, is deservedly popular. Expect a fair dose of Marin scenery but also an astounding array of company, including toddlers on tricycles. It's all great fun.

The trail begins at the end of Tennessee Valley Road, amid farms and a well developed parking area. Simply walk along the paved, gated road which trends slightly downhill along Tennessee Creek. Most of the surrounding countryside is open and grassy, except for a few alders along the creek.

About ⅓ of the way along, the arrow straight path comes to a charming little ranch. There the pavement ends but the trail remains straight and wide. Several springs and side creeks make parts of the lower trail and the surrounding grass rather muddy in winter.

The ranch can also be seen from the Hill 88/Wolf Ridge Trail.

Conversely, of course, Wolf Ridge can be seen towering above the Tennessee Valley Trail. The Coastal Trail from Wolf Ridge meets the Tennessee Valley Trail a mile from the Tennessee Valley trailhead.

It's an extremely short 2 miles from the parking area to the beach, as the families toting picnic baskets and all manner of paraphernalia will attest. Tennessee Beach and Tennessee Cove, named after an old shipwreck, offer a superb afternoon of sand, surf and scenery, if not solitude. The trek back to your car is slightly uphill but almost as easy as the journey in.

3. GREEN GULCH TRAILS/MUIR BEACH
(Golden Gate Nat. Rec. Area.)

Length: 5 miles (or less)
Water: None
Access: Paved, very winding roads
Season: All
Difficulty: Moderately difficult
Elevation: 0 to 1031 feet
Use: Non-motorized
Ownership: Golden Gate Nat. Rec. Area.
Phone: (415) 388-2596

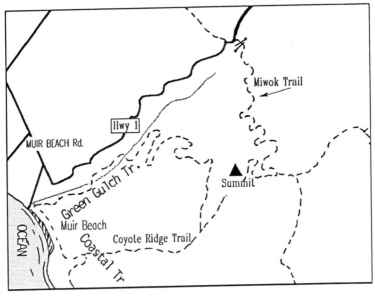

Directions: *Exit Hwy 101 at Hwy 1 just north of Sausalito. Follow Hwy 1 towards Stinson Beach. The upper (Miwok) trailhead is on the left, around a point, ½ mile past the Mt. Tamalpais turnoff. Parking is extremely limited and traffic may be heavy. The main trailhead is at Muir Beach. Take the Muir Beach turnoff and proceed to the parking area. Many users compete for spots in the large parking lot in summer. The trail is across the creek, south of the parking lot.*

Hwy 1, from Tamalpais Junction northward, is one of the

world's great scenic drives. It is not for the faint hearted, however. The two lane route makes you work for every mile. It dips up, down, in, out and every other imaginable direction as it ribbons its way along cliff tops far above the ocean.

The vast Pacific panoramas begin shortly after the turnoff to Mt. Tamalpais and Muir Woods. There, the road comes over a crest and begins a long descent towards Muir Beach, down Green Gulch. The surrounding hills, belonging to Golden Gate National Recreation Area and Mt. Tamalpais State Park, are riddled with spectacular hiking possibilities.

To thoroughly explore on foot the area's magnificent peaks and valleys, follow the Miwok Trail from the road crest, along Green Gulch or Coyote Ridge, to Muir Beach. This is a 5 mile route, one way. Have someone pick you up at Muir Beach to avoid having to reclimb Coyote Ridge, which rises from sea level to over 1000 feet. Even via this one way, mostly downhill course, you'll do plenty of climbing.

The Miwok Trail crosses Hwy 1 about ½ mile past the Mt. Tamalpais turnoff. Look for a trail sign and a gated road taking off south, where the highway rounds a little point. The trail also continues north of the road. In either case, parking is limited and walking along the road can be frightening.

The trail begins as a fairly level, closed off road, in a eucalyptus grove. It soon breaks out into the open and climbs rather steeply. Vistas here are mostly east, of Tamalpais Valley, Marin City and Sausalito.

The path contours around the heads of a series of very deep ravines as it steadily ascends. The terrain is not only steep but, like most of the hills north of San Francisco, grassy and largely treeless except for scattered Douglas-fir, blue oak and toyon.

The trail reaches a 1031 foot summit after 1¾ miles, with outstanding, 360 degree views from the barren, flat crest. It then descends gradually to the upper end of the Green Gulch Trail. From there, hikers can either continue along Coyote Ridge or drop down to Green Gulch.

The Coyote Ridge and Green Gulch routes are equidistant, equally scenic and both end at Muir Beach. Coyote Ridge explores the hills immediately above the ocean while Green Gulch visits a little inland valley. Unfortunately, no feasible loop takes in the Miwok, Coyote Ridge and Green Gulch Trails. The best one can do is two out of three.

For a 4 mile loop beginning and ending at Muir Beach, take the Green Gulch Trail out and the Coyote Ridge Trail back, or vice-versa. In either case, the Green Gulch Trail follows a road uphill to the left on the far side of the creek. Continue straight ahead where the Coyote Ridge Trail takes off uphill on the right.

The path continues up the narrow green valley for about a mile. At one point, it's necessary to go through a closed gate and cut across to the valley's opposite side. The Zen monastery which owns the property welcomes hikers as long as they respect their private property. Past the gardens, at monastery headquarters, the trail loops uphill to the right, leaves the valley, and makes a series of steep switchbacks to Coyote Ridge.

No matter which path one takes, and no matter what the order, your trip should end in a picnic lunch at Muir Beach. There are worse ways to conclude a day's hiking.

4. MATT DAVIS/COASTAL LOOP
(Mt. Tamalpais State Park)

Length: 3 miles (6 mi. loop)
Water: None
Access: Winding, paved roads
Season: All
Difficulty: Easy
Elevation: 1500 to 2000 feet
Use: Hikers only
Ownership: Mt.Tamalpais St. Pk
Phone: (415) 388-2070.

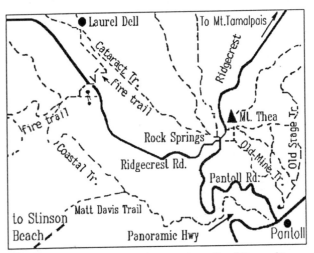

Directions: *Leave Hwy 101 just north of Sausalito and follow Hwy 1 to the Mt. Tamalpais/Panoramic Highway turnoff. Proceed to the Pantoll Ranger Station. The Matt Davis/Coastal Trail takes off at the north end of the parking lot. After crossing the road, the trail climbs the hill west of Pantoll Road and north of Panoramic Highway. The gated road above Panoramic Highway, east of*

Pantoll Road, is Old Stage Trail. Follow it to the Old Mine Trail for the far end of the loop.

I hesitate, generally, to write about trails which closely hug roads. Especially when the roads are among the most scenic any where. And even more so when the trail crosses the road in a least three places.

I could not, however, bring myself to omit this lovely little loop on the west slope of Mt. Tamalpais. A quick hike down from the road to the Coastal Trail, with its vast expanses, or from the road to redwood lined Cataract Creek, reveals variety and solitude unattainable by auto.

The hike begins at the Pantoll Ranger Station of Mt. Tamalpais State Park. The road to Pantoll, Panoramic Highway, follows an exposed, scenic ridge up from Hwy 1. At Mountain Home, it enters a heavily forested area which lasts to Pantoll. At the busy Ranger Station, the road emerges from the woods and begins a winding descent to Stinson Beach. Also at Pantoll, the Pantoll Road takes off along a crest above the ocean. It leads to the summit of Tamalpais and to the town of Bolinas.

We suggest following the Matt Davis Trail from Pantoll, which leads out across the grassy heights, 1500 feet above the ocean. The level path crosses occasional forested pockets but mainly contours around the precipitous slopes and hillsides. Look for outstanding vistas of the coast, Bolinas Lagoon and the Point Reyes peninsula.

After a mile or so, the Coastal Trail takes off to the right while the Matt Davis Trail descends to Stinson Beach. Stay on the Coastal Trail for another 1½ miles, until you come to a ¼ mile long fire road leading back up to the road. To smooth the connection with the Laurel Dell Trail, on the other side of the road, look for a short side trail off the fire road, to the left, which comes out directly opposite the Laurel Dell Trail.

To reach this road crossing by car, take Pantoll Road to Ridgecrest Road and turn left, towards Bolinas, rather than right towards the Tamalpais summit.

From Ridgecrest Road, between the Coastal Trail and the Laurel Dell Trail, look for stunning views of the ocean in one direction, the heavily forested valley of Cataract Creek in the other, with Alpine Lake reservoir to the northeast. Follow the gated road comprising Laurel Dell Trail, downhill to the creek.

On reaching the valley bottom, the path runs along the creek for almost ½ mile before crossing it at Laurel Dell. As the name implies, Laurel Dell is a grassy opening surrounded by redwoods, Douglas-fir and, along the creek, aromatic bay laurel trees.

To save almost a mile, wade across where the Laurel Dell Trail first meets the creek, and pick up the Cataract Trail on the east bank. Follow it to the right to omit Laurel Dell and return to Pantoll.

This leg is fairly level, climbing gradually through the woods back up to Ridgecrest Road, near the Pantoll Road junction. The crossing of Ridgecrest Road, 1½ miles above Laurel Dell, is the high elevation point at 2000 feet. From there, the path drops 500 feet in ¾ of a mile on the way back to Pantoll.

This last leg, while the steepest, is all downhill. The route follows the Old Mine Trail from Ridgecrest, through alternating Douglas-fir patches, grassy openings and rocky crests. Eventually, it runs into the Old Stage Trail which it follows for the last few hundred yards to the Ranger Station.

5. BOOTJACK TRAIL
(Tamalpais State Park/Muir Woods Nat. Mon.)

Length: 2 ½ miles
Water: Lots
Access: Winding, paved roads
Season: All
Difficulty: Moderate
Elevation: 250 to 1300 feet
Use: Hikers only
Ownership: Tamalpais St. Pk./Muir Woods Nat. Monument.
Phone: (415) 388-2070, 388-2595

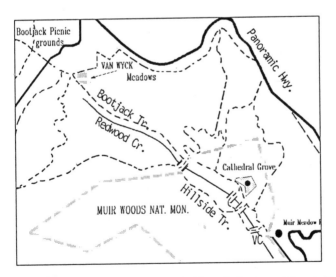

Directions: *Leave Hwy 101 at Hwy 1, just past Sausalito. Follow Hwy 1 to Panoramic Highway. Proceed to the Bootjack Picnic Area*

*for the upper trailhead. Turn off Panoramic onto Muir Woods Road
and follow it to Monument Headquarters for the lower trailhead.*

Few American counties boast three National Park Service units
within their boundaries, let alone a county as small as Marin. Yet
all three areas, Point Reyes National Seashore, Golden Gate National Recreation Area and Muir Woods National Monument,
richly deserve their protected federal status.

Muir Woods is smallest of the three. The Monument protects a
magnificent stand of mature coastal redwoods, growing along an
inland creek. While Northern California abounds in sheltered redwood canyons, giant tree groves are uncommon in the Bay Area.

The park is named in honor of John Muir, the famous natural-
ist and writer. Founder of the Sierra Club, Muir is largely responsible for Yosemite becoming America's second National Park.

From the visitor center and gift shop at Monument Headquarters, a paved trail, with charming little foot bridges, leads along
the creek among the somber pillars. Visitors tend to be respectful
and it's a lovely experience.

Nevertheless, to fully experience Muir Woods, we suggest the
2½ mile Bootjack Trail, which begins in Mt. Tamalpais State Park
and follows Redwood Creek to Monument Headquarters. Parking
is easier to come by at the upper trailhead and much more solitude is available. Since the trail drops 1000 feet, the return trip
may be a little steep for some.

From the parking lot at the Bootjack Picnic Area, cross the
road and follow the well marked path steeply downhill. You'll find
yourself almost immediately in the woods, amid steep canyon
walls, giant boulders and a rushing creek. This upper area is
more Douglas-fir than redwood dominated, but still beautiful. The
Douglas-fir is accompanied by ever present tanoak, a shade lover
abounding in moist, north coast canyons. Look also for sweet
smelling bay laurel and sweet tasting evergreen huckleberry.

After ½ mile, the trail drops into Van Wyck Meadow, a grassy
expanse with a myriad of trail crossings. Below Van Wyck, the
route re-enters the woods. It continues to descend gradually for
another ¾ mile, then levels off as the percentage of redwoods in-
creases. It's 1½ miles from the trailhead to the Monument
Boundary and the beginning of the paved trail.

Beginning at the Muir Woods end, the Bootjack Trail continues
along the creek's east bank where the paved trail ends at the
fourth bridge. As is the case throughout the region, side trails
abound, connecting every conceivable point to every other conceivable point.

Despite the crowds and the paved walk, the lower mile is prettiest, with its giant, often hollowed out trees. The hollowing results from frequent fires in this generally dry, brushy region
(more so uphill than in the canyons). Evidence of past fires may
be observed along the trail's entire length.

Dipsey—MattDavis

6. STEEP RAVINE TRAIL
(Mt. Tamalpais State Park)

Length: 2 miles
Water: Lots
Access: Curvy, 2 lane roads
Season: Any
Difficulty: Moderately difficult
Elevation: 450 to 1450
Use: Hikers only
Ownership: Mt. Tamalpais State Park
Phone: (415) 388-2070

Directions: *Top—Leave Hwy 101 just north of Sausalito and follow Hwy 1 to the Mt. Tamalpais turnoff (Panoramic Hwy). Continue to the Pantoll Ranger Station. The trailhead is at the west end of the parking lot.*

Bottom—Proceed on Hwy 1 past Muir Beach and around two canyon-mouth switchbacks. The trailhead is a mile beyond the second switchback, immediately before the road crosses Webb Creek. There's parking for one or two cars. A quarter mile down the highway, parking is a little better at the turnoff to the Steep Ravine Environmental Camp.

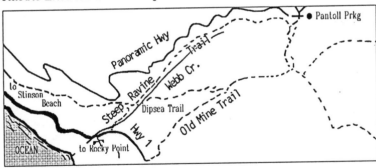

This is a typical coastal redwood trail, following a beautiful red-wood lined creek out to the ocean. While the north coast abounds in such paths, this is one of the nearer to San Francisco and among the prettier.

With a road at either end, hikers have the choice of traveling down-up or up-down. Or a pickup might be arranged to eliminate one direction. Or one of many alternate side loops might be taken in one direction.

We'll begin at the Pantoll Ranger Station, headquarters for Mt. Tamalpais State Park. Not necessarily recommended as a starting point, Pantoll can be mobbed in summer and on weekends. The road to Pantoll, while lovely, isn't quite as attractive as Hwy 1, which ranks among the world's great scenic drives. Pantoll may be better for walking to than driving to.

The Steep Ravine Trail begins at the far end of the Pantoll parking lot. The closed road immediately left of the Steep Ravine trailhead connects to the Old Mine and Dipsea Trails. For those interested in a loop route with one leg on the ridge, away from the redwood canyon, take the Old Mine Trail to the Dipsea Trail and the Dipsea Trail back to the Steep Ravine Trail. Or take the Old Mine Trail to Hwy 1 and follow the road ½ mile back to Steep Ravine. Or...

Steep Ravine lives up to its name, rising (or dropping) 1000 feet in 2 miles. While not killingly steep, it provides a workout. From Pantoll, the path drops almost immediately into the woods and down to the crashing little creek. The redwood canopy closes in overhead and a shadowy world of sun flecks, ferns and sparse understory vegetation unfolds.

Aside from redwood, look for abundant Douglas-fir, blue oak, laurel, red alder and tanoak. Red alder is largely a creek bank species in northern California. In Washington and northern Oregon, it becomes the major upland hardwood. Tanoak, of course, is the principal associate of redwood while blue oak is a more upland oriented, sun loving species.

About ⅔ of the way down, the path meets the Dipsea Trail (which comes in from the south), crosses a little footbridge, and briefly follows the Dipsea Trail out into the sunlight to the north. Continue north here for the trail to Stinson Beach. To rejoin the Steep Ravine Trail, loop back to the left as soon as possible and head into the canyon. The spot can be a little confusing, especially from the Hwy 1 end.

The trail eventually emerges at Hwy 1. Unfortunately, the rocky spot is 450 feet above the ocean. While the road offers spectacular vistas, the trees are too dense along the trail to reveal much, it would be a shame to come this far and not stick a toe in the surf.

To continue the journey, follow Hwy 1 north a few hundred feet, to the gated turnoff to the Steep Ravine Environmental Camp. The ¾ mile road snakes downward to a rock point (called Rocky Point), enclosing a series of tidepools. The grassy beaches are home to a small campground and some rustic cabins. It's a charming spot for studying marine wildlife.

Panoramic Hwy, beyond Pantoll, parallels Steep Ravine to the north. For a good overview of the ravine, drive down the road aways from the Ranger Station. The trail, being down in the woods, offers a vastly different environment from that seen from the car window. It deserves exploration on foot.

7. MT. TAMALPAIS SUMMIT
(Mt. Tamalpais State Park)

Length: 3 miles
Water: A little
Access: Steep, winding, paved roads
Season: All
Difficulty: Moderately difficult (up)
Elevation: 1400 to 2200 feet
Use: Non-motorized
Ownership: Tamalpais State Park
Phone: (415) 388-2070

Directions: From Hwy 101, take Hwy 1, just north of Sausalito, past Tamalpais junction, to Panoramic Highway. For the lower trailhead, park at Bootjack Campground and follow the Bootjack Trail north, up the hill. For the upper trailhead, turn right at the Pantoll Ranger Station, onto Pantoll Road. Turn right again on Ridgecrest Blvd. The trailhead is just before the summit parking area, where the road divides into a one-way loop. Parking is limited at the trailhead, much better ¼ mile up at the East Peak trailhead.

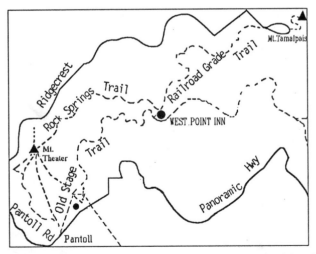

The impact of this trek up Marin County's principal landmark is lessened by the fact that one can drive to the same place. The path ends at a road just below the summit. Still, it offers commanding views of the Marin hills and San Francisco Bay, plus an intimate peek at the mountain's varied ecosystems.

Despite rising 800 feet in three miles, this isn't a particularly steep or difficult trail. Nevertheless, I suggest "unclimbing" the peak, rather than climbing it, by starting at the top and hiking down.

The drive up Mt. Tamalpais to the upper trailhead and the summit beyond is fabulous, with changing vistas at every turn. The road alternates between forest and grassland, sheltered canyon and ridge. The highway ends at a parking area, where a ½ mile loop trail assaults the rocky, 2571 foot peak, capped by a stone lookout. Get the loop trail out of the way before starting on the main trail.

The longer trail begins (or ends), at a gated dirt road, ¼ mile down from the summit parking area, where the road divides into a one-way loop. It's 1 ½ miles from the trailhead, along the Old Railroad Grade Trail, to West Point Inn.

This portion of the route is open and brushy, with views of the summit and the bay. The path is lined with occasional Douglas-firs, plus Bishop pine, canyon live oak, toyon, coyote brush and a little madrone. Wildflowers abound, especially in spring.

West Point Inn, a stately old stone lodge, marks the halfway point. The walk-in facility offers coffee and snacks on an irregular basis, as well as shelter from the cold. It's a fascinating establishment.

Several trails converge at the Inn. To continue to Bootjack and Pantoll, switch over to the Old Stage Trail. The Rock Springs Trail also comes in at West Point Inn. It leads to Bootjack and Pantoll via the Mountain Theater, a slightly longer route.

Below the inn, the terrain becomes a little more varied, with side creeks, rock outcroppings and canyon heads. The downhill gradient remains about the same. Most interesting in this section is a beautiful little creek crossing amid a large, silvery green, serpentine rock formation. Just above the creek, on a little hillock, is a beautiful cypress grove, the only one on the trail.

As the trail approaches the Bootjack Picnic Area, the Bootjack Trail comes in on the right, from Mountain Theater. A service road from the picnic ground meets the trail at the same spot. To reach the Bootjack parking area, turn left, downhill, onto the Bootjack Trail. It's ¼ mile to the highway. For Pantoll, continue straight on the Old Stage Trail for another ½ mile.

The summit of Mt. Tamalpais, and most of this trail, lies outside the State Park boundary, on land owned by the Marin Municipal Water District. Aside from the Water District property, the county owns extensive park and open space lands. The nearest Open Space Preserve to Mt. Tamalpais is the immediately adjacent Blithedale Ridge area. For information, stop by the Marin Civic Center.

8. BACK RANCH TRAIL
(China Camp State Park)

Length: 2 miles
Water: No
Access: Good, paved highway
Season: All
Difficulty: Moderately difficult
Elevation: 90 to 950 feet
Use: Non-motorized only
Ownership:China Camp St.Pk
Phone: (415) 456-0766

Directions: Take Hwy 101 to the first or second San Rafael exit. From the Central San Rafael exit, follow Third Street east to Point San Pedro Road. From the Civic Center Exit, follow the state park signs to North San Pedro Road. The two roads form a loop.

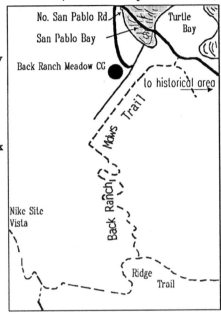

The trailhead is immediately before (or after), the turnoff to Back Ranch Campground. Park at the high spot in the road where an island called Turtle Back juts out into the marsh. The trail to Back Ranch Campground and beyond is fairly obvious, on the side of the road away from the Turtle Back.

There's much more to do besides hike trails in this fascinating state park, minutes from downtown San Rafael. The best place to begin is not the trailhead but a couple miles down the road, at the Historic Area. The latter is an authentic fishing village, used by the Chinese from Gold Rush days until acquired by the state in 1977. The state has added only a few interpretative displays. This isolated site's fascination is enhanced by its proximity to downtown San Rafael.

Away from the village, the quiet road along San Pablo Bay also contrasts with the nearness to San Rafael. A row of hills separates the city from the road and bay. At Turtle Back Island, near the trailhead, paths explore the vast marsh areas adjacent to parts of the bay.

The Back Ranch Trail climbs a steep hill with views of San Pablo and San Francisco Bays, the marsh and Turtle Back. It passes through a number of ecosystems, representing more interior forest communities than other Marin trails.

It's possible to cut ¼ mile off the trail by beginning at the Back Ranch Campground. This is a good option only if staying at the campground. A night at the walk-in camp, including parking in the adjacent lot, costs $6.00. Parking on the road and walking the extra distance is free.

From the road, the trail wanders back to the campground area over open grasslands at the marsh's edge. Occasional spreading valley oaks dot the grassy fields.

The woods start in the campground, along the creek and continue to the end of the trail. They consist largely of laurel, black oak, blue oak and a few madrones. The creek is lined mostly with red alder. Higher up, look for Douglas-fir and canyon live oak, with manzanita, coyote brush and toyon in brushy areas.

Above the campground, things become quite steep for a mile or so as the trail switches relentlessly upward. Views of the bay and marsh become better and better, with occasional glimpses of the structures atop the hill.

After 1½ miles, the path hits the ridge top. Turn right for the remainder of the trail. It's a little over ½ mile along the ridge to the abandoned Nike site and vista point. We suggest turning back at that point. The view from the Nike site is superb. Although oriented towards the bay, there are also panoramas of the surrounding hills. It's a terrific place for sunrises. Or sunsets.

China Camp Village (Chapter 8)

9. BOLINAS RIDGE TRAIL
(Golden Gate Nat. Rec. Area)

Length: 2 miles
Water: No
Access: Good, paved roads
Season: Any
Difficulty: Easy
Elevation: 375 to 500 ft.
Use: Hikers only
Ownership: Golden Gate Nat. Rec. Area.
Phone: (415) 663-1092

Directions: Take the central San Rafael exit off Hwy 101. Proceed west several miles, bearing right on Sir Frances Drake Boulevard. Past Samuel P. Taylor State Park, the road jumps out of the woods, over a barren hilltop, and down to the town of Olema. The trailhead is located at the hilltop, with parking along the road.

Alternatively, take Hwy 1 from Sausalito to Olema and turn right on Drake Boulevard.

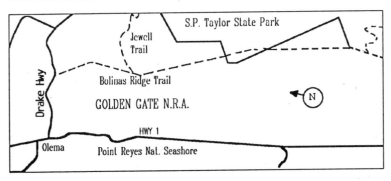

Why does this trail belong to Golden Gate National Recreation Area when it adjoins Point Reyes National Seashore? You'll have to ask the National Park Service. It's a lovely, instructive trail no matter who owns it.

The story of the Point Reyes Peninsula, which this trail looks down upon (or across to), is the story of the San Andreas Fault. The peninsula, cut off from the mainland by the fault, is geologically unrelated to the adjacent terrain. The Point's huge granite block has migrated hundreds of miles north from Southern California parent rock.

The San Andreas Fault, of course, is a 1000 mile crack in the earth, running through the Southern California desert and up the central Coast Ranges. It goes out to sea just south of San Francisco and hits land again at the south end of the Point Reyes Peninsula, forming Bolinas Lagoon. From there, it runs through the Olema Valley into Tomales Bay. Both the valley and the bay are unnaturally long, narrow, and straight. At one point, I read, two Olema Valley creeks run side by side in opposite directions.

Olema was the epicenter of the 1906 San Francisco earthquake, considered the worst in U.S. history. The quake resulted from massive horizontal movement along the fault. The severed ends of a road near Olema, cut in half by the 1906 quake, ended up 20 feet apart. Tomales Point was shoved 16 feet north.

Beyond Tomales Bay, the fault again takes to the waves, hitting land briefly again at Bodega Head and again, much less dramatically, along the Sonoma Coast.

The Bolinas Ridge Trail examines the San Andreas Fault better than any other pathway. Bolinas Ridge, along whose crest the trail runs, forms the east side of the Olema Valley.

The barren, grassy upland continues to be an active cattle ranch, even though the land now belongs to the National Park Service. It is an easy, level trail offering spectacular views of the Olema Valley and Tomales Bay.

The best way to reach the trailhead is from the town of Olema, "gateway" to Point Reyes on Highway 1. If you've come from San Rafael, this means overshooting your mark by a mile. But Olema is worth a quick soda pop stop to orient to the area. We presume you wouldn't come all this way without taking in some of the National Seashore's magnificent roads and trails. Bolinas Ridge is a good starting place.

The trailhead is located about a mile up Sir Frances Drake Boulevard from Highway 1. Look for a gate on the right (south), at the crest of the hill. There's a signed walk-through 50 feet east of the gate. After going through the fence, hike back to the road you'd be on if you had entered via the gate. The road is the trail.

The vistas don't appear immediately. The path climbs very gradually as it winds among rolling hills, occasional rock outcroppings, widely scattered oaks and herds of cattle. The picturesque oaks present an open grown habit, with short, thick trunks and extremely wide crowns.

The tree and farm lined Olema Valley soon appears on the right, with the blue expanse of Tomales Bay to the north. The bay is lined on both sides by yellow, grassy hills identical to those you're standing on. Mt. Tamalpais decorates the southern vista.

To the east, the ridge slopes down to Lagunitas Creek, a redwood canyon in Samuel P. Taylor State Park. The prominent, barren summit beyond the creek is Barnabe Peak, accessible by Taylor State Park's Barnabe Trail. Look for its trailhead on the left on Frances Drake Boulevard, just past the gated Devils Gulch/Horse Corral Road and Deadman Creek. The trail rises 1300 feet in 2½ miles.

It's 1¼ miles along the Bolinas Ridge Trail to the Jewell Trail intersection. The latter dips 500 feet down to Lagunitas Creek and makes a good turnaround point. If you crave more of Bolinas Ridge, keep going until you get bored. Since the trail continues for 6 miles, it'll easily outlast you. You can pick up the far end at a gated trailhead a few miles south in Olema Valley or at Shafter Bridge, 2½ miles past Taylor Park headquarters. If you're truly a glutton, it's possible to walk another 15 miles, to Mt. Tamalpais.

10. PALOMARIN/COASTAL TRAIL
(Point Reyes National Seashore)

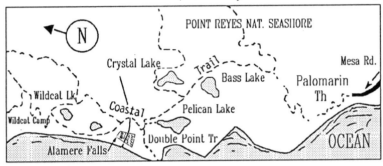

Length: 4 miles
Water: Lots and lots
Access: Narrow, paved roads
Season: All
Difficulty: Easy to moderate
Elevation: 350 to 600 ft.
Use: Non-motorized
Ownership: Point Reyes National Seashore
Phone: (415)663-1092

Directions: *Take Highway 1 to the Bolinas turnoff, an unmarked road a couple miles north of Stinson Beach. The road is difficult to miss, being the first route west, immediately north of Bolinas Lagoon. Just outside the town of Bolinas, turn right on Mesa Road and follow it to the end. If you miss the Bolinas turnoff, turn onto Horseshoe Hill Road from Hwy 1, then right onto Bolinas Road and right again onto Mesa Road.*

This southernmost Point Reyes trail offers several convenient destinations. From the trailhead, it's 2½ miles to Bass Lake, 3½ to Pelican Lake, 4 to Double Point and 5½ to Wildcat Beach. If you're making more than a day of it, it's 8 miles to Arch Rock at the end of the Bear Valley Trail and 15 to Limantour Road. We suggest Double Point as the best day-hike destination.

From the Palomarin trailhead, the Coastal Trail packs astonishing variety into its first 4 miles, not to mention some magnificent coastal panoramas. Of course the entire Stinson Beach area is a sightseeing haven. Hwy 1, contouring along the coast from Muir Beach, is one of the most spectacular ocean drives on the Pacific Coast. It's extremely winding, however.

Mesa Road, from the quaint village of Bolinas, winds past tree shaded homes and farms onto the yellow, open hills above the sea. Past the Point Reyes Bird Observatory, the pavement ends at the Palomarin trailhead. Parking is ample and the path follows an old, gated road through a eucalyptus grove, out onto the bluffs.

This is an excellent wildlife observation area. Look especially for hawks, osprey, falcons and a number of water birds. The public is invited to watch banding operations at the Bird Observatory, noted for sightings of the rare hooded warbler. Harbor seals can also be seen, along with gray whales in season.

The trail contains an inordinate amount of zig-zags and up-downs. It follows the shoreline at first, then swings inland through a series of gulches, creek canyons and terraces.

The vegetation changes constantly, depending on the elevation, water supply and shelter from ocean winds. Look mainly for grass, bush lupine, coastal sage and coyote brush. Bishop pine and Douglas-fir is also scattered around, as is blue oak, coffeeberry and toyon.

One unique feature of the Point Reyes Peninsula is the absence of redwoods, a common and highly noticeable mainstay of the Northern California coast. A couple of groves occur in the Palomarin area but are not visible from the trail.

A mile or so from the trailhead, the path cuts around a huge canyon, with lush greenery along the creek and hills soaring overhead. The path contains a few steep spots in this section, as elsewhere. At one point, it cuts inland through a small, sheltered gorge lined with ferns and canyon liveoak.

Immediately beyond, the trail intersects the Lake Ranch Trail, passes a couple ponds and finally arrives at Bass Lake, this chapter's elevational high point. In short order, the path also skirts Crystal and Pelican Lakes. The lakes, all about 10 acres, nestle on upland terraces. Look for waterfowl or fish for sunfish and bass.

I'm told the swimming is especially good at Pelican Lake. Since I visited in January, I passed on the opportunity to test its waters, even though it was a beautiful day with temperatures in the 60's. It's certainly the prettiest of the three lakes, and closest to the ocean.

Beyond Pelican Lake, the trail loops back towards the ocean and the Double Point Trail takes off to the left. This 4/10 mile side path leads to a rocky promontory. Double Point is the best place to view often photographed Alamere Falls, which drops over a cliff onto the beach. The trail later passes over the top of the falls.

11. BEAR VALLEY TRAIL
(Point Reyes National Seashore)

Length: 4 miles
Water: Lots
Access: Good, paved roads
Season: Any
Difficulty: Easy
Elevation: 0 to 400 ft.
Use: Non-motorized (see text)
Ownership: Point Reyes Nat. Seashore
Phone: (415) 663-1092

Directions: From Hwy 101, take the central San Rafael exit and proceed west to Sir Frances Drake Blvd, which veers right. Drake Blvd. ends at the town of Olema. There, turn right onto Hwy 1 and left immediately after onto Bear Valley Road. Follow the signs to the Bear Valley Visitor Center. The trailhead is at the far end of the large parking lot. Hwy 1, which leaves Hwy 101 just past Sausalito, also leads to Olema.

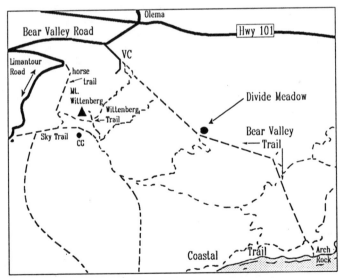

This is possibly the easiest trail within Point Reyes National Seashore. While mostly a quiet walk through the woods along a creek, it is not without charm and boasts some worthwhile highlights. Arch Rock Beach, the path's terminus, merits a visit.

The trail is remarkably similar to the Tennessee Valley Trail in Golden Gate National Recreation Area.

The huge Bear Valley Visitor Center, at the trailhead, should be included on any Point Reyes itinerary. Their trail mileage map was especially helpful, as were flyers on vegetation, geology, birds, climate and wildlife. Nearby interpretive trails and exhibits include the Earthquake Trail, exploring the San Andreas Fault zone in the Olema Valley, the Kule Koklo Indian exhibit and the Morgan Horse Ranch.

Whatever else you do, spend a few minutes on the short (½ mile) Earthquake Trail. It is ¹⁄₁₀ mile from the parking area and restroom across from the Visitor Center, to a secluded little footbridge over Olema Creek. The spot happens to be the exact epicenter of the 1906 San Francisco earthquake. A series of poles shows the exact line of slippage, in which the entire Point Reyes Peninsula jumped 16 feet northward.

For the Bear Valley Trail, park at the far end of the Visitor Center lot. The path begins just past the Morgan Horse Ranch, at a locked gate. It enters the woods almost immediately, following a little creek.

The most notable feature of this shaded, coastal canyon is the absence of redwoods. While redwoods dominate most sheltered areas of the Northern California Coast, they avoid the Point Reyes Peninsula's granitic soils.

In the absence of redwoods, Douglas-fir (which itself is capable of 200 to 300 foot heights), becomes the dominant species, as it does in many low and middle elevation areas of the West. Look also for tanoak, bay laurel and creek bank alder.

The Bear Valley Trail is berry heaven. I've never tasted salal berries but understand some people like them. Elderberry abounds and its sour, purple fruit makes excellent wine and jam.

Evergreen huckleberry is closely related to blueberry except the berries are smaller and a little tangier. Blackberry and thimbleberry form bramble patches along much of the path. The latter is a raspberry whose stem stays on the plant when the fruit is picked.

It's 1½ miles from the trailhead to Divide Meadow. Prior to the meadow, the creek had been flowing east, away from the ocean, towards Olema Valley. Beyond the meadow, the trail picks up Coast Creek, which it follows to the ocean.

Between the trailhead and Divide Meadow, three paths take off northward, all of which lead to the Sky Camp/Mt. Wittenberg area. All are quite steep. Divide Meadow, 100 feet higher in elevation than the trailhead and 400 feet higher than the beach, is a large, grassy opening surrounded by a dense forest. There's no ocean view but it's a fine picnic spot.

Below the meadow, the trail continues pretty much as before, except the creek flows in the opposite direction and glimpses of the ocean pop up here and there. The path crosses a couple more side routes, including the Glen and Baldy Trails and the Coastal Trail. The latter peels off north about ⅛ mile from the beach and south just before the beach.

A short path climbs down to the beach and Arch Rock. Arch Rock's arch can be crawled through at low tide but not at high tide.

Horses are not permitted on weekends or holidays.

12. MT. WITTENBERG/SKY TRAIL
(Point Reyes National Seashore)

Map: See Chapter 11
Length: 2 miles (4 mile loop)
Water: No
Access: Two lane, paved road
Season: All
Difficulty: Moderate
Elevation: 650 to 1336 feet
Use: Non-motorized
Ownership: Point Reyes National Seashore
Phone: (415) 663-1092

Directions: From Hwy 101, take the central San Rafael exit and go west on Fourth St. and Red Hill Ave. to Sir Frances Drake Hwy. Bear right on Sir Frances Drake and continue to the intersection with Hwy 1 at Olema. Or pick up Hwy 1 just north of Sausalito and proceed to Olema that way. Immediately past Olema, turn left onto Bear Valley Road. Turn left again, a mile or so later, onto Limantour Road. Look on the left for the parking area and wooden fence marking the Sky trailhead, 3 miles from the Bear Valley/Limantour junction.

One usually can't go wrong hiking to a park's highest point. Despite the astonishing beauty of other trails at Point Reyes National Seashore, the rule definitely applies here. In my opinion, Mt. Wittenberg offers the park's best day-hike, although its panoramas are often obscured by fog and bad weather.

Timing is crucial if you plan to spend only a couple hours on the trail. Afternoons are best, after the fog burns off. In winter, the park boasts occasional warm, sunny days, but check the weather report the day before so you don't end up fighting your way through a hurricane.

The trailhead is reached via Limantour Road, a lovely route which climbs, then descends Inverness Ridge, backbone of the Point Reyes Peninsula, of which Mt. Wittenberg is the keystone.

The rock forming Mt. Wittenberg is similar to the beige sandstone (Franciscan Formation), underlying most of the northern California Coast Ranges. While it looks Franciscan, however, it is several million years younger—Cenozoic rather than Mesozoic—and of a type more common south of San Francisco Bay.

As noted in other chapters, granite is found along the northern California coast only in isolated fragments west of the San Andreas Fault, including the Point Reyes Peninsula. Elsewhere, it normally forms the highest peaks of the range. At Point Reyes, however, it turns up only at the tip of Point Reyes and at Tomales Point. Mt. Wittenberg contains no granite.

Before starting out, pick up a Trail Map at the Bear Valley Visitor Center. It's a little more detailed and accurate than the park brochure. However, not all its distances agree with those on the trail signs. For instance, the sign at the Sky Trail/Horse Trail junction claims it's 1.2 miles back to the trailhead while the Trail Map insists it's only .7 miles. My gut feeling sides with the map.

In either case, at the Sky trailhead, follow the gated, dirt road forming the Sky Trail. You'll find it on the left, with the narrower Bayview Trail heading downhill on the right. It's .7 (or 1.2), somewhat steep miles up the Sky Trail to the Horse Trail, located $1/10$ mile past the junction with the Fire Lane Trail. It sounds confusing but the area is extremely well signed.

I took the long way around, via Sky Camp, hoping the fog would lift, which it eventually did. Either prong at the Horse Trail/Sky Trail junction will suffice.

The Sky Trail begins in a rainforest of Douglas-fir, Bishop pine, tanoak, liveoak, salal, huckleberry, toyon, coyote brush, etc. Keep an eye out also for cypress and knobcone pine and note the lack of redwoods. Redwood, the dominant species of the northern California coast, is largely absent from the peninsula.

The forest mainly covers the northern slopes of the higher elevations. Much of the peninsula is devoid of trees, with the only vegetation being grass. Even in forested areas, frequent openings reveal astonishing vistas.

From the Horse Trail/Sky Trail junction, it's a level ½ mile along the Sky Trail to Sky Camp. The walk-in campground perches on a beautiful meadow, 1000 feet above the surrounding lowlands. You'll find pit toilets, picnic tables, fire grates—and bear poles on which to hang your belongings.

To continue on the Sky Trail, follow the unmarked uphill fork, just past the toilets. It winds in and out of the woods for ½ mile, to a four-way intersection on a grassy ridge. Three of the converging paths there are the Sky Trail and one is the Meadow Trail. Follow the signs to Mt. Wittenberg, uphill to the left.

The short, uphill connecting path emerges, after .4 mile, on a vast, barren saddle where the Sky Trail charges downhill to the Bear Valley Trail and the Mt. Wittenberg Trail takes off on the left.

It's 1.6 miles to this spot, by the way, from the Bear Valley trailhead, near the Visitor Center, as opposed to 1.7 miles from the Sky Trail trailhead (via Horse Trail—2.1 miles via Sky Camp). However, the route from Bear Valley gains 350 feet more in elevation than does that from the Sky trailhead.

You have arrived, you'll find a short, very steep way trail, up through the grass, to Mt. Wittenberg's 1407 foot summit. The actual Wittenberg Trail skirts around the peak to the west.

The mountaintop consists of a large, grassy flat, with views east and south. The west and north are blocked by trees. Since there's not much to see to the south, the only real vista is of the Olema Valley around the town of Olema. The slightly lower Wittenberg Trail offers better views of the remainder of the region.

The best view of Mt. Wittenberg, conversely, may be had from the Olema Store.

The first half of the level, 1 mile Mt. Wittenberg Trail, heading back towards the Sky trailhead, looks down on Sky Camp and across to Limantour Beach, Limantour Estero and Point Reyes.

About halfway along, it crosses to the north side of the ridge and into the woods. From there on, the trek is anti-climactic. It's ¾ mile to the Horse Trail junction, another .4 steep miles down the Horse Trail (left), back to the Sky Trail, and either .7 or 1.2 miles from there to your car.

Mt. Wittenberg trail. Point Reyes.(Chapter 11)

13. ESTERO TRAIL
(Point Reyes National Seashore)

Length: 4 miles
Water: Lots
Access: Good paved roads
Season: Any
Difficulty: Easy
Elevation: 0 to 200 ft.
Use: Non-motorized only
Ownership: Point Reyes Nat. Seashore
Phone: (415) 663-1092

Directions: *From Hwy 101, take the central San Rafael exit and proceed west, bearing right onto Sir Frances Drake Hwy. Or take the Hwy 1 exit just past Sausalito. Both routes lead to the Hwy 1 town of Olema. Just past Olema, Frances Drake Hwy continues westward onto the Pt. Reyes Peninsula. Follow it to the paved, one lane Estero Road and turn left. The trailhead is well marked near the end of Estero Road.*

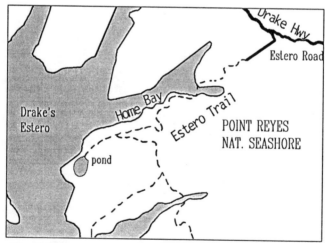

This trail explores the bays, salt marshes and wetlands of the Point Reyes Peninsula's interior. The bleak, beautiful country abounds in wildlife.

While this is one of the National Seashore's more remote trails, I once visited on a December weekday and counted 16 cars at the trailhead. The entire park is deservedly popular but can be crowded on summer weekends.

Estero Road, to the trailhead, is a one lane, paved route with a few rough spots. It traverses rolling cattle and sheep country to the well developed trailhead area, with its restrooms and parking lot.

One catches a glimpse of Drakes Estero from the road, but not from the trailhead. The trail climbs a grassy hill and skirts a rocky knob before coming out high above the Estero's Home Bay arm. "Estero," of course, is spanish for estuary, a salt water bay formed at a river mouth.

Once the shimmering bay comes into view, the path slowly descends. The country remains lonely and barren, with many rock outcroppings. However, a scattering of Bishop pines and exotic Monterey pines begin to turn up near the water. The path meanders through a pine plantation, crosses a little bridge, and slowly works its way up the low bluffs on the bay's south side.

Be sure to observe the estuarian wetland habitat. Look for great egrets, blue herons and loons. You'll also find great-horned owls in the pines and hawks circling overhead. The bay itself is a bountiful oyster bed.

After 2½ miles, the Estero Trail makes a 90 degree turn left, connecting to Drake's Head, Limantour Estero and Limantour Beach. The Sunset Beach Trail continues ahead where the Estero Trail turns left. It's 1½ miles along the Sunset Beach Trail to a small pond above Sunset Beach. Views of the Estero and the Ocean are fabulous from these low bluffs, with, as the name suggests, some of the most glorious sunsets you're likely to witness.

14. TOMALES POINT
(Point Reyes National Seashore)

Length: 4¾ miles
Water: None
Access: Long, winding, paved roads
Season: All
Difficulty: Easy
Elevation: 375 to 80 ft.
Use: Non-motorized
Ownership: Pt. Reyes Nat. Seashore
Phone: (415) 663-1092

Directions: Leave Hwy 101 at the central San Rafael exit. Proceed west, bearing right onto Sir Frances Drake Hwy, and follow it to Hwy 1. Or pick up Hwy 1 from Hwy 101, just beyond Sausalito. Past the Hwy 101 town of Olema, just before Pt. Reyes Station, turn left onto Sir Frances Drake Hwy, where it continues

*towards Pt. Reyes. Turn
right, off Drake Hwy, onto
the Pierce Point/McClures
Beach Road and proceed to
the Pierce Ranch trailhead.*

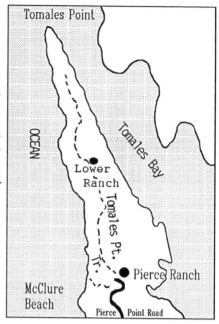

Of the many trails riddling Point Reyes National Seashore, this may be the most beautiful. It explores not Point Reyes itself but Tomales Point, a lonely spit of land between Tomales Bay and the Pacific which forms the northern tip of the Point Reyes Peninsula.

Point Reyes itself, several miles away, impressively juxtaposes high cliffs, barren slopes, shoals, sea lions and a picturesque lighthouse. The trail to the point and the Lighthouse Visitor Center is quite short, however.

Tomales Point, on the other hand, lies away from the more trafficked areas. A visit to this "other" point is a major undertaking. While not a difficult trek, it's 4¾ miles from trailhead to tip. This exposed sliver of land can be quite windy and much colder than the rest of the park.

Things change dramatically at the turnoff between Frances Drake Hwy and Pierce Point Road. The former, the National Seashore's main road, snakes over the ridge of forested peaks forming the peninsula's backbone. It then winds past low lying bays and estuaries before climbing Point Reyes' high bluffs.

Lonely Pierce Point Road (the sign says McClures Beach), on the other hand, winds among rolling ranchlands where cattle graze on naked, grassy hills. Views of sea and bay abound.

Frances Drake Hwy is particularly scenic following the western shore of Tomales Bay near the town of Inverness. The latter is quite picturesque, with many fine dining establishments, including two Czech restaurants.

Near the end of Pierce Point Road, a Tule elk herd can usually be seen. Once abundant on the Peninsula, the species has recently been reintroduced.

The road ends at the McClures Beach trailhead and Pierce Ranch. Park at the ranch, not the beach parking area, for Tomales Point. It's ¼ mile from the ranch to the beach parking area. The beach trail winds for ½ mile down a sandy gully.

To find the Tomales Point Trail, walk around the ranch to the west (left), following the old dirt road. The first mile skirts the cliff tops on the ocean side. This is naked country, vegetated by grass, bush lupine and little else. Gullies and coves shoot down 100 feet or so to the beach.

Eventually, the path works its way to the crest between the ocean and the bay, affording views of both. The exceptionally linear shape of the 15 miles by one mile Tomales Bay results from the San Andreas Fault, which runs along its middle. The bay, adjacent Olema Valley, and Bolinas Lagoon on the Peninsula's south side, are all shaped by the fault.

Three miles along the trail, a second unit of Pierce Ranch is passed. Founded in 1869, the dairy ranch operated until 1980.

The point lies 1¼ miles past the far ranch. Although getting lost would be difficult, the path in this section grows a little faint, petering out well before the land runs out. The actual point consists of a series of granite cliffs and outcroppings. Along the Northern California coast, granite occurs only in rare patches west of the San Andreas Fault.

Climb out as far as you feel comfortable but be careful. Losing your footing would be both easy and disastrous. Contain your adventurousness in wet or windy weather.

15. LOWER STEVE'S TRAIL
(Annadel State Park)

Length: 2 miles
Water: Very little
Access:Paved roads
Season: Any
Difficulty: Moderately easy
Elevation: 350to 850 feet
Use: Non-motorized
Ownership: Annadel State Park
Phone:(707) 539-3911 or 938-1519

Directions: Take Hwy 101 to Hwy 12 at Santa Rosa. Follow Hwy 12 east to Mission Blvd or Los Alamos Road (still in Santa Rosa) and turn right. Turn left on Montgomery from Mission or right onto Melita, which runs into Montgomery, from Los Alamos. The park entrance is well marked off Montgomery. Proceed

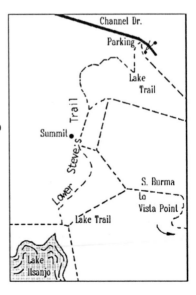

over the channel and bear left through the toll booth to the parking lot at the road end. The trailhead is at the southeast end of the parking area. A $5.00 day use fee is assessed in summer.

Santa Rosans should be envied for having Annadel's quiet, wooded hills and lakes so close to town. While the park is located just off a residential neighborhood, the trail and lake are surrounded by higher peaks which largely block the view of urban Santa Rosa. Interesting ecological variety adds to the park's attractiveness.

The Lower Steve trailhead is situated at the far end of the farthest parking lot. The Lake Trail takes off at the same spot, up a dirt road along a wooded canyon. The narrower Lower Steve's Trail climbs a steep hill immediately to the right. While both routes lead to Lake Ilsanjo, Lower Steve is ½ mile shorter.

The park brochure describes the Lake Trail as much easier than the Lower Steve Trail. I didn't find the latter very difficult at all, however, except perhaps the first ¼ mile. The first portion of the Lake Trail, along the gully bottom, visits a few redwoods.

The Lower Steve's Trail winds steeply up a shaded north slope forested by young Douglas-fir, bay laurel, black oak and madrone. The path soon levels, following a gentle contour up to an easy crest.

After a mile, the Louis Trail comes in on the left, connecting back to the Lake Trail. Beyond this junction, the Lower Steve's Trail enters an open, grassy area fringed in blue oak, valley oak, manzanita and canyon liveoak. The first three are sun loving species while canyon liveoak likes rocky, thin soil areas.

The path rises gently through the meadow, past rock outcroppings and picturesque, open grown oaks with spreading crowns. It's 4/10 of a mile from the Louis Trail junction to the junction with the Burma Trail, which also leads back to the Lake Trail.

At this second junction, the trail crests and a lovely panorama unfolds, of a vast, spreading meadow and Lake Ilsanjo in the distance. The basin breaks to the right, while a row of higher peaks, topping off at 1900 feet, forms a barrier to the south.

Lake Ilsanjo lies 8/10 of a mile from the crest. The charming little tule lined reservoir is named for a couple who once owned the property, Ilsa and Joe. (Cute, huh?) It's a fine picnic spot.

Trails fairly riddle the park and most skirt the lake. For variety, take the Lake Trail back to the parking lot. Pick it up immediately left of where the Lower Steve's Trail meets the lake. The Lake Trail is more in the woods and crests at a little higher elevation.

About 4/10 of a mile up the Lake Trail from the lake, the South Burma Trail takes off to the right. If you're not yet hiked out, it's two miles along the South Burma Trail to a scenic vista at an elevation of 1350 feet. The vista looks down the canyon to Lake Ilsanjo and beyond to the Santa Rosa Valley.

16. BALD MOUNTAIN TRAIL
(Sugarloaf Ridge State Park)

Length: 2½ miles
Water: Very little
Access: Good, paved roads
Season: Any
Difficulty: Difficult, extremelly difficult near the summit.
Elevation: 1300 to 2729 ft
Use: Non-motorized only
Ownership: Sugarloaf Ridge
St Pk
Phone:(707)833-5712
or 938-1519

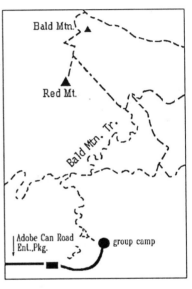

Directions: From Hwy 101 at Santa Rosa, take Hwy 12 east to Adobe Canyon Road. Follow the road past the toll booth to the Group Camp at the very end. If the Group Camp is in use, park in the lot immediately past the toll booth, on the left. That's the main trailhead, although that path is slightly longer than the one from the Group Camp. A $5 day use fee is assessed in summer.

This spectacular trail climbs the high ridge of the Mayacmas Mountains, between Santa Rosa and the Napa and Sonoma Valleys. While the climb can be fairly difficult, the vistas and the vegetation offer great variety. Although often very hot in summer, the trail can be delightful other times of the year. I went in January, on a gorgeous, 65 degree day.

There are actually two mountains to be climbed within Sugarloaf Ridge State Park, Bald Mountain and Hood Mountain. Adobe Canyon Road passes both trailheads while winding along the redwood lined canyon of upper Sonoma Creek. The drive is worth the trip in itself. Stop at the Vista Point for a view of a 25 foot waterfall (in winter and spring) on Sonoma Creek.

The Hood Mountain (Goodspeed) Trail is about the same length as the Bald Mountain Trail. The former tends to be more in the woods, although it passes an impressive outcropping at Gunsight

Rock. Bald Mountain, as the name suggests, is more open, with better panoramas. While Hood is a foot higher than Bald, its trailhead is 400 feet lower, making the path considerably steeper.

From the Bald Mountain trailhead just past the toll booth, it's ¼ of a mile up a grassy expanse to the junction with the trail from the group camp, on the right. If coming from the group camp, you'll meet the junction after a couple hundred feet. In either case, head uphill.

Little Bald Mountain, to the south, and Brushy Peak, to the east, can be seen along this first trail segment. Little Bald is the dome shaped, barren peak to the south, just outside the park.

At 2275 feet, it's a tiny bit higher than, but much prettier than, Brushy Peak, rising within the park. Bald, Little Bald and Brushy Peak are all aptly named.

Beyond the trail's initial grassy flat, the route climbs a series of fairly steep switchbacks, through a hardwood forest of madrone, blue oak, black oak, bay laurel and canyon liveoak. This sun baked south slope displays little understory vegetation and a history of repeated fires. Look for young Douglas-fir, which does best in a slightly shaded situation, creeping into the understory.

After ¾ mile, the path comes out on an old paved road. Turn right, uphill for the summit. I find trails following paved roads a bit disconcerting as I always ponder how much easier driving would be.

This middle trail section is much brushier than the first section. Like Brushy Peak, it is choked with manzanita, coyote brush, ceanothus, chamise and the red berried toyon. It begins with good views of Hood Mountain but soon swings around to the east slope, peering out over Brushy Peak and Little Bald. Look for a pretty little pond early on, and some deep gullies farther up. This is a good wildflower area in spring.

Approaching the Red Mountain/Headwaters Trails (to the left), almost 2 miles from the trailhead, the path swings around to the north face of Red Mountain. Note the better developed woods here, reflecting better moisture retention and cooler temperatures than on the south slope. You'll run into a few maples, alders and buckeyes here, above the Sonoma Creek headwaters. The main Bald Mountain summit soon comes into view.

The pavement ends a little over 2 miles from the trailhead, at the saddle between Red and Bald Mountain. Red Mountain is a 2549 foot high serpentine outcropping covered with telephone microwave installations.

Above the saddle, the path grows very steep as it climbs the bald part of Bald Mountain. The views improve dramatically as the path makes its way around the peak's west and north sides. Immediately north of the summit, the trail joins another trail. To reach the top, swing briefly up the path on the right.

In addition to the Sonoma Valley, Napa Valley and Valley of the Moon, a myriad of landmarks are visible from the summit. To the northwest, Mt. St. Helena anchors Napa Valley and the May-acmas Range's northern end. Farther north, in winter, the nearest snow capped peaks (depending on the snow line), are Snow and Goat Mountains in the Mendocino Range.

To the south and west, various smog filled valleys of the San Francisco Bay area can be seen. And on the eastern horizon, on a clear day, rises the snow capped line of the Sierra Nevada, on the far side of the Sacramento Valley.

17. SKYLINE TRAIL
(Skyline Wilderness County Park)

Length: 2½ to 4½ miles
Water: Lots
Access: Paved highway
Season: All
Difficulty: Easy to moderate
Elevation: 200 feet to 1000 feet
Use: Non-motorized
Ownership: Napa County Parks
Phone: (707) 252-0481

Directions: Leave I-80 at Vallejo, proceeding west on Hwy 37. Turn north (right), onto Hwy 29 and follow the 4 lane route to Napa. Get off at the Hwy 121/Imola exit and head east on Imola, past the intersection where 121 turns north, to the park entrance.

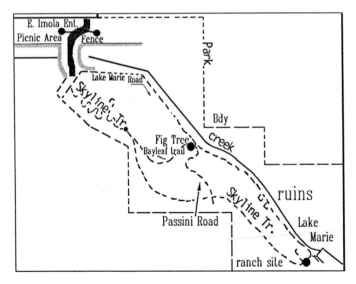

A $3 day use fee is assessed year round.

Although this is the only county owned trail herein, it more than holds its own. I am pleased to include this gem both because of its scenic attractiveness and the high quality of the Napa County management. A nearby county, with a "thing" about outsiders, requested I omit their parks. Not to worry.

While Skyline Park offers a network of beautiful footways through quiet, rolling hills, some things about it amused me. I trust Napa residents won't mind my mentioning them.

First, the trailhead is closer to a McDonalds than any wilderness oriented path I've ever been on (which I consider a plus). Second, the trail's first ⅛ mile has a 6 foot chain link fence on either side. In 100 years, all trails will probably be similarly constructed.

Third, the entire park was overrun with salamanders (rough-skinned newts, I think). During my seven mile trek, I encountered more of these creatures than in my entire life previously.

The Area Locator inset on the park brochure is a little difficult to interpret, since it's oriented with north on the bottom and doesn't show Hwy 29. For the record, Hwy 121 follows Imola Road from 29 to Soscal Road. It then turns north on Soscal through Napa. The brochure's trail map is remarkably accurate and detailed.

From the parking lot, walk across the little footbridge and up the hill to the picnic area. Turn right on the gravel road beyond the picnic area and follow it to a bridge over a creek on the left. You'll see a trailhead sign at the bridge and the beginning of the chain link fencing. This first portion of the path runs between two pretty little ponds, both outside the park boundary.

The fences end, and the countryside opens out, at the lower end of Lake Marie Road (which is closed to vehicles). For the Skyline Trail, follow the side road running uphill to the right. The actual trail, near the hilltop, is well marked.

It's 4½ miles to Lake Marie, at the far end of the park, via the Skyline Trail. Along Lake Marie Road, the lake lies 2½ miles away.

The Skyline Trail's first ½ mile ascends a steep hillside dotted with solitary, wide crowned blue oaks and bay laurels. Near the junction with the Bayleaf Trail, at the top of the hill, the path crests at just under 800 feet. This is an area of expanses, sheltered hardwood clumps and picturesque, moss covered stone fences. Vistas of the surrounding valleys and higher peaks, with glimpses of San Pablo Bay in the distance, are impressive.

At Bayleaf junction, the Skyline Trail swings right and dips downhill for a while, following the park boundary. The path's high point can be seen in the distance. It crests a mile ahead at 800 feet (on a hill whose 900 summit lies outside the park) and yet again after another 1½ miles atop a 1000 foot knoll.

A mile can be cut off the route by following the Bayleaf Trail through a beautiful, bay laurel lined ravine, back to the Lake Marie Road. Continuing on the Skyline Trail yields views and terrain similar to the earlier portions. Despite a few ups and downs, the going is generally easy. The last 1½ miles closely parallels Lake Marie Road before emerging at the lake.

Just prior to the lake, the trail crosses an old home site, amid views of Marie Creek canyon and a grove of California buckeyes. The aptly named Buckeye Trail also passes the spot.

Lake Marie, surrounded by steep, green summits up to 1700 feet high, was completely dry when I visited. Still, the little reservoir makes a worthwhile destination.

The Lake Marie Road back to the parking area offers experiences different from the Skyline Trail. Paralleling well uphill of the creek, it is lined with madrone, oak, alder, bay laurel, toyon and fern. A creek bank trail, far below, may be picked up at the far end of the dam or at Fig Tree.

Between the Lake and Fig Tree, the path passes a couple of old cabin bases, cut into the hillside. The immense, gnarled Fig Tree, a park focal point, marks the road's halfway point. Beyond, the terrain opens out, with views of the ponds and barns near the entrance area.

Back at the trailhead, the picnic area's concrete slabs are building foundations for what once was a dairy staffed by Napa State Hospital patients. The hospital grounds are immediately adjacent and once included much of the park. The dairy was closed amid much scandal, following a lawsuit by a local rancher.

18. COYOTE PEAK TRAIL
(Napa Valley State Park)

Length: 1½ miles
Water: Oodles
Access: Paved highway
Season: Any
Difficulty: Mostly easy
Elevation: 450 to 1170 feet
Use: Hikers only
Ownership: Napa Valley State Park
Phone: (707) 942-4575

Directions: The park is on Hwy 29, just south of Calistoga. Once inside the park, proceed past the visitor center, over the creek, and park at the day use area on the right. Follow the well marked Redwood Trail. Entry to the park costs $5 in summer. The trail may also be reached by turning right immediately past the visitor center, towards Richey Creek Campground. That trailhead is on *the left, just past the restroom, at the beginning of the one way loop.*

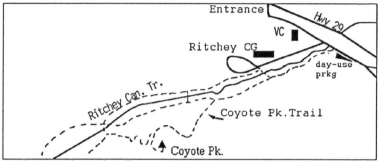

This gentle path offers an exercise break to Napa Valley tourists who might have overdone their wine tasting. While Coyote Peak lacks the grandeur of nearby Mt. St. Helena, the park's shaded paths explore one of California's most inland redwood canyons. The trail then ascends the low peak for a pleasant valley vista.

The park is centered around Richey Creek and a network of trails surrounds its narrow canyon. While you'll save ½ mile by using the campground trailhead, parking there is limited. The situation at the day use area, near the visitor center, is much better.

From the campground trailhead, the path dips down to and across the creek, joining the Redwood Trail on the far side of the rushing little brook. The first trail sign is located across the creek.

While this is a redwood canyon, Douglas-fir is the dominant tree, along with ever present tanoak. Redwoods are few and far between. In spring, many herbaceous plants may be observed along the creek, including ferns, Solomon's seal and trillium.

The Coyote Peak Trail takes off to the left after ½ mile. It climbs easily up a couple side gullies, then levels off and contours around the north side of the summit. A short, somewhat steep and rocky side trail leads to the actual peak. The entire trail remains largely in the woods throughout, with a few brushy openings. Views from rocky summit are obscured by dense brush and hardwoods. The creek valley is seen best, with only glimpses of the much larger Napa Valley.

19. MOUNT ST. HELENA
(R.L. Stevenson State Park)

Length: 5 miles
Water: Zip
Access: Winding, paved, 2 lane hwy
Season: All
Difficulty: Moderately difficult
Elevation: 2000 /4343 ft
Use: Hikers only
Ownership: R.L Stevenson State Park
Phone: (707) 942-4575

Directions: From Hwy 101, take Hwy 12 west from Santa Rosa
to Calistoga Road.
Proceed to the end, just
north of Calistoga. There,
follow the signs to
Lakeport, turning left
briefly onto Hwy. 128,
right onto the cutoff to
Hwy 29, and left onto 29.
The latter winds steeply
uphill for several miles.
Where it starts back

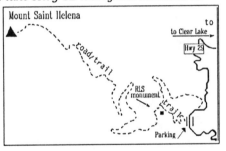

down, park at the State Park parking area on the left (west). The
trailhead sign is a hundred feet up a dirt road.

St. Helena may be the one Bay Area peak everyone dreams of
scaling. At 4343 feet, the bald summit towers above the surrounding Mayacmas Range. It stands spectacular guard over the
adjacent Napa Valley's quiet vinyards.

And don't worry—unlike Washington's Mt. St. Helens, St. Helena is not likely to erupt.

The steep, first gear road up the pass, from the Napa Valley
town of Calistoga, may cause some anxiety. But ever improving
views of the valley and St. Helena more than compensate. Most of
the highway climbs through barren grasslands, broken only by
scattered hardwood clumps. Near the summit, however, the road
enters a dense Douglas-fir forest. That's where the trailhead is located.

These woods are extremely interesting. Along the trail's first
mile, Douglas-fir, tanoak, blue oak, black oak and bay laurel represent the common Bay Area upland forest. Farther up, ponderosa pine makes perhaps its southernmost coast range appear-

ance. It is accompanied by knobcone pine, an odd, inland mountain dweller to the north but absent from the Bay Area.

Several forest zones meet on St. Helena. Immediately past the park, towards Clear Lake, the inland Sierra Nevada forest takes over and coastal species such as tanoak and blue oak vanish. There, acres of ponderosa pine are accompanied by incense cedar and the high desert western juniper. You probably wouldn't have to look very hard for sugar pine or white fir, either.

Of particular interest along the St. Helena Trail, was California torreya, a shrubby species I'd read about but never seen. I thought the first one I saw was a grand fir until, on touching it, the tips of its evergreen needles embedded in my hand.

References describe torreya's range as "upland, middle elevation forest understories in the central Sierra and Coast Ranges." Despite my inexperience with the species, this Yew family member is not particularly rare. Also called California nutmeg, it's unrelated to that spice.

The trail's first mile climbs steeply up a densely wooded canyon. Just before emerging from the woods, it passes a small stone monument to Robert Louis Stevenson. Stevenson, it seems, built a crude cabin on the spot in 1880 and lived there with his wife. His stay inspired "The Silverado Squatters and parts of Treasure Island." The cabin site, a tiny earth fill in the middle of a gully, struck me as bleak, lacking water, sunlight or vistas.

Above the monument, the path joins a wide gravel road and breaks out of the woods. Turn left, uphill onto the road. The next couple miles follow a huge switchback on the mountain's south side. You probably noticed it from the highway. Views of the Napa Valley and the rocky cliffs of the adjacent Palisades are particularly impressive.

The Palisades are a series of faulted, uplifted lava flows, as is St. Helena. In fact, the Mayacmas Range's entire east end is a small volcanic island unrelated to the surrounding region. Sedimentary, not volcanic rock underlies the bulk of northwest California.

Oddly, while St. Helena is composed of volcanic rock, it isn't a volcano. The source of it's lava is unknown and the uplift making it a mountain came much later. The nearby and equally isolated Clear Lake volcanic area is much younger.

Beyond the switchback, the trail swings around the peak's east face and continues to climb through grass and brush. Look for ceanothus, manzanita, pine, canyon liveoak, and an occasional bay laurel and torreya. Many rock outcroppings are passed, some quite impressive. Despite the elevation, snow rarely lingers or accumulates. The trail can be very hot in summer so bring water.

Though long, the path isn't particularly steep. The gradient is remarkably even and the miles go quickly by. You'll soon find yourself atop the roomy, level summit with its buildings and huge platform. A map identifies the surrounding landmarks. In addition to the Palisades and Napa Valley, look for Lake Berryessa, the Sacramento Valley and the Sierra to the east. Snow Mountain adorns the north horizon (along with Shasta and Lassen on clear days). The San Francisco area, Bald Mountain and Mt. Diablo lie to the west and south.

20. CACHE CREEK/MARSH TRAIL
(Anderson Marsh State Historic Park)

Length: 1½ miles (3 mile loop)
Water: None
Access: Paved highway
Season:Any
Difficulty: Easy
Elevation: 1320 to 1400 feet
Use: Hikers only
Ownership: Anderson Marsh State Park
Phone: (707) 994-0688

Directions: From the Bay Area, follow Hwy 29 past Calistoga to the town of Lower Lake. From I-5, take Hwy 20 west from Williams to Hwy 53, then turn south. From Hwy 101, take Hwy 20 east from Calpella or Hwy 175 east from Hopland to Lower Lake. The park is on Hwy 53, just north of Lower Lake and the 53-29 junction. Park at the little ranch west of the road. The visitor center, in the house, is open three days a week. If the gate is closed, park on the highway. The unsigned Marsh Trail follows a dirt road bearing left, behind the barns.

This unusual trail begins at a visitor center staffed by some of the nicest people I've run across. Since the park interprets Indian culture and archaeology as well as natural history, many volunteers boast a Native American heritage. They do a commendable job.

Stop by the visitor center on Friday, Saturday and Sunday until 4 p.m. A call ahead or good timing will result in a guided tour of the ranch and park by a trained docent.

From the old barns, home to several adorable donkeys, the Marsh Trail to the Pomo village is easily located. A couple gaps in the fence, alongside the barns, lead to a closed dirt road. Bear left across the flat grasslands, towards a little knoll ½ mile away.

There are as yet no trail signs in this new park. A quarter mile from the ranch, the trail makes a sharp left turn and a side road takes off right. Stay left.

The reconstructed Pomo Indian village, with its reed huts and fire pits, is used for interpretative programs. The park also en-

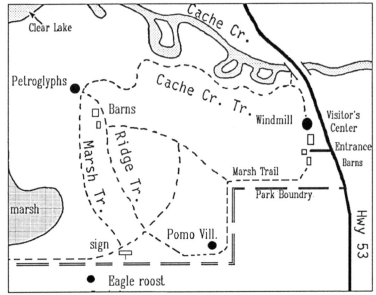

compasses what Archaeologists believe to be some of California's oldest human habitation sites.

Past the Pomo village, the road bears gradually away from the park boundary and crosses another road. Turn left at the junction for the Marsh Trail or continue ahead for the Ridge Trail.

A couple hundred feet beyond this junction, on the Marsh Trail, you'll come to a second junction, at a sign about bald eagles. Just past the sign, on the path leading towards the marsh (not on the Marsh Trail, which bears to the right from here), look for a huge, lone ponderosa pine on the high ridge to the south (left). Eagles usually perch in its top branches in winter.

There is little difference between the Ridge Trail and the lower Marsh Trail. The two parallel one another a couple hundred feet apart and offer almost identical views. The Marsh Trail does not enter the marsh and you'll want to explore the far end of the Ridge Trail whichever path you take. These are extremely easy walks and and side trips require little effort.

The marsh, on Clear Lake's edge, is home to ducks, grebes, coots and hawks, as well as bald eagles. Clear Lake, not visible from the park, is the largest natural Lake entirely within California. Cache Creek, passed shortly, is the lake's main outlet and empties into the Sacramento River.

Aside from birds, garter snakes, toads, muskrat, fox, beaver and other animals inhabit the vast wetlands. Its rushes and sedges are breeding grounds for catfish, bass, crappie and bluegill, as well as salamanders and pond turtles.

Both the Ridge and Marsh Trails follow a low ridge rising 30 or 40 feet above the surrounding flats. The ridge is covered with rock outcrops and scattered brush, blue oaks and valley oaks.

Where the two paths meet at the far end, double back up to the old barns. Several rocks in the vicinity contain Indian petroglyphs, or scratched designs. They are difficult to see, however, due to lichen and moss. Look for wooden stakes and metal survey markers downhill from where the two trails unite to form the Cache Creek Trail.

Beyond the ridge, barns and petroglyphs, the trail cuts across a swampy field of grass and thistles. Five successive drought years have dried it out considerably. From there, the path skirts a couple of oxbows adjoining Cache Creek. Oxbows are old meanders left as stagnant backwaters when the creek cut across them to form a new channel. Look for ducks and cottonwoods.

The trail ends up almost bumping into the highway. Near the only access to Cache Creek's main channel, it cuts right and returns to the ranch, emerging at the windmill behind the house.

21. DORN NATURE TRAIL
(Clear Lake State Park)

Length: 1 mile
Water: None
Access: Paved highway
Season: All
Difficulty: Easy
Elevation: 1400 to 1500 feet
Use: Hikers only
Ownership: Clear Lake State Park
Phone: (707) 279-4293

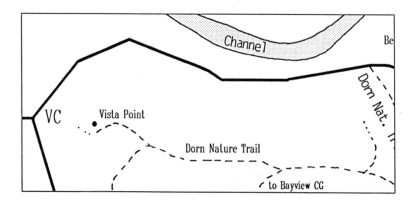

Directions: From the San Francisco area, take Hwy 29 past Lower Lake to Soda Bay Road. From I-5, take Hwy 20 west from Williams to Hwy 53. Follow 53 south to 29 and turn right. From Hwy 101, take Hwy 20 from Calpella or Hwy 175 from Hopland and turn right on 29. From Lower Lake on 29, turn right on Soda Bay Road and continue to the park entrance. From Kelseyville, take Main Street to Gaddy Road (both left), and turn right on Soda Bay Road. Drive through the park to the swimming area and walk up the gated road in winter. In summer, park at Lower Bayview Campground. The trailhead is at the far end of the campground, on the right. A $5 day use fee is assessed in summer.

While the Dorn trail may be too short for this book, it offers an opportunity to discuss Clear Lake, the largest natural body of water entirely within California. The park brochure claims the trail is 3 miles long. Although they're undoubtedly correct, I estimated less than a mile from the Lower Bayview Campground to the Lake Overlook.

A couple other things in the brochure didn't jibe. Its trail diagram seemed to bear little relationship to what I encountered on the ground. Also, Soda Bay Road, shown as Hwy 128, is actually Hwy 281.

An explanation of the area begins well away from the park, on Hwy 29. It's impossible not to notice the immense, domed peak towering above the lake's south shore. The peak is 4200 Mt. Konocti, principal summit of the Clear Lake volcanic area. Dating back only a couple million years, it is considered dormant rather than extinct.

The tiny Clear Lake volcanic area is unrelated to and much younger than the Sonoma volcanic area immediately south, whose highest point is Mt. St. Helena. It is also unrelated to any other California volcanic areas.

A lava flow across Cache Creek, the lake's main outlet to the Sacramento River, contributed to the lake's formation. So did a great landslide which blocked its original drainage westward into the Russian River. The lake today flows into both the Sacramento and Russian Rivers, the latter much more than the former.

Highway 20 from I-5 to Clear Lake, winds through a beautiful canyon dotted with valley oak and redbud. It's particularly lovely in spring. At one point, the road crosses a low pass. Although creeks paralleling the road flow in opposite directions on either side of the pass, both end up in Cache Creek.

The area between Clear Lake Oaks and Lower Lake ranks among the nation's most productive mercury mining areas. Mercury concentrates in sediments just beneath the periphery of volcanic regions.

Soda Bay Road from Hwy 29 skirts Mt. Konocti, then turns west along the lake. The north facing south shore here is steep, rocky and densely forested. Quaint houses clutter the hillsides, giving a European look.

The road passes a large peninsula jutting almost across the lake. The peninsula is the only south shore locale free of volcanic overburden. Beyond, Soda Bay, named for an underwater carbonated spring of volcanic origin, laps against Clear Lake State Park's east shore.

Before hitting the Dorn Trail, stop at the much shorter Indian Nature Trail, just past the entrance booth and park office. The short, self guiding path interprets local vegetation and Pomo, Miwok and Wintuk Indian culture. Stop also at the visitor center, if it's open. The building and grounds are exquisite.

The Dorn Nature Trail is riddled with trailheads. Since the path winds all over the park peninsula, doubling back on itself a couple times, it's difficult to get lost. For the most straightforward route, I suggest starting at the Lower Bayview Campground. The road to the campground is gated at the swimming area in winter. If so, park and walk up the road ¼ mile. The trailhead is just past the campground, on the right.

To reach the Lake Overlook from the Lower Bayview trailhead, turn left at the first junction, where the sign says "To Upper Bayview." At the next junction, turn right on the Dorn Trail. A short jog downhill to the right at the next junction, where the sign also says "Dorn Trail," leads to The Overlook. The Overlook's rocky knob, amid woods of valley oak, bay laurel and manzanita, is neither the trail nor the park's highest point.

The view is excellent, however. The 70 square mile lake, with a surface elevation of 1320 feet, dominates, of course. Below to the left, the visitor center is nestled on a grassy flat between two creeks. Beyond, low lying hardwood forests spread westward along the shore. Behind that, farm and ranch land, mountains and volcanoes reach to the horizon.

Forests in the the Clear Lake basin are typical of the inland Sierra Nevada, Klamath and Mendocino Mountains and differ from those of the coastal mountains and Bay Area. Blue oak, tanoak, Bishop pine and redwood stop at the basin's western and southern boundary. They are replaced by ponderosa pine, juniper, incense cedar and sugar pine. Douglas-fir, black oak and valley oak grow in all areas.

In summer, cap your hike off with a quick swim, although the shallow lake tends to be warm and algae filled. Fishing for bluegill, bass and crappie is superb.

22. BLIND BEACH/COASTAL TRAIL
(Sonoma Coast State Beach)

Length: 2 miles
Water: No
Access: Two lane, paved roads
Season: All
Difficulty: Easy
Elevation: 0 to 100 feet
Use: Hikers only
Ownership: Sonoma Coast St. Bch
Phone: (707) 875-3483 or 875-3382

Directions: From Hwy 101, take Hwy 116 west at Rohnert Park, south of Santa Rosa. Or take Hwy 12 from Santa Rosa, west to Hwy 116. The two roads meet at Sepastopol. Continue west on 116 to Hwy 1. Turn south on Hwy 1, over the Russian River Bridge, and proceed less than a mile to Goat Rock Road. Take Goat Rock Road to the Blind Beach parking area. The trail parallels the road to the west for ¼ mile, and may be picked up at any point prior to the parking area.

Even though the entire length of this beautiful trail can be seen from roads, the trail and road experiences differ significantly. The isolated Sonoma Coast has a unique appeal, whether explored close-up on foot or from a car window.

We suggest the 2 mile trail from Blind Beach to Shell Beach, although the same path continues another 2 miles to Wrights Beach. The Blind Beach parking area offers a spectacular view of Goat Rock, a large, grass topped sea stack at the mouth of the Russian River. Adjacent Goat Rock Beach occupies the river's south bank while the town of Jenner perches on a steep north bank hillside.

A network of trails wind down from the Blind Beach Parking area to the top of the bluffs. While fun to explore, and while they eventually join the main path, they can be a little dangerous. This is an area of gullies, washouts, much rain and high winds.

The safer main trail begins west of and immediately before the Blind Beach parking area. It parallels the road southward, crossing a couple fences via wooden stiles. About ¼ mile from the parking area, it crests over a bulbous hill. Leave the path here, for a quick side trip to the top of the large round knob. The view is stupendous.

From the knob, the huge, southward expanse of a flat, grassy terrace can be seen ending in a series of low bluffs above the beach. The trail beyond the knob swings from the road to the top of the bluffs. It is marked by a series of wooden posts in the grass. The bluffs are followed to Shell Beach.

One may, of course, begin at Shell Beach and work back to Blind Beach, but I believe the southbound route is more dramatic. Shell Beach is well marked a mile south of the Hwy 1/Goat Rock Road junction. It offers excellent tide pool observation, surf fishing and shell collecting.

The 2 miles of trail between Shell Beach and Wrights Beach follows Hwy 1 a little too closely. The path here is an old gravel road passing several houses. At Wrights Beach, the trail emerges on a gated but unsigned road at the highway turnoff. A narrow path drops from there to the beach and picnic area. Getting your car to the picnic spot costs $5 in summer.

While visiting the region, continue south from Wright's Beach, 5 miles to Bodega Head. The head is also part of Sonoma Coast State Beach.

A narrow spit of beach, a lagoon and the town of Bodega Bay adorn the head's tiny peninsula. The head itself consists of a dramatic granite outcropping with contorted cliffs dropping into the sea. Bay Flat Road leads there from Bodega Bay.

The head is an extremely compact version of Point Reyes and the lagoon and beach are actually the San Andreas Fault fracture zone. The head is composed of rock unrelated to that of the rest of the region.

23. GERSTLE COVE/COASTAL TRAIL
(Salt Point State Park)

Length: 1½ miles
Water: No
Access: Paved highway
Season: Any
Difficulty: Easy
Elevation: 0 to 150 feet
Use: Non-motorized

Ownership: Salt Point State Park
Phone: (707) 847-3221 or 865-2391

Directions: *From Hwy 101, turn west onto Hwy 12 at Santa*
Rosa. At Sebastopol, turn right onto Hwy 116 and follow it to Hwy
1. Hwy 1 may also be reached from Hwy 101 just north of
Sausalito but that route is long and very winding. Either way,
proceed north on Hwy 1 past the Salt Point Sate Park entrance.
Just beyond an open meadow, with a wide shoulder for parking,
Hwy 1 curves downhill and across a creek, to Stump Cove.

The trailhead is just beyond the meadow, at a gated road on
the left (west). There's room only for 2 or 3 cars. Parking is better
along the wide shoulder near the meadow.

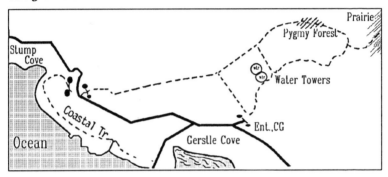

Although the gentle trail never strays far from Hwy 1, exploring
this lovely piece of the Sonoma Coast on foot yields many rewards. The road, for the most part, remains in the woods while
the path follows the shore atop low, barren bluffs dotted with grotesque rock outcroppings.

The walk ends at Salt Point and Gerstle Cove. The latter is a
shallow bay forming one of California's few underwater nature re-
serves. We recommend ending, rather than beginning at the exquisite cove because it makes a better climax than a starting
point and because there's a parking fee at that end in summer.

As with many chunks of coastal California, the story of Salt
Point is also the story of the San Andreas Fault. The famed fissure, cleaving California from the Salton Sea northward for nearly
1000 miles, disappears into the Pacific just south of San Francisco. It hits land again at Point Reyes and briefly at Bodega
Head. Its last landfall, on the Sonoma Coast, runs just east of
Salt Point State Park. Much less dramatic than at Pt. Reyes, the
fault is marked in the Sonoma area by the unnaturally straight
orientation of portions of the Garcia and Gualala Rivers. It leaves
California for good just above Point Arena.

As noted in other chapters, rock west of the fault is unrelated
to that east of the fault and correlates with material in southern
California. The white, oddly rounded outcroppings dotting the flat

tableland above the beach along this trail, are Cenozoic sand-stone similar to that at Mt. Wittenberg on the Point Reyes peninsula.

The trail is actually an old gated road, with the north end unsigned. It hits the highway a few hundred yards north of the North Trail trailhead, although the park brochure shows the two trailheads directly opposite. One may, in fact, begin by crossing the road opposite the North Trail trailhead, at the open meadow area. Follow the trail down to the main path or head to the right, towards the creek. It's difficult to become lost.

After winding past Stump Cove along Miller Creek, the route slowly swings south along the bluffs described earlier. It drops down almost to the water in a couple places. On the bluff tops, look not only for picturesque rock outcroppings but vegetation consisting largely of grass and bush lupine. I noticed a fair amount of wildlife, including rabbits, deer and a number of predator birds including osprey.

At it heads south, the path gains a little elevation, then drops back down almost to the ocean as it crosses Warren Creek. A half mile beyond, it bumps into the pavement just before the Salt Point/Gerstle Cove Parking area. The only sign marking this end of the route proclaims simply "No Dogs."

A short path leads to Salt Point from the far end of the parking lot and views of the cove may be had from just about anywhere. Snorkelers in the vegetation crammed cove can observe abalone, bull kelp, anemone, sea urchins, etc.

24. NORTH TRAIL
(Salt Point State Park)

See map, chapter 23
Length: 2½ miles
Water: No
Access: Paved highway
Season: Any
Difficulty: Moderate
Elevation: 350 to 1000 feet
Use: Non-motorized
Ownership: Salt Point State Park
Phone: (707) 847-3221 or 865-2391

Directions: *From Hwy 101 at Santa Rosa, take Hwy 12 west to Sebastopol and turn right (west) onto Hwy 116. Follow 116 to Hwy 1 at the Russian River mouth and turn north (right). Use the first park entrance, on the east side of the highway. Proceed just past the toll booth to the first parking area. Do not enter the* *campground. The trailhead is unmarked, at the east end of the parking area, at a gated fire road.*

This trail, just off the spectacular Sonoma coast, offers a quiet walk through deep woods with, unfortunately, no ocean vistas. The general forest, the pygmy forest and the upland prairie it visits, however, provides some fascinating lessons. The path's first 1½ miles also provides a fair workout.

The San Andreas Fault's northernmost landfall runs through this section of the coast, although it's less apparent than at Point Reyes or Bodega Head. The difference in rock type east and west of the fault is better observed on the grassy terrace above the beach, on the Gerstle Cove/Coastal Trail also described herein.

The recommended North Trail trailhead, at the park's east entrance, involves a toll booth and a $5 summer parking fee. The true North Trail trailhead is actually a mile north, where Hwy 1 begins a switchback down to Stump Beach Cove. That trailhead, at a gated road, is well signed, with plenty of free parking on the wide shoulder.

The trailhead from the park entrance is a mile shorter and boasts a restroom and drinking fountain. That's why we recommend it.

From the parking lot, follow the gated fire road uphill for ¼ mile, until you cross a side trail on the left. That is the first actual trail marker. Proceed straight, following arrows pointing to the "pygmy forest." A half mile farther, at a junction by two water towers, another sign directs hikers to the left for the pygmy forest. You'll return via the right hand path. From the water towers, it's ¼ mile to yet another junction, with a turn to the right.

This first mile climbs rather steeply through Douglas-fir, Bishop pine, tanoak, a few redwoods and many species in the Heath family, including madrone, azalea, evergreen huckleberry, rhododendron and manzanita.

The trail levels off 1½ miles from the trailhead and the forest changes dramatically. Such fascinating "pygmy forests" are not uncommon along the northern California coast. Trails at Vandamme and Jug Handle State Parks, described in other chapters, also visit pygmy forests. The one at Vandamme, just south of Mendocino, can be driven to.

Pygmy forests occur on level uplands near the coast, where heavy rains leech nutrients out of the soil and deposit them a few feet down in a hardpan layer. Neither tree roots nor water are able to penetrate this layer.

Trees on such areas become dwarfed, the extent of the dwarfing correlating to the depth of the hardpan. At Vandamme, trees in some parts of the pygmy forest are less than two feet tall. At Salt Point, they're closer to 10 or 20 feet tall. A break in the hardpan or a steep slope or gully enables the normal forest to resume.

Although the transition to pygmy forest is very abrupt at Salt Point, it can be much more gradual. The species composition, as well as the tree size, differs from the surroun... Bishop pine, redwood and Douglas-fir both ... pygmy forest. Rhododendron, huckleberry an... being dwarfed in the pygmy forest, seem to thriv... few golden chinkapin.

At Salt Point, cypress (probably Sargents) and l... appear confined solely to the pygmy forest. Lodgepol... ...or shore component along the Oregon coast. In Cal... ...a, its coastal occurrences are widely scattered and pretty much limited to pygmy forest areas.

The trail, as noted, levels off at the pygmy forest. Beyond, it hits a barely noticeable high point before starting gradually downhill. Two miles from the trailhead, you'll meet yet another junction. The right hand path loops back down to the water towers and the parking lot while the left hand path continues ¼ mile to the high prairie.

The prairie, while pretty, is not very interesting. Most such openings along the coast are created by fire or deliberate clearing for cattle. This one, while a fine picnic spot, is completely surrounded by forest with no views of the ocean.

To return quickly to the parking lot, double back to the last junction and follow the steep left hand path, away from the pygmy forest.

25. FERN CANYON TRAIL
(Vandamme State Park)

Length: 3¼ miles
Water: Lots
Access: Paved highway
Season: Any
Difficulty: Easy to moderate
Elevation: 50 to 550 feet
Use: Hikers only
Ownership: Vandamme State Park
Phone: (707) 937-5804

Directions: Turn onto Hwy 1 from Hwy 101 at Leggett, near the Avenue of the Giants' south end. The park is a few miles past Mendocino, just north of Little River. Follow the road from the entrance, through the campground, to the unpaved parking area. The trail follows the gated dirt road. A $5 day use fee is assessed in summer.

This is one of three state parks along the beautiful Mendocino coast featuring trails up redwood canyons. All three begin near

...ean, two lead to pygmy forests and two offer pathways named Fern Canyon Trail. Vandamme boasts both a Fern Canyon and a pygmy forest.

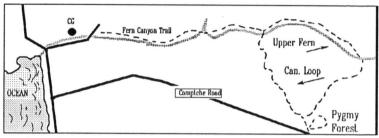

This Fern Canyon Trail, beginning at a dirt parking area, follows the deep, damp gorge for two miles. The wide path along the fern lined canyon is virtually level. Redwood, Douglas-fir, western hemlock, tanoak and alder line the beautiful, fast flowing creek and covers the hillsides. Ferns, as the name implies, decorate the rock walls and dark side canyons.

Two miles up, the trail crosses the creek and climbs steeply uphill for ¾ of a mile before leveling off. In this drier, upland area, the redwoods fade away and Bishop pines, along with a few chinkapin and other upland species, move in. Other species remain.

This upper trail is actually a loop route. 1¼ miles from the creek crossing, it meets a junction. Continue ahead for the loop's 2¼ mile far end. Turn right for a ¼ mile trek to the pygmy forest nature trail.

The short pygmy forest trail is wonderfully presented and easily reached by car. To drive there, take Hwy 1 past the park entrance to Comptche Road. The site is well marked, about 4 miles up.

The pygmy forest trail follows a raised wooden walkway through the vegetation choked, fragile, often swampy tract. Dwarf cypress, Douglas-fir, Bishop pine and lodgepole pine dominate. Huckleberry, salal, azalea and rhododendron, far from being dwarfed, seem to thrive. Redwood, while apparently absent here, will grow in such areas.

The gradual transition to pygmy forest begins on the trail from Fern Canyon. The wooden walkway, however, penetrates its most stunted area, with trees less than 2 feet high. See the North Trail/Salt Point chapter (24) for more information.

26. CANYON TRAIL
(Russian Gulch State Park)

Length: 3½ miles
Water: Gallons
Access: Paved highway
Season: All
Difficulty: Easy
Elevation: 50 to 300 feet
Use: Hikers only
Ownership: Russian Gulch State Park
Phone: (707) 937-5804

Directions: *Leave Hwy 101 at Leggett. Take Hwy 1 past Fort Bragg to the park entrance. Follow the park road under Hwy 1 and through the campground to the east end parking area. The trail follows the gated road along the creek.*

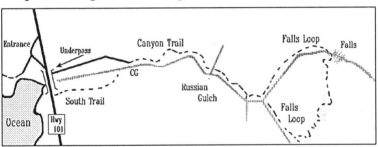

This beautiful little trail has the same name as, and is virtually identical to, the trail at Vandamme State Park, a few miles south. Some maps show Russian Gulch's Fern Canyon Trail as simply Canyon Trail. While Vandamme's Fern Canyon leads to a pygmy forest, this path ends at a lovely waterfall.

Either before or after walking the Canyon Trail, spend time on the 6/10 mile Headlands Trail, well marked near park headquarters. It explores the bluffs, rocks and tidepools around the mouth of Russian Gulch.

The paved Canyon Trail follows a dark, moist canyon for 2½ miles, amid towering redwoods, Douglas-fir, hemlock and red alder. Ferns decorate the shadiest and moistest areas, side gullies and rock outcroppings. The path winds a little while following the fast flowing creek but gains little elevation.

Western hemlock, a constant companion of redwood farther north, becomes more and more sporadic southward, fading out below Point Arena. Hemlock and tanoak are slower to invade than other species so their presence indicates a quite mature forest.

The trail's pavement ends at the junction with the Falls Loop. The left hand trail from there leads to the falls in 1 mile. The right hand route arrives in 2 miles. The shorter path remains down in the canyon while the longer climbs the hillside.

The 36 foot falls are exquisite. More of a steep cascade than a sheer drop, the water forms a beautiful pool at the base. It's a wonderful spot to linger and enjoy the Mendocino coast's secluded grandeur.

27. ECOLOGICAL STAIRCASE
(Jug Handle State Park)

Length: 4 miles
Water: Very little
Access: Paved highway
Season: Any
Difficulty: Moderately easy
Elevation: 0 to 650 feet
Use: Hikers only
Ownership: Jug Handle State Park
Phone: (707) 937-5804

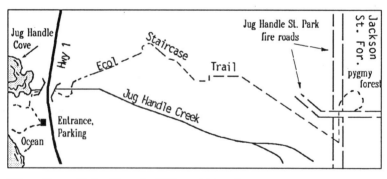

Directions: *Take Hwy 1 off Hwy 101 at Leggett. Continue past Fort Bragg to the park entrance. The trailhead is to the right of a large interpretive sign.*

This is among the most interesting and best presented, if longest, self-guided nature trails I've encountered. Before starting out, stop at the headquarters building and invest 25 cents in a guide brochure. Since it is essential to the trail, I won't repeat the information therein other than to summarize the subjects covered.

Both guide and trail interpret the geology and ecology of a series of marine terraces rising above the Pacific. In this extremely geologically active region, the terraces are composed of sediments once on the ocean bottom. The brochure's explanation of this, and of the changing ecology from level to level, is outstanding. Equally outstanding is its discussion of coastal pygmy forests. The path ends at such a forest.

Finding the trailhead is a little complicated, although not difficult. From the parking lot, walk over to the interpretive display. There, take the trail to the right, leading to the bluffs above the creek mouth.

Spend a few minutes at Jug Handle Cove, with its low cliffs, beach and windswept Monterey pines, Bishop pines and Sitka spruces. The bumpy-coned, yellowish Monterey pines are not native to the area. You're standing about a mile short of the southernmost extent of Sitka spruce's range.

Instead of hiking down to the beach, follow the trail along the bluffs and under the highway bridge. From there, the path drops steeply to the creek, crosses a pretty little foot bridge, and climbs up the far side. The route then swings east and takes off in earnest.

I was surprised to encounter grand fir along this trail. While the brochure didn't find their presence unusual, I've observed them nowhere else along the California Coast.

This low and middle elevation species is a principal western Oregon forest associate. In the Klamath Mountains, and down the main Mendocino crest, it interbreeds with Sierra white fir. Along the California and Washington coasts, the species becomes an extremely minor component. Its southward range extends to Sonoma County.

The fact that I'd never before seen a grand fir in redwood country emphasizes a basic rule of ecology: Never infer anything from the absence of a species. Or, just because you don't see it, that doesn't mean its not there.

The trail guide also refers to "Bolander pine" which, it suggests, grows only in pygmy forests. This sent me scurrying to the reference books. Bolander pine, it turns out, is an archaic name for lodgepole pine. This tree, while extremely widespread throughout the Rockies and West Coast, is indeed confined to pygmy forests in this area.

The Staircase Trail climbs for 3 miles beyond the bridge. The ascent is gradual, for the most part, with a few steep spots. Beyond a large, coyote brush fringed meadow above the creek crossing, it enters the woods and pretty much remains there.

The upland trail, well above Jug Handle Creek, runs largely out of the redwoods, although they are far from absent. For the most part, you'll find Bishop pine, Douglas-fir, tanoak, hemlock and alder. The path's first half is fairly densely wooded while the latter portion gradually transitions to pygmy forest.

The trail runs into a dirt road 3 miles from the trailhead. To continue, turn left along the road and follow the signs to the pygmy forest loop. The road marks the state park boundary and the loop lies within in Jackson State Forest.

See the North Trail chapter for more discussion of pygmy forests.

28. LOOKOUT TRAIL
(Standish-Hickey State Park)

Length: 1½ miles
Water: No
Access: Paved highway
Season: May—October
Difficulty: Moderate
Elevation: 950 to 1600 feet
Use: Hikers only
Ownership: Standish-Hickey State Park
Phone: (707) 925-6482 or 946-2311

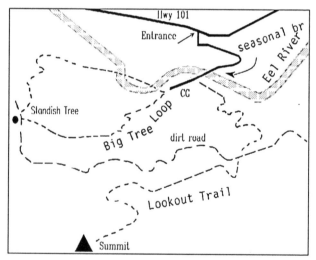

Directions: *Turn off Hwy 101 at the park entrance, just north of Leggett. Proceed past the entrance gate, down the hill to the river and over the bridge to Redwood Campground. The trailhead is on the left, just across the river. Continue into the campground, bearing right, to the day use parking area, and walk back to the trailhead.*

A $5 parking fee is assessed in summer. While this is a little steep, the hike down to the trailhead from the entrance station is *even steeper, should you choose to cut expenses by walking into the park.*

Of the parks lining the Avenue of the Giants region along the Eel River, Standish-Hickey focuses most closely on the river itself. Among California's most scenic waterways, the unpredictable Eel cuts a wide, steep sided gorge from the Yolla Bolly Wilderness, through the rugged redwood country, to Eureka's Humboldt Bay.

The blue/green river, with its wide banks and towering bluffs, cuts a particularly deep, curvy swath through Standish-Hickey. Nearby Humboldt Redwoods State Park contains more river frontage but the canyon there is much more benign.

Standish-Hickey's Lookout Trail offers a somewhat strenuous workout leading to a panorama of the Eel River redwood country. The path is a compact version of the Grasshopper Trail at Humboldt Redwoods. While the latter reaches a 3300 foot summit in 6 miles, Standish-Hickey's offering attains its 1600 foot overlook in a much easier 1½ miles.

The Eel's dominance becomes apparent just past the park entrance when the road drops over a huge bluff to the river's gravel banks. Opposite, Redwood Campground occupies a shaded flat beneath a handsome redwood grove.

All the park's bridges spanning the Eel are taken down in winter, rendering the path inaccessible. On a February visit once, the tiny bridge was pulled up onto the far bank. It didn't look like it would reach even ⅕ of the way across the raging waters. Fortunately, the river drops dramatically in summer. It can also rise dramatically in winter, as the high water marks from the infamous 1964 flood, painted on the cliffs above Hwy 101, attest.

From the trailhead, the path follows the river a short distance, climbing along the edge of a high bluff. The already outstanding views improve as the route turns inland and inscribes a series of steep switchbacks up the shaded hillside.

Things level off somewhat above the Page and Gates logging road, although the path remains fairly steep. The next mile wanders up a ridge, through the upland redwood/Douglas-fir forest blanketing much of northwest California. There are few vistas here.

Eventually, the trail enters private property, amid horizons expanded by logging clear cuts. The summit offers a commanding overview. Although the actual river is not visible, the canyon, Hwy 101, and the open flats of the Leggett Valley can be seen below.

29. BIG TREE TRAIL
(Standish-Hickey State Park)

Length: 1 to 3 miles (2 to 6 mile loop)

Water: Some
Access: Paved highway
Season: May thr. Oct.
Difficulty: Moderate
Elevation: 950 to 1500 feet
Use: Hikers only
Ownership: Standish-Hickey State Park
Phone: (707) 925-6482 or 946-3211

Directions: Turn off Hwy 101 at the park entrance, immediately north of Leggett. Inside the park, proceed straight, taking the steep road down to the Eel River. Cross the river to Redwood Campground and follow the roads to the right, to the parking area. The trailhead is well marked at the parking area.

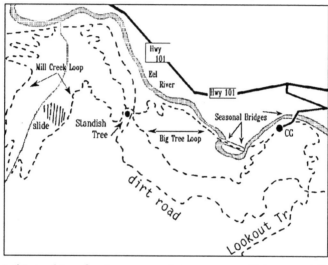

A $5 parking fee is assessed in summer. This recent fee increase can be avoided by parking on the highway and walking into the park. Nevertheless, I suggest paying it. It's a very steep, avoidable hike down the bluffs to the trailhead. On a hot day, you'll need to save your energy.

The Eel River ranks high among California's scenic experiences. From the Yolla Bolly Mountains, through the rugged Avenue of the Giants redwood country, to its gaping mouth at Eureka's Humboldt Bay, it cuts a spectacular, if unpredictable, swath. The river is noted for fast flowing, blue/green water and wide banks imprisoned within steep, unstable walls.

Most state parks along the Avenue of the Giants are centered around the Eel and Hwy 101 largely follows its course. The canyon through Standish-Hickey State Park is particularly deep and curvy and many park trails explore its bluffs and beaches.

Past the entrance area, the park road descends a sheer bluff to a gravel bank below. The road is gated in winter, when the bridge across the river is removed. From the entrance area during a February visit, I could see the span pulled up on the far shore. It was difficult to imagine it crossing the immense waterway.

Fortunately, the river drops dramatically in summer. The bridge is then laid across, providing access to the main park trails and to Redwood Campground, situated in a lovely redwood grove at the water's edge.

From the day use parking lot, follow the Big Tree Trail a few hundred feet to a junction and take the left fork. The path parallels the river a short way, then climbs the steep bank into the Redwood/Douglas-fir forest blanketing the region's vast upland areas. This section offers outstanding river views. The gentle ascent, with a few steep spots, follows a ridge past a couple side creeks.

This loop trail's far side is rejoined after a mile, just below the Page and Gates logging road. The Miles Standish Tree towers from inside a log fence, at the edge of a meadow above the road.

The 221 foot redwood is the park's largest. Its namesake, the famous Pilgrim, lived in Massachusetts in the 1600's and probably never heard of the Eel River. The Standish family, donors of much of the park's land (along with the Hickey family) did, however.

From the Standish Tree, follow the loop's other leg back to the parking area. If you're in an energetic, exploring mood, the much more strenuous, 4 mile Mill Creek Loop begins at the Standish Tree.

For this route, continue around the tree fence and up the road to the left. The route crosses the meadow and enters the woods, climbing steadily to an immense landslide above Mill Creek. It then drops abruptly to the creek and climbs just as abruptly up the far slope to the trail's highest point.

Mill Creek, like the Eel, courses through a lovely, narrow canyon. Crossing is rarely a problem in summer but the water can rise significantly. Beyond Mill Creek, the path follows a high ridge, then plunges steeply back down to the river. It emerges near the creek mouth at Page and Gate Road.

Either return to the Standish Tree via the road or turn right, just past the creek mouth, back onto the Mill Creek Loop. The latter is a little steep at first but runs for a considerable distance through the large, open Big Tree Meadow.

From the Standish Tree, the Big Tree Trail's return fork swings down to the river and follows the shore through Cabin Meadow. The path soon runs out of room as it bumps into a perpendicular bluff.

Fortunately, a redwood log spans the river here, leading to the swimming area at Hickey Campground. Another log bridge, anchored at the opposite end of the little gravel peninsula, quickly takes you back across to your car.

30. TANOAK SPRINGS TRAIL
(Richardson Grove State Park)

Length: 2 miles (4 mi. loop)
Water: Plenty
Access: Four lane highway
Season: All seasons
Difficulty: Moderate
Elevation: 600 to 1500 feet
Use: Hikers only
Ownership: Richardson State Park
Phone: (707) 247-3318 or 946-2311

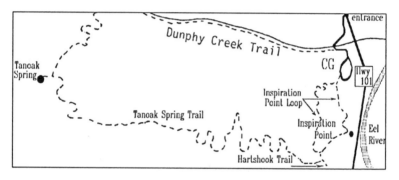

Directions: *Leave Hwy 101 at the Richardson Grove exit, just north of Leggett. From the entrance, follow the main park road past the office and over Dunphy Creek to the Madrone Campground. Take the right hand campground loop road to the second restroom. The trailhead sign, which says "Lookout Point Trail," is on the right, near the restroom sign. It may be necessary to park away from the trailhead to avoid a campground fee.*

The other end of the loop trail starts just past the park office, where the pavement curves across Dunphy Creek. It, too is well marked.

This pleasant loop, through the redwoods above the Eel River, offers an interlude of relaxation and exercise in the famous Avenue of the Giants recreation area.

I started by the restroom, at the Lookout Point trailhead, since passing a major highlight early on tends to motivate me. On the other hand, much can said for ending the loop, rather than beginning it, at the restroom trailhead, with its wash basins and drinking fountain.

Presuming you begin, not end, at the campground restroom, follow the Lookout Point Trail 50 feet or so to the junction with the Lookout Point loop's return end. Stay left and continue 1/3 of a mile to Lookout Point.

This first segment sidehills gently up from the campground amid soaring redwood and Douglas-fir, along with much smaller tanoak, bay laurel and huckleberry. The sparse understory probably results from the dense forest canopy. Fairly recent looking fire scars on the larger trees, however, offer another clue regarding the lack of understory.

After climbing through a fern-lined gully, the path passes Lookout Point, with its vista southward of the Eel River canyon. The view isn't very wide and the spot, atop the river bluffs, looks like it was hacked from the dense surrounding vegetation. I'm sure the opening is natural, of course.

Beyond Lookout Point, the path climbs a little more steeply. In 1/4 mile, the Hartsook Trail comes in on the left. Follow it a couple hundred feet to where the Tanoak Springs Trail takes off to the right. The next 1/2 mile is the trail's steepest, but at least you're finally on the right path.

Above the Hartsook junction, the Tanoak Springs Trail inscribes a series of switchbacks to the ridge top. The forest thins considerably here and the redwoods fade out in the thinner soil. The ridge top woods of Douglas-fir, oak and madrone continues unbroken, however. There are no panoramas beyond Lookout Point.

The path gradually tops out and, 1 1/4 miles from the trailhead, slowly starts back down. Tanoak Springs, the far end of the loop, lies at the 2 mile point.

While not spectacular, the spring offers a satisfactory destination. Water volume varies depending on the season but rarely exceeds a trickle. The little mud hole, nestled in a wooded depression, is surrounded by tules, cattails and bulrushes.

Look for the junction with the Dunphy Creek Trail just before the springs. It's 2 miles to the Dunphy Creek trailhead and 1/4 mile (or less) along the road from there back to the restroom.

The Dunphy Creek route drops rather sharply at first, down a large, wooded gully to Dunphy Creek. There it levels off, following the wide creek through the heart of Richardson Grove's redwood stand. You might consider starting, not finishing, with the beautiful, tranquil, 1 3/4 mile creek walk.

31. USAL CAMP/LOST COAST TRAIL
(Sinkyone Wilderness State Park)

Length: 5 miles
Water: Lots
Access: Narrow, dirt road
Season: All
Difficulty: Moderately difficult
Elevation: 0 to 1100 feet
Use: Hikers only
Ownership: Sinkyone State Park
Phone: (707) 986-7711 or 946-2311

Directions: Take Hwy 101 to Leggett. Turn onto Hwy 1 and proceed to County Road 431, at mile post 90.88. The turnoff can be a little difficult to find and the sign tends to disappear. Turn right (north) up the narrow dirt road and follow it 6 miles to Usal Camp. Past the park boundary, proceed over the bridge and into the campground. The trailhead is well marked in the campground, at a large bulletin board.

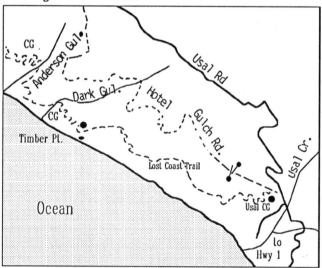

The 16 mile Lost Coast Trail, between Bear Harbor and Usal Camp, may be the scenic blockbuster of the California Coast. The 4.3 miles south from Bear Harbor, which passes a couple superlative redwood stands, is a little easier going than the path north from Usal Camp. The 5 mile northward trek from Usal Camp, discussed here, is easier to reach by car but the trail is steeper and rises to over 1000 feet. In either case, temperatures rarely rise above 70 degrees, even when it's over 100 immediately inland.

Just finding Usal Road from Hwy 1 is an accomplishment. The sign marking the unobtrusive intersection tends to disappear. Bear in mind that the spot where Hwy 1 visually—and dramatically—bumps into the ocean and swings sharply left, is 5 miles from where it appears to do so on the map. That's because the road parallels the ocean before meeting it, through a sheltered valley ⅛ mile inland.

Usal Road takes off where Hwy 1 enters the valley, just before the town of Rockport. The ocean's proximity is immediately apparent as the dirt road climbs the bluffs and peers down on the beach. The six mile route is muddy in winter and a 4x4 may be required. In summer, it can be a little intimidating as it's very narrow, winding and steep in spots. But a passenger car should make it easily.

The road to Usal Camp offers an outstanding scenic drive. After snaking in, out, up and down through the woods for a several miles, it comes out on a ridge, 800 feet above the ocean, with a commanding view of Usal Creek and the cliffs of the Lost Coast. The last mile descends to the Usal Camp area.

Beyond the Usal Creek bridge but before the campground, a beach access road takes off left, through a wide meadow. Immediately past the campground, the gated Hotel Gulch Road takes off north. For variety, consider returning on this road/trail. Horses, banned from the Lost Coast Trail, are permitted on Hotel Gulch Road, marked as the "horse trail."

From Usal Camp, the Lost Coast Trail climbs 500 feet in its first mile, in a series of switchbacks, to the ridge between the ocean and Hotel Gulch. From here north, except at creek crossings, the path follows the crest of an astonishing series of cliffs and bluffs, some of which drop almost perpendicularly, over 1000 feet, into the surf.

If you get the feeling that powerful forces created this area, you're right. The King Range/Sinkyone area is among the West Coast's most geologically active. Observing the abrupt, soaring cliffs and jagged peaks, it's easy to imagine the westward moving continental plate smashing into and over the east moving Pacific sea floor.

For the next 1½ miles, the path proceeds with only minor ups and downs. It hits the bluff rim here and there and occasionally wanders into the Douglas-fir and redwood forest. Mostly, however, it crosses steep, open grassy prairies. Between mile 2½ and 3, it gains another 500 feet elevation, topping out at 1100 feet.

Between mile 3 and Timber Point, the path levels off and Hotel Gulch Road can be seen up the hill in several places. To reach it for an alternate return loop, cut cross country. The road crests about 200 feet higher than the trail, then drops into Hotel Gulch for its last 1½ miles.

Timber Point rises 1000 feet above the ocean and Dark Creek. Despite its name, the area has been logged off, leaving the vista unobscured.

From Timber Point, the path abruptly drops into Dark Creek over a series of sharp switchbacks. It bottoms out fairly high above the Pacific. Beyond Dark Creek, the route contours at the 300 foot level for the final ½ mile to Anderson Gulch.

The recommended day-hike ends at Anderson Creek's lovely but seldom used campground. Well inland (¼ mile), it's possible, if a bit wet and rocky, to follow the creek to a black sand beach. The campground occupies a small meadow in a narrow canyon.

Immediately past Anderson Gulch, the path rises 900 feet in ½ mile. We suggest you come prepared to spend the night if you plan to proceed from here.

Fogged in Lost Coast/Sinkyone, view from Usal Road.(Ch.31)

32. BEAR HARBOR/LOST COAST TRAIL
(Sinkyone Wilderness State Park)

Length: 4¼ miles
Water: Lots
Access: Very narrow, steep, winding dirt road

Season: Any
Difficulty: Moderate
Elevation: 0 to 800 feet
Use: Hikers only
Ownership: Sinkyone State Park
**Phone: (707) 986-7711 or
946-2311**

*Directions: Leave Hwy
101 at Garberville or
Redway and proceed west
through Redway, towards
Briceland and Shelter Cove.
Beyond Briceland, follow
the signs to Whitethorn.
The pavement ends just
past Whitethorn. A few
miles farther, at Four
Corners, a road marked
"steep and winding" takes
off left. Follow this route
(trailers and motor homes
not advised), to the Needle
Rock area. See the text
below for further trailhead
directions.*

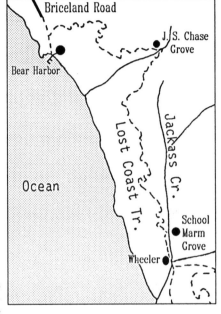

No other trail in this
book provides such an en-
joyable trailhead drive. The
plunging roller coaster road, barely more than a car width wide,
circles wildly from a wooded ridge, 1400 feet above the ocean, to a
secluded ranch on a grassy terrace near the beach. The drive isn't
for everyone and can be treacherous in wet weather. I found it the
height of exhilaration.

The ranch is now a small state park visitor center. Nearby
trails lead to the beach, the bluffs overlooking Needle Rock and
north to Whale Gulch (see the Needle Rock/Lost Coast Trail
chapter). The visitor center volunteer was exceptionally friendly.

Past the ranch, the road is barred by an imposing gate, a sign
saying the road is washed out 1.4 miles ahead and another sign
informing that it's 2.7 miles to Bear Harbor. The gate isn't locked
and the washout consists of an easily forded, 3 foot wide stream.

The drive from Needle Rock to Bear Harbor continues narrow
and winding but is better than the road down from Four Corners.
After a second unlocked gate and the creek crossing, the road
takes a short, steep, rutted uphill run. Beyond, it's clear sailing
to the grassy trailhead area, ¼ mile from Bear Harbor.

The short, charming path to Bear Harbor passes several campsites along a eucalyptus lined creek. Bear Harbor itself consists of a sheltered, grass and alder cove with a little footbridge across the creek. Masses of domestic flowers and vines cover the site. The main trail takes off inland, to the left, just before the bridge.

From Bear Harbor, the path follows a deep gulch uphill for ½ mile, then circles back to the bluff tops, at an elevation of about 700 feet. This is the path's steepest section. The views south are breathtaking.

The trail's highlight comes a mile farther down, where it again cuts inland, maintaining a level contour to Dyers Gulch. This wide canyon contains probably the area's most impressive redwood grove.

South of the grove, the route swings back towards the coast, occasionally meeting the cliff edge, occasionally winding back into the woods, occasionally traversing grassy prairies. Some 3½ miles from the traihead, it drops 500 feet in a series of switchbacks, to the East Fork of Jackass Creek. Running through the East Fork's School Marm Redwood Grove, the path follows the creek to Wheeler Camp, on Jackass Creek proper.

The remnants of an old sawmill and town can be seen at Wheeler. The mill was active from 1950 to 1960. Immediately beyond, Hotel Gulch Road's north terminus joins the trail.

Past the road junction, the trail follows the creek almost to the beach before swinging south along some low bluffs. We recommend the beach below Wheeler as a turnaround spot for day-hikers.

It's almost 12 miles from Wheeler to the trail's southern anchor at Usal Camp (See the Usal Camp/Lost Coast Trail chapter). The route north from Usal is steeper, much more difficult and more dramatic than that south from Bear Harbor, cresting at 1100 feet. It's also easier to reach but lacks the Bear Harbor segment's redwood groves.

For high drama, of course, the towering cliffs south (and north) of Bear harbor compare favorably to virtually any area of the California Coast. Among the Pacific rim's most geologically active areas, the advancing continental plate riding up and over the opposingly advancing ocean floor is easily pictured in the King Range/Sinkyone/Lost Coast region. The power of the land-sea collision is obvious.

33. NEEDLE ROCK/LOST COAST TRAIL
(Sinkyone Wilderness State Park)

Length: 2¾ miles
Water: OK
Access: Very long, steep dirt road

Season: Any
Difficulty: Easy
Elevation: 0 to 200 ft
Use: Hikers only
Ownership: Sinkyone St Pk
Phone: (707) 986-7711 or
946-3211

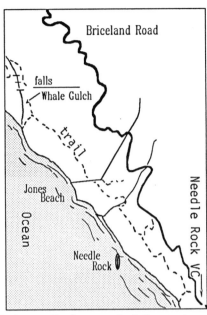

*Directions: Take Hwy 101
to Redway or Garberville
and proceed through
Redway towards Briceland
and Shelter Cove. Turn left
past Briceland, at the
Whitethorn turnoff. The
pavement ends just beyond
Whitethorn. A few miles
later, take a soft left at the
junction at the top of the hill,
onto the road marked "steep
and winding." Motor homes
and trailers are not advised.*
The trailhead is well marked, between the barn and visitor center
at Needle Rock.

On a map of California, the massive coastline bulge south of
Eureka and west of the Avenue of the Giants, appears empty and
inaccessible. Several roads penetrate the area, however. While a
couple roads are of surprisingly high quality, most are long, winding and poor. From any road, the King Range/Sinkyone/Lost
Coast region ranks among the Golden State's remote spots.

The towering Lost Coast cliffs and the ruggedness of the King
Range's peaks affirms that this may be California's most geologically active area. Nearly perpendicular bluffs rise 1000 feet from
the water in places. Nearby Kings Peak soars to over 4000 feet
within 3 miles of the coast.

Several circumstances account for the region's drama. First,
Cape Mendocino, California's westernmost point, lies just north.
From Cape Mendocino, the immense Mendocino Fracture Zone
projects into the sea. It ends well past Hawaii. The entire California coast to the south pivots around this fracture zone. The
equally active San Andreas Fault lies just offshore and is believed
by some to hit land briefly at Shelter Cove, just north of the Needle Rock area.

It's also easy to imagine the Lost Coast resulting from a collision between the westward advancing continent and the eastward
moving ocean subfloor. This is an oversimplification, of course, as
the continental mass extends offshore for several miles.

I found the roller coaster ride into Needle Rock extremely exhilarating. From a wooded intersection at 1500 feet elevation, the narrow, dirt route careens down like a party streamer, ending at a secluded ranch. Perched atop a low, grassy terrace, the ranch house is now a state park visitor center.

The Needle Rock/Lost Coast trailhead is well posted between the barn and the house. Before heading out, walk to the edge of the bluff for a view of needle rock and the coast. Whale Gulch, this chapter's destination, is clearly visible 2½ miles north. There, the terrace ends and 800 foot sea cliffs shoot upward.

The actual trail begins back towards the trailhead from the Needle Rock vista point. Its northward journey starts with a plunge into a ravine and up the other side. At the bottom, it's a few hundred feet to a black (and brown) sand beach. The next mile passes similar gullies and creeks.

At Jones Beach Camp, 1 mile from the trailhead, a short path leads down the creek to the beach. North of Jones Beach, the trail cuts inland for ½ mile, following the alder lined Whale Gulch Creek. The creek parallels the coast here, separated from it by a low, narrow ridge.

At the ridge's far end, a side trail climbs through a narrow gap down to Whale Gulch Beach, a pretty little sandy cove. This, for all intents and purposes, is the end of the trail.

It's possible, with some difficulty, to continue along the main trail into Whale Gulch's narrow, rocky gorge. Less than ¼ mile up, the creek drops over a 30 foot waterfall. The path however, clings to the canyon 100 feet overhead and the falls cannot be seen. Attempts to view the falls could lead to serious injury.

Shortly beyond the falls, the path bumps into the creek and dead ends. The map, however, shows the trail crossing the creek and climbing out of the canyon in a series of switchbacks. While the State Park District Office assured me that the trail was completed from Whale Gulch to Chemise Mountain and Shelter Cove, the Ranger at Sinkyone claims they're in error. Theoretically, one could, with considerable uphill scrambling, connect with the northward path. This is not recommended.

34. KING CREST TRAIL
(King Range Nat. Conservation Area)

Length: 2½ miles
Water: No
Access: Long, very poor, unpaved roads
Season: Any, but be aware of the snow line
Difficulty: Difficult
Elevation: 3000 to 4087 feet

Use: Hikers only
Ownership: BLM
Phone: (707) 822-7648

Directions: Leave Hwy 101 at Redway or Garberville and cross the Eel River to Redway, following signs to Briceland and ShelterCove. Five miles before Shelter Cove, turn right at the summit of the 25 mile, paved, 2 lane road. From there, follow signs along Horse Mountain and Saddle Mountain Roads, pointing to Kings Peak and the King Crest Trail.

Five miles up the well graded, dirt Horse Mountain Road, turn left and proceed 7 miles on

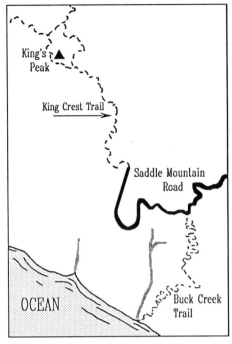

Saddle Mountain Road. These last miles are very narrow and winding. Littered with rocks and boulders, they contain steep upgrades with loose, gravely surfaces. Only 4 or 5 cars may be squeezed into the trailhead.

Throughout my trail excursions, I've noted what I call "ultimate hikes." Thus, the Caribou Lakes Trail was singled out as the ultimate northwest California glacial lake trail, while the Mt. Shasta/Horse Camp Trail is the ultimate high mountain trek. Until Kings Peak, however, my quest for the ultimate coastal trail had been frustrated.

Kings Peak, reached via the King Crest Trail, is America's loftiest coastal promontory. One can stand atop this mountain and curl their toes over the edge of a steep gully. A step forward would result in a 4087 foot tumble into the Pacific.

The peak projects from the coast's most remote back country. The King Range National Conservation Area hides 25 miles due west of the popular Avenue of the Giants section of Hwy 101. Shelter Cove, at the range's southern end, is reached by a reasonably good, paved road. After conquering Kings Peak, Shelter Cove, highlighted by the aptly named Black Sands Beach, offers a lovely place to unwind, picnic or camp.

A dispute exists as to whether a rift zone across the Shelter Cove peninsula is the last land fall of the San Andreas Fault. Although the rift moved significantly during the 1906 San Francisco earthquake, much of it was vertical. The San Andreas Fault, responsible for the quake, is noted for exclusively horizontal movement. Also, Shelter Cove is not aligned with the main fault. Most geologists consider this a side fault of the San Andreas.

The dirt road north from the Shelter Cove winds through logging areas and past a couple small BLM campgrounds. Ocean views from 2000 to 3000 feet up add a special quality. Extensive tracts adjacent to the road burned in the 1987 forest fires.

Glimpses of Kings Peak pop up in the drive's middle section. Farther up, Saddle Mountain completely blocks it. Saddle Mountain's round, forested, roaded profile contrasts with Kings Peak's pointed, brushy, deeply gullied summit.

Like most northern California coastal mountains, the King Range is composed of graywacke, a beige sandstone lacking bedding planes. The range, possibly the West Coast's most geologically active, has risen 66 feet in the last 6000 years. This also ranks among California's rainiest spots, although summers are hot and arid and the area is extremely fire prone.

The last few miles to the trailhead are pretty bad. Four wheel drive, or at least high ground clearance, is very helpful, if not essential. You may run into snow in winter, although the typical snowline lies well above the trailhead's 3000 foot elevation.

Just reaching the remote trailhead is a major accomplishment. From there, the trail drops several hundred feet, crossing the saddle between Saddle Mountain and adjacent Kings Peak. The first mile is forested with Douglas-fir, tanoak, madrone and canyon liveoak. The elevation, a little too high for redwood, is near tanoak and madrone's upper limit as well.

The eroded, chaparral covered south face of Kings Peak soon appears through the woods. At the saddle where the path begins its relentless climb, peer down Shipman Creek Canyon to the blue ocean.

The entire trail seems laid out to dramatize the unfolding panorama. Only the coast to the northeast cannot be seen prior to the summit. The best views are southwest and east. After emerging from the woods, the steep trail cuts through dense fields of manzanita and whitethorn ceanothus. Douglas-fir pops up here and there, especially on the shadier north slope.

I noted much brush overhanging the trail, so be careful. Whitethorn spines can put your eye out. The trail soon loops over the ridge and around to the north side. A little rockier and less brushy than the south face, the trail grows ever steeper in this section. Making the hike in February, I encountered much snow. In the form of lingering patches on the trail bed, it fortunately didn't obscure the route.

Tightroping along snowbank tops, however, increased the difficulty. A half-mile from the summit, atop the ridge, the Maple Camp Trail peels off to the right. The main path then swings again to the north slope. Several hundred yards from the top, another side trail takes off to the right.

It is 3 horizontal miles from the top of Kings Peak to the ocean. The gully tumbling from the summit to the water culminates in Big Flat Creek. For its final ½ mile, the creek meanders through an extremely isolated sand flat.

North of the summit, the coastal view is blocked by the remainder of the jagged King Range. The vista south, of the Sinkyone/Lost Coast area, is spectacular.

On my February visit, an endless row of snowcapped peaks adorned the eastern horizon. Highest and most obvious (I think), was Leech Lake Mountain, a 6500 foot upwelling just west of the Yolla Bolly Wilderness. Mt. Solomon and South Yolla Bolly, inside the Wilderness, are also visible. The southernmost snow capped peak, Snow Mountain, caps the Snow Mountain Wilderness west of Willows.

On the return hike, the trail forks a few hundred feet before the trailhead. Take the upper route, to the right, or you may end up lost somewhere on Big Flat Creek.

35. BUCK CREEK TRAIL
(King Range Conservation Area)

See map, chapter 34
Length: 2½ miles
Water: No
Access: Very long, poor dirt roads
Season: Any (but note snow line)
Difficulty: Very difficult (up-hill)
Elevation: 0 to 3200 feet
Use: Non-motorized only
Ownership: BLM
Phone: (707) 822-7648

Directions: Leave Hwy 101 at Redway or Garberville and proceed west on the paved, 2 lane Shelter Cove Road. Five miles before Shelter Cove, turn right (north) onto the dirt Horse Mountain Road, following signs to Kings Peak and the King Crest Trail. They'll eventually lead up Saddle Mountain Road to a well marked, cramped trailhead.

There's not much to be said about this trail except that it's steep—steeper by far than any other in this book. Fortunately, with a little car juggling, one can avoid the uphill portion of the hike.

The imposing King Range, elaborated on in the King Crest Trail chapter, ranks among California's ruggedest, most remote and most geologically active areas. Kings Peak, immediately north of Buck

Creek, soars 4000 feet above the beach in a scant 3 miles. This is the West's steepest coastal rise.

The drive to the trailhead is remarkable. Many locations on Horse Mountain and Saddle Mountain Roads peer 3000 feet down to the ocean's blue expanse.

Horse Mountain Road, while curvy, is wide and of fair quality. Saddle Mountain Road becomes much narrower and rockier, with very steep, loose upgrades. Four-wheel drive, while not essential, helps.

The trailhead lies part way up a steep, shaded grade, at a gated side road. Parking is extremely limited and turning around can be challenging.

It's hard to believe this trail was a road. Endless extremely tight, short switchbacks corkscrew ever downward. Most of the way, it remains in an upland woods of Douglas-fir, madrone, tan-oak and canyon liveoak with rare canopy breaks. Infrequent grass, brush or slide scar openings offer views from Shelter Cove and the Lost Coast, north to Cape Mendocino, California's westernmost point.

The trail ends at a secluded home site, marked by a free standing chimney, at the mouth of alder lined Buck Creek. Nearby lies a secluded beach cove and a small canyon.

Unless you're determined to prove something, don't try to hike back up the trail. It's a level 5 miles along the wide beach to the north end of Shelter Cove Road at Black Sands Beach. Leave a car here before starting out or arrange a pickup.

36. GRASSPHOPPER TRAIL
(Humboldt Redwoods State Park)

Length: 6 miles
Water: Very little
Access: Paved Hwy
Season: Any (see text)
Difficulty: Moderately difficult
Elevation: 350 to 3379 feet
Use: Hikers only (see text)
Ownership: Humboldt Redwoods State Park
Phone: (707) 946-2311

Directions: Leave Hwy 101 at the Founders Grove/Honeydew exit (or the Weott exit), and follow the Avenue of the Giants south. Past Weott and Park Headquarters, turn west (right), into the Garden Club of America Grove parking area. Take the path down to the beach and cross the river if the bridge is up. You'll see a trailhead sign on the far bank.

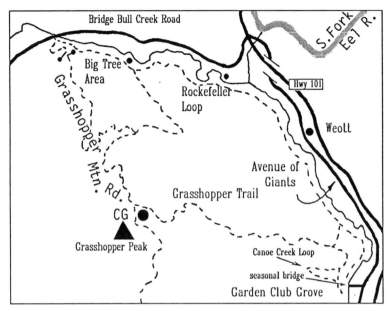

Sprawling Humboldt Redwoods State Park is the centerpiece of the Eel River's Avenue of the Giants recreation area. The park boasts many miles of trail through some of California's most magnificent redwoods and along the spectacular Eel canyon.

Most trails closely parallel either the Avenue of the Giants or the paved Bull Creek Road. While these exquisite paths merit exploring, this book focuses on trails significantly removed from automobile routes.

Both the Avenue of the Giants and Bull Creek Road rank among America's most scenic drives. The Avenue offers vistas of the Eel, with its deep, unstable canyon and towering redwoods. Stop by the visitor center at Park Headquarters.

Bull Creek Road, paved but more remote, winds lazily among some of California's tallest trees. Short trails through the Rockefeller Grove and Big Tree Area highlight the drive. Bull Creek is well marked at the Hwy 101 exit. Follow the signs for Honeydew.

Well away from these roads, the 6 mile Grasshopper Trail offers a rewarding challenge in anybody's book. During winter, when the trailhead is inaccessible due to high water in the Eel, a less scenic alternate trail leads to the same spot. We'll describe it shortly.

Of several summer river crossings at Humboldt Redwoods, the Garden Club Grove offers the best parking, without the $5.00 parking fee charged in many other California State Parks. Also, the trail on the opposite bank is most easily found. All crossings use immense redwood logs, anchored at both ends and planed flat on one side. Seeing these "bridges" on the bank in winter, one can't imagine them spanning the rushing waters. The flow drops dramatically in summer.

Once across the Eel from the Garden Club area, the path climbs the steep, loose bank to a ledge along which the River Trail runs. Since the dirt bluffs are extremely unstable and change from year to year, the park is occasionally forced to recut the path.

After climbing the bank, head north (right), towards the Canoe Creek Loop, Burlington Campground and Grasshopper Camp. The first ½ mile follows the bluff top above the river.

The path soon passes a one mile side trail, the Canoe Creek Loop, which explores a pretty little redwood canyon. The Grasshopper Trail begins where the River Trail meets the far end of the Canoe Creek Loop. Take the middle, well signed path.

For 5 miles, the Grasshopper Trail climbs at a fairly uniform rate. While it hugs the ridge, it largely remains in the woods. A few grassy prairies break the monotony with views of the ever receding canyon below.

As the path rises, the redwoods, with an understory of bay laurel, tanoak and maple, slowly yield to Douglas-fir. Douglas-fir, though less majestic than redwood, can also reach immense heights. The tallest coastal Douglas-firs exceed 300 feet.

At Grasshopper Trail Camp, where you may wish to spend the night, the trail ends just below the summit. A very short jog south, along Grasshopper Road, takes you out of the woods to the chaparral covered summit, with its fire lookout. The lookout is manned during fire season.

The gated Grasshopper Road, open in winter and to horses, offers an alternate route to Grasshopper peak. Take Bull Creek Road to the bridge over Bull Creek. Immediately past the bridge, Grasshopper Road takes off to the the left. Parking is plentiful.

This route offers less sense of wilderness than the other trail. The wide, often unshaded roadway traverses many logged, second growth areas. The Squaw Creek crossing is lovely.

While ½ mile shorter, Grasshopper Road climbs at a far less steady pace than the trail. Much of the elevation gain is concentrated in the 2 miles past Squaw Creek. This stretch is arduous.

However one arrives, the vista from the 3379 foot summit will not soon be forgotten. The river cannot be seen, except in a couple spots, but the canyon and freeway can. Eastward, beyond the canyon, rise the often snowcapped summits of the Yolla Bolly Wilderness.

And yes, the ocean is visible, through a "V" at the mouth of the Mattole river. Kings Peak, whose 4087 foot summit soars upward a scant 3 miles from the Pacific, blocks the coastal view to the south.

Fishing at the Eel River. Humbolt Redwood State Park.(ch.36)

37. JAMES IRVINE TRAIL
(Prairie Creek Redwoods State Park)

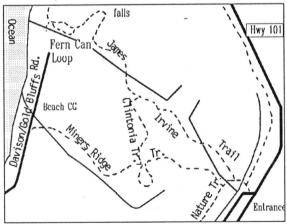

Length: 4 miles
Water:Plenty

Access: Paved, major hwy
Season: Any
Difficulty: Moderate to easy
Elevation: 0 to 300 feet
Use: Hikers only
Ownership: Prairie Creek. State Park
Phone: (707) 488-2171 or 445-6547

Directions: Turn off Hwy 101 at park headquarters, north of Orick. The trailhead is well marked, across from the visitor center. Davison Road, leaving 101 a few miles south, is a winding gravel route leading to the trail's far end. Both entries have toll booths which are manned in summer. Parking fee is $5.00 a day.

This may be one of the loveliest coastal redwood canyons in California. The lush, 4 mile trail is not only beautiful, it offers a variety of side routes and ends at one of northern California's longest and most remote beaches.

It all begins at Prairie Creek Redwoods State Park's visitor center. Along with Jedediah Smith and Del Norte Redwoods, Prairie Creek is one of three state parks embedded in Redwood National Park. Hopefully, the original plan to unite them all will be realized eventually. Meanwhile, I nominate Prairie Creek as the prettiest and best presented of the parks. It certainly boasts the best trails.

The visitor center lies at the edge of a huge field which a herd of giant Roosevelt elk calls home. Several short trails explore Prairie Creek from there. For the James Irvine Trail, follow the Nature Trail from the sign opposite the visitor center.

Almost immediately, the path descends into a lush canyon of towering redwoods, Douglas-fir, alder, rhododendron, salal, huckleberry and other damp- site, north coast denizens. Ferns are everywhere, which is why the lower end of the Irvine Trail is called Fern Canyon.

The James Irvine Trail peels off to the right, 3/10 of a mile down the Nature Trail. While the route follows a canyon to the ocean, the paralleling stream, Godwood Creek, flows inland towards Prairie Creek for the first mile. The path then crosses a barely perceptible "divide" and heads downhill rather more seriously, along Home Creek.

The 4 mile canyon presents a dark world of towering trees, churning side creeks and grottoes, mosses and pretty little foot bridges. The walls grow ever more rocky and narrow as the ocean is approached.

The scenery culminates a mile from the sea, where the trail takes a long swing up a little side creek to visit a steep sided, fern draped grotto housing a beautiful waterfall. Below the fall, the path rejoins Home Creek, passes a little meadow, and emerges onto the beach.

After the trail ends at a large interpretative sign, walk back upstream a short way, following the creek rather than the path, to fully experience Fern Canyon. Below the canyon, the creek flows out over the sand, through a beautiful little alder forest, before merging with Boat Creek. The merged creeks find their way to the sea shortly thereafter.

A little picnic area graces the mouth of Fern Canyon and the Irvine Trail's terminus. It is located at the end of Gold Bluffs Beach Road, at the trailhead for the Gold Bluff Beach Trail. For more information on the isolated Gold Bluff area, see the Gold Bluffs Beach Trail chapter. Few other California beaches extend unbroken for 7 miles.

To reach the Irvine Trail's beach terminus by car, follow Davison Road, beginning a few miles south of park headquarters, to where it dead ends. This gravel route's first few miles are steep and winding, but the last 3 miles, along the beach at the foot of the Gold Bluffs, are highly recommended.

The 4 mile Miner's Ridge Trail to Gold Bluffs Beach also begins at the Nature Trail, shortly past the Irvine trailhead. It climbs from 140 feet to 600 feet elevation in 2 miles, following an old mining road along the ridge crest. Rarely leaving the woods, it offers few vistas. The forest is much like that along the Irvine Trail except the redwoods are a little smaller and the percentage of Douglas-fir is greater.

It is 1½ miles north, up Davdson/Gold Bluffs Beach Road, from the Miners Ridge far terminus at the Beach Campground, to the James Irvine/Fern Canyon area.

For a shorter loop (by a mile), combining the Irvine and Miners Ridge Trails, hike to the beach on the Irvine Trail. On the return trek, cut over to the steep Clintonia Trail, which peels off to the right, near the Irvine Trails highest point. It joins the Miners Ridge Trail after ¾ mile. From there it's 2 miles downhill to park headquarters.

38. GOLD BLUFFS BEACH TRAIL
(Prairie Creek Redwoods State Park)

Length: 2 miles
Water: Oceans
Access: Long, gravel road
Season: Any
Difficulty: Ridiculously easy
Elevation: Sea level
Use: Hikers only
Ownership: Prairie Creek Redwoods State Park

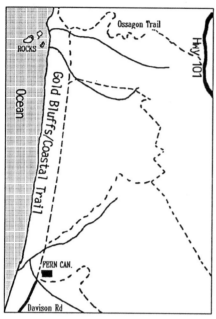

Phone: (707) 488-2171 or 445-6547

Directions: From Hwy 101, 3 miles north of Orick, turn west onto Davison Road and follow the gravel route to its end. The trail begins across the creek. The trailhead is roomy, with much parking and a picnic area. A $5 day use fee is collected in summer.

Because the Pacific Coast is extremely rocky, with jutting headlands and cliffs, sandy beaches tend to be small and difficult to reach. Trails along the coast, therefore, usually contour high above the water, dropping down only occasionally. This trail, however, follows at sea level for some 3 miles and may be the easiest in this book.

The Gold Bluffs Beach Trail follows at the base of the Gold Bluffs, a 7 miles long series of... well... gold colored bluffs in Prairie Creek Redwoods State Park. The reddish tan cliffs aren't very high, less than 100 feet in most places. They're made of compacted beach sand which was mined for its gold content in the 1850's. Reached only by a steep, winding, gravel road and hidden from Hwy 101 by massive redwood forests, Gold Bluffs Beach feels like a private little universe. Douglas-fir and redwood forests cling to the bluff tops and occasionally meander out onto the beach along creeks and canyons. While the area gets a little crowded in summer, that only underscores the fact that many people single it out as a personal "special place."

After Davison Road finally hits the beach and becomes the Beach Road, it parallels the base of the bluffs for 3⅓ miles, ending at a little picnic site at Fern Canyon, which is also the far end of the James Irvine Trail. The latter ranks among California's nicest redwood-canyon-to-the-beach trails.

The trailhead begins at a creek crossing, in a lovely alder grove. The trail is actually a continuation of the road, now closed to vehicles. It is generally routed through low, brush covered sand dunes in a narrow, sheltered strand well back from the water.

You'll find little variation between Boat Creek, near the trailhead, and Butler Creek 2 miles up. For much of the mile between Butler and Ossagon Creeks, the path follows Butler Creek through sand and forest. Past Ossagon Rocks, the beach narrows considerably and the trail may be impassible at high tide. Ossagon Rocks and the pretty little alder grove lining the mouth of Ossagon Creek makes an ideal turnaround point.

39. OSSAGON TRAIL
(Prairie Creek Redwoods State Park)

See map on chapter 38
Length: 1½ miles
Water: Lots
Access: Paved Highway
Season: Year Around
Difficulty: Almost difficult
Elevation: 0 to 700 feet
Use: Non-motorized only
Ownership: Prairie Creek St. Park
Phone: (707) 488-2171 or 445-6547

Directions: The trailhead is on Hwy 101, south of Klamath, at mile post 132.9, on the west side of the road. The small sign is easily missed and parking is non-existent, except for wide spots on the shoulder a few hundred feet up and down the highway. Be very careful walking along 101.

Everyone loves secluded redwood canyons which charge down to the sea. The Northern California coast abounds with such trails through many such canyons. The best begin at a highway and end at a hidden beach.

The Ossagon Trail ranks among the nicer examples of this genre. The path is short and beautiful, if a little strenuous, and there isn't a road within miles of the beach.

Presuming you find the trailhead, at a narrow, densely wooded spot on Hwy 101, find a parking place and make it onto the path; you won't be disappointed. I parked at the trailhead but my car jutted precariously onto the pavement.

While the trail drops 700 feet in 1½ miles, the bulk of the descent is concentrated into the middle ¾ mile. The first mile is almost level, climbing ever so slightly through a damp forest of redwood, Douglas-fir, salal and abundant huckleberry. While these redwoods hardly fall into the "fabled giant" category, the ground below is covered with shamrock-like redwood sorrel, with its purple underside.

The wide path soon begins its plunge, swinging around a little side gully, then over to the deep gorge above Ossagon Creek. This middle section would be rated as "difficult," were it longer. In wet weather, it can be slippery. The redwoods peter out as the coast is approached.

Note the lack of tanoak and western hemlock, mainstays of the redwood coast. Hemlock occurs down to Marin and tanoak abounds everywhere near the coast. Unlike some other coastal species, however, these two are extremely fire sensitive.

Redwoods are largely impervious to fire while the reproduction of Douglas-fir, madrone and oak is actually stimulated by it. The shade loving tanoak and hemlock, on the other hand, take decades to re-invade following a fire.

Lodgepole pine, a principal associate of the southern Oregon coast, also extends to Marin. Below Crescent City, it is widely scattered and often limited to upland pygmy forests. Western red cedar is also widely scattered south of Coos Bay, Oregon. North of there, it is unavoidable. I saw neither species along the Ossagon Trail but noted a few red cedars on the highway near the trailhead.

Be aware of elk tracks along the path. Prairie Creek State Park is proud of its Roosevelt elk herd. In fact, we encountered a bachelor herd of about a dozen males grazing along the lower end of the path. Their immense size can be intimidating but they're pretty docile. If you fail to observe the huge beasts here, you should find some near park headquarters.

Be aware, too, of ocean noises. In the main canyon, it can be deafening. Step a few feet into a side gully, however, and an eerie silence immediately closes in.

The trail levels off, briefly, at a charming side creek with a wooden foot bridge and a railroad tie staircase. Below, alder and Sitka spruce take over and the forest occasionally opens into grassy hillsides. A magnificent view of the beach and creek mouth unfolds from atop the Gold Bluffs.

The last few hundred feet are steep but rewarding. Ossagon Creek, emerging from its dank gorge, spills out onto the sand through an enchanted, park-like, alder and grass woods. Beyond lie the beach and the Ossagon Rocks, a couple of huge boulders embedded in the sand. This is an excellent picnic spot.

The north bound Coastal Trail comes in at the alder grove, where the Ossagon Trail hits bottom. The path continues south, emerging from the woods onto the dunes and continuing at the base of the bluffs.

It's a fair distance to the beach, off the trail, from the point where the trail breaks onto the dunes, through vast expanses of gullies and dune grass. Ossagon Rocks make great climbing.

40. HIDDEN BEACH/COASTAL TRAIL
(Redwood National Park)

Length: 4 miles
Water: Lots
Access: Paved hwys
Season: Year around
Difficulty: Easy
Elevation: 50 to 600 feet
Use: Hikers only
Ownership: Redwood
National Park
Phone: (707) 464-6101

Directions: Follow Hwy 101 to the Lagoon Creek interpretative area, for the north trailhead, or to Requa Road, off 101, for the south trailhead. Both are roomy and well developed. Requa Road is a little steep. Bear left near the end of Requa Road for the trailhead and to avoid the CCC and radar

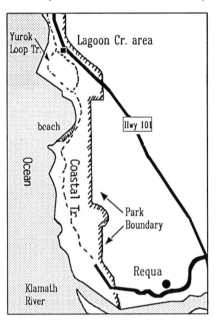

compounds. The trailhead is located at the vista point.

From either direction, this path has much to recommend it. First, it's easy. Second, traveling south to north lands you at a restroom and drinking fountain. That direction's only drawback is that the view from the south trailhead renders the rest of the trail a little anticlimactic.

The north trailhead may be found at the Lagoon Creek interpretive area, just south of False Klamath Cove on Hwy 101. Heading south from Crescent City, the highway emerges from the woods and high cliffs and drops down to the beach at False Klamath Cove. It's a dramatic spot.

Lagoon Creek boasts a little pond, the amenities mentioned and an interpretive display. Waterfowl and rush/sedge ecosystems may be observed in the little pond. The well marked trail begins as an old road. Follow left and don't accidentally get onto the Coastal Trail on the right.

The path contours 30 or 40 feet above the ocean for the first mile. Beyond Hidden Beach, it begins a slow climb to over 600 feet at the south trailhead. Vegetation ranges from redwood,

Douglas-fir and alder along the creeks to Sitka spruce and brush on the coastal bluffs. The scene can change abruptly, from dungeon-like jungles where the sun never shines to grassy fields and hillsides. The area is much more open than other trails nearby.

At a junction ½ mile from Lagoon Creek, one may follow the Yurok Loop Trail back to the north trailhead, making a one mile loop. I found the return half of the loop boring and a little too brushy. Beyond the junction, on the Coastal Trail lies 3 miles of isolated north coast beaches, coves and towering cliffs.

Near the end of the line, far above the churning sea, the trail' makes its way over barren, windswept slopes, immediately below a military compound. Finally, rounding a bend, ¼ mile from the south trailhead, the mouth of the Klamath River appears in the distance.

The Klamath ranks as Northern California's second longest river after the Sacramento, draining much of the Klamath/Trinity mountain system. The Trinity River joins the Klamath on the Hoopa Indian Reservation.

The wide Klamath mouth cuts an impressive canyon. Steep, sharply eroded mountains, covered by black forests, rise up on three sides. A huge sand bar blocks the river's path to the sea, but the waterway makes short work of it, charging through in a pretty much straight course. It's worth a drive up Requa Road for a look.

41. LAST CHANCE/COASTAL TRAIL
(Redwood National Park)

Length: 3 miles
Water: Lots
Access: Paved road from highway
Season: Any
Difficulty: Moderate
Elevation: 225 to 900 ft.
Use: Any
Ownership: Redwood NP
Phone: (707) 483-3461

Directions: Leave Hwy 101 at Enderts Beach Road, just south of Crescent City. Continue to the end and park at the roomy trailhead. See text for comments on the south trailhead at Hwy 101's mile-post 16.

This section of the California Coastal Trail lives up to its last chance" name. To continue northward, one must switch over to the Oregon Coast Trail.

An area of great ecological flux, this is an excellent place to observe Northwest Coast forest communities. Sitka spruce can be found on the more storm battered sites. While widespread to the north, the state tree of Alaska is limited to exposed, coast facing slopes south of Coos Bay, Oregon. It eventually peters out along the Mendocino coast. Redwood, Douglas-fir and western hemlock prefer more sheltered inland areas.

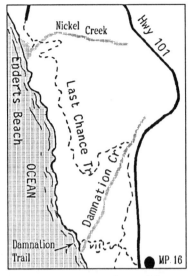

The redwoods end abruptly just north of the state line but thrive around Crescent City. Lodgepole pine, by contrast, a major Sitka spruce associate in Oregon, occurs only on widely scattered sites along the California coast. The majestic western hemlock, another Northwest mainstay, fares a little better, extending southward to Marin County.

From Hwy 101 at Crescent City, a huge cliff can be seen rising to the south. Enderts Beach Road takes off just before the bluff and climbs it a short way. The trail, actually an old road, starts where the road ends.

You'll find a large map and interpretive sign at the trailhead. The map is oriented with north on the bottom and south on top. It confused me at first.

While we're discussing the National Park Service, I wish they would realize that the US is not on the metric system and that government efforts to officially switch have been abandoned. They persist in giving metric elevations and distances, with the real numbers in parentheses as an afterthought.

The Last Chance Trail follows the top of a steep cliff for mile. Where a short trail takes off right, down to Enderts Beach, the main path loops around alder lined Nickel Creek and begins a very long, steep climb upward and inland to the bluff tops.

Things level off after 1 mile, as the path picks up the old road bed of Hwy 101. The bluff tops offer a few vistas although most are screened by trees. The trail here winds through a lush, second growth Douglas-fir, redwood and alder forest, with an understory of salal and huckleberry.

After 2 miles, the route slowly bends east and drops into the Damnation Creek Basin, containing one of the north coast's more impressive old growth redwood stands. The creek crossing, 4 miles from the trailhead, makes a good turn around spot. The beautiful, fast flowing stream may be difficult to cross, since the culvert was washed out in 1987.

It's 1 mile from Damnation Creek to the unsigned south trailhead on Hwy 101. If starting there, or continuing on instead of returning to Enderts Beach, be aware that the park's free "Map and Guide" offers scant information on the Last Chance Trail south of Damnation Creek. Their 50 cent "Trail Map," while more detailed, is inaccurate. A free newspaper, called "Visitor Guide," best shows these trailheads and connections.

The best place to pick up the Last Chance Trail from the south is from the Damnation Creek Trailhead, at mile-post 16 on Hwy 101. The actual post was knocked over when I last visited. Look for a wide parking area and MP 15.96. From MP 16, the Damnation Creek Trail swings north among giant redwoods, then veers west and begins descending a series of tight switchbacks.

The Damnation Creek Trail drops 1000 feet in 2 miles, to the mouth of Damnation Creek. It intersects the Last chance Trail ¾ of a mile down. The wide Last Chance Trail dead ends at Hwy 101, at MP 15.5. Immediately before, the Coastal Trail breaks away, crossing Hwy 101 at MP 15.6. Parking is extremely limited at MP 15.6, marked only by signs reading "CT." It is a little better at MP 15.5.

42. BLACK BUTTE
(Siskiyou Wilderness Area)

Length: 5 miles
Water: OK
Access: Long, very poor
 roads (Youngs Val); fair, shorter dirt roads.
Season: June — October
Difficulty: Moderate
Elev.: 4800 to 5400 ft.
Use: Non-motorized only
Ownership: Siskiyou NF
Phone: (503) 592-2166

Directions: *Youngs Valley—take Hwy 199 south from Grants Pass into California and turn left up Knopke Creek Road. Follow it to the "T" junction just before Sanger Lake, where the road levels off. Turn right at the junction and proceed up the extremely poor road to the gated wilderness boundary. There's plenty of parking. It's a 1 mile walk down the closed road to the actual trailhead.*

Black Butte—take Hwy 199 to Cave Junction and turn up Caves Hwy. Turn right onto Holland Loop and right again on Bridgeview/ Takilma Road. Continue past the Happy Camp turnoff through

Takilma. Turn left at the fork, up 4904, right at the junction with 4906 (becoming 053), and proceed to the very roomy trailhead.

SISKIYOU WILDERNESS AREA

Route 4903-053

Black Butte

S. Fk. Illinois R.

Butte Trail

Polar Bear Trail

South Fork Trail

to Twins Valley

Youngs Peak

Black

Knopke Creek/ Youngs Valley Road(trail)

The most mountainous mountains in the Siskiyous can be explored on this trail. It penetrates the snow capped crags which pop into view as you enter the Illinois Valley from Grants Pass. The group of summits rise above the head of the South Fork of the Illinois River, just past the California line.

Young's Peak is the cluster's most interesting because it lies in three National Forests and its slopes drain into the Smith, Klamath and Rogue Rivers. The group's loftiest point is Preston Peak at 7300 feet. Its eerie black pyramid, alas, is not easily visible, except from mountaintops. The area has recently been set aside as part of the Siskiyou Wilderness.

The Black Butte area shows much evidence of past glaciation with numerous steep-walled cirque basins. There are relatively few lakes, however. The upper valley of the Illinois River's south Fork, furthermore, once contained far more than the usual hanging mountain glaciers which carved the cirques. Rather, it shows evidence of a valley glacier. Look for a round bottomed valley with hanging valleys spilling in from the sides.

Trailheads adorn either end of the Black Butte Trail, with about 30 miles of driving on dirt and gravel between. It's probably easier to walk out and back over the same route than to leave cars at both ends. The Black Butte end is easier to reach but the drive to either end is spectacular.

Unfortunately, accurate trail maps of this area are difficult to come by. The paths on the ground bore little relation to those on my National Forest map. That map didn't agree with two other's and all three were wrong. The map herein is based on aerial photos.

There's no mistaking Black Butte; a narrow, pointed projection towering above the surrounding area. If you have a little time, continue down the road a mile past the trailhead to the first creek, noting the Brewer spruce along the way. The creek flows out of a small, steep walled cirque which bears exploring. Follow the creek through a narrow canyon into the cirque. Instead of a lake inside, there's a little marsh. Look for insect eating darlingtonia plants.

From the trailhead, the Black Butte Trail circles around Black Butte's mysterious, rocky crest across a serpentine soil area. Look for an open, park-like forest of Jeffrey and western white pine. The view of the Illinois, far below, is spectacular.

After 1 mile, you'll come to a side trail dropping steeply downhill to the right, into a grassy basin. By continuing straight (along the Polar Bear Trail), you'll end up in Twin Valley. Consisting of a

Black Butte, Siskiyou Wilderness Area. (Chapter 42)

pair of meadows, Twin Valley lies 1 mile away, over a sharp ridge.

Technically, the Black Butte Trail begins at this junction. It's much rougher than the more established Polar Bear Trail and in places is only partially constructed and difficult to follow. Despite a few quite steep ups and downs, it's surprisingly level, considering the terrain.

In a little over a mile, the Black Butte Trail emerges at the Youngs Valley Trail, actually an old jeep road. The path left ventures into a lovely little cirque, then becomes horrendously steep. To the right, it hugs a rock wall above the valley, opposite a sheer, glacially polished rock face.

Pretty soon, you'll find yourself stepping across the headwaters of the Illinois River. Look for the upper end of the South Fork Trail. Not long after, at a small saddle, you'll finally reach the road into Youngs Valley. Turn right and follow it for 1½ miles to the road end at the Wilderness boundary. Or turn around and return to your car. Or hike a mile to the left for Youngs Valley. Or...

43. RASPBERRY LAKE
(Siskiyou Wilderness Area)

Length: 5 miles
Water: Lots
Access: Long,poor dirt road
Season: June — October
Difficulty: Difficult
Elevation: 4600 to 5400 ft.
Use: Non-motorized only
Ownership: Klamath NF
Phone: (916) 493-2243

Directions: Take Hwy 199 south from Grants Pass into California and turn left up Knopke Creek Road. Follow it to the "T" junction just before Sanger Lake, where the road levels off. Turn right at the junction and proceed up the extremely poor road to the gated wilderness boundary. There's plenty of parking.

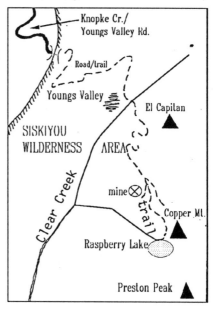

Everything went wrong the day I visited Raspberry Lake but I don't regret any of it. Don't bring a toddler, however. But do bring a camera to this remote pool at the base of Preston Peak, the black pyramid forming the Siskiyou Mountains' second highest peak.

Getting to the trailhead isn't easy but it's an adventure and extremely scenic. For a rougher, even more scenic road, follow the Waldo Lookout Road to the trailhead instead of Knopke Creek Road, past Sanger Peak and Sanger Lake.

From the trailhead/overlook where the gated road drops into Youngs Valley, the views of Preston Peak an El Capitan are breathtaking. Clear Creek, running through Youngs Valley, is a major tributary of the Klamath River. You used to be able to drive through Youngs Valley, across Clear Creek, to the old chrome mine—if you had four wheel drive. The trail from the mine was only 1 mile long. These days, you walk in from the gate at the pass.

The actual trail begins 3½ miles from the pass, at the end of the high road through the mine area. It is poorly maintained, very rocky and badly marked. We put up a few blazes but that was 16 years ago.

The path hits the lake at the top of a tremendous rock fall. I was carrying a pack when I visited so the scramble down was harrowing. Once down, I left the pack at the lake, climbed back up and carried my 3 year old daughter down. I then made my way up and down yet again, gallantly but stupidly, to carry my wife's pack for her. I then collapsed in exhaustion until morning.

Covering some 30 acres, the lake is beautiful and deep with good campsites and excellent fishing. Preston Peak disappears as you drop into the basin but a smaller, equally inspiring summit rises sharply out of the lake's eastern shore.

44. DEVIL'S PUNCHBOWL
(Siskiyou Wilderness Area)

Length: 5 1/2 miles
Water: Lots
Access: Long dirt and gravel road
Season: June —October
Difficulty: Very difficult
Elevation: 3400 to 4750 feet
Use: Non-motorized only
Ownership: Klamath NF
Phone: (916) 493-2243

Directions: *Take Hwy 199 from Crescent City to Little Jones Creek Road, just north of Patrick's Creek Resort. Follow the blacktop about 15 miles to the Bear Basin turnoff (14N04). Turn*

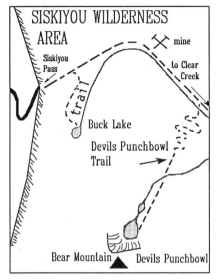

SISKIYOU WILDERNESS AREA

Siskiyou Pass

mine

to Clear Creek

trail

Buck Lake

Devils Punchbowl Trail

Bear Mountain   Devils Punchbowl

left and follow the winding, gravel road to the low quality Siskiyou Pass Road. Turn left again and proceed to the parking area at the Wilderness boundary. If you reach the South Fork of the Smith, you've missed the Siskiyou Pass turnoff.

Despite its low elevation and location in a range fairly devoid of lakes, Devil's Punchbowl ranks among the most awesome glacial cirque lakes anywhere. Isolation and a long, extremely arduous trail heightens the experience. Situated in the remote western Siskiyous, not a single road crosses the range's crest for 30 miles south of Siskiyou Pass. The area is famous for its many bigfoot sightings.

It used to be possible to drive two miles beyond Siskiyou Pass, although the road was pretty poor. Beyond the Buck Lake trailhead, a mile down, it became pretty much undriveable. But that's all academic these days, with the new Siskiyou Wilderness Area. Now you walk from the pass.

A mile past the parking area, you'll pass a primitive camp at the Buck Lake trailhead, on Doe Creek. From there, an easy mile trail leads to Buck Lake, a delightful little pool in a small cirque. While worth a visit, it doesn't compare to Devil's Punchbowl, 3 grueling miles away. The flatter Buck Lake setting is more amenable to camping than the rock lined Punchbowl.

The closed Siskiyou Pass Road ends at an old mine. From there, a trail continues on to Clear Creek and the Klamath River. A half-mile down, a side trail crosses a huge log over the creek and climbs the opposite hillside. It begins with an endless series of steep switchbacks which challenges even the most experienced hiker.

Should you make it to the ridge above the switchbacks, the view is breathtaking. The black pyramid of Preston Peak, second highest in the Siskiyous at 7300 feet, rises immediately south. Southwest lies the craggy summit of Bear Mountain, the trail's destination. Just below the Bear Mountain summit, a "V" notch can be discerned in the towering rock face. The Punchbowl is inside.

Although the trail remains steep even after the switchbacks, the last mile is so beautiful, you're unlikely to notice its difficulty.

It crosses cascading creeks and floral meadows, scrambles over rock faces, winds around the edge of a small, clear lake and penetrates the "V" canyon described earlier.

The main lake consists of 30 acres of crystal water, surrounded by perpendicular cliffs up to 1000 feet high. Prettier even than some of the best lakes in the Marbles and Trinity Alps, such beauty is unexpected at an elevation of only 4700 feet. I don't believe the Devil had anything to do with creating this enchanted spot.

While I made it in and out in the same day, an overnight stay is advised. There are few good campsites, however. What the shore lacks in brushiness, it makes up in steepness. Fishing, however, is excellent and the lake is surprisingly popular. The bottom is mostly rock and the water tends to be icy and invigorating.

Preston Peak. Elevation 7,304 ft. (Chapter 43)

45. BEAR LAKE
(Siskiyou Wilderness)

Length: 2½ miles
Water: No
**Access: Steep, mostly
blacktopped road**
Season: June—October.
**Difficulty: Easy to
moderate**
Elevation: 4800 to 5600 ft.
Use: Non-motorized only
Ownership: Klamath NF
Phone: (916) 493-2243

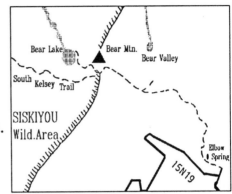

Directions: *Take Hwy
96, the Klamath River Road, to road 15N19, 8 miles past (or
before) Happy Camp, just south of Clear Creek. Turn here and
follow the signs to the Bear Lake/South Kelsey Trail. The curvy
road is steep in spots but paved for 8 of its 12 miles. A ¼ mile
spur leads to the trailhead. Parking is ample.*

If any range gives a sense of the "backbone" of the northern
California coast, it is the remote western Siskiyous. A proper vantage point reveals a swollen chain of red tips oozing up from the
lush emerald blanket of coastal jungle. None of the major peaks
are visible from main highways. This is Bigfoot Country, as a sign
outside Happy Camp announces.

The 10 mile drive along the Klamath, from Happy Camp to the
trailhead, is rewarding in itself, with its whitewater riffles, crashing side creeks and vast stone faces. As road 15N19 climbs above
the canyon, one can peer down on the river, east to the Marbles
or south to the Salmon Mountains. Near the road end, Red Hill
and Bear Peak pop into view. The trail leads to both. Red Hill is
particularly easy to identify.

The red is mostly weathered serpentine, a black granitic rock
poor in calcium minerals. Serpentine tends to occur in bands
paralleling the coast. It abounds in the western Siskiyous.

From the trailhead, the path follows an old road for a few hundred feet into woods of white fir, red fir, Douglas-fir, sugar pine
and incense cedar. Beyond the flower (monkshood) lined creek,
through the tiny meadow at Elbow Springs, the trail re-enters the
woods for ½ mile or so. This is the only fairly steep spot but it's
soon past.

The trail then breaks out onto the ridgetop. Look for Preston

Peak, the western Siskiyous' highest at 7300 feet, to the north. Sawtooth Mountain can be seen just south of Red Hill. There's also an outstanding view of the trailhead area. The ridge's sparse forests of western white pine, Jeffrey pine and Brewer spruce belie its serpentine underpinnings. Brush species include manzanita, snowbrush and Sadler oak.

A stone cairn on the right indicates what is supposed to be a trail into Bear Valley, a huge glacial cirque with a beautiful meadow at the bottom. Although indicated on the map, I found no such path. The lake lies one cirque over, in Little Bear Valley.

The path finally skirts the barren, brushy summit of Bear Peak, then drops a colossal 800 feet in ½ mile, into Little Bear Valley. I looked for a path to the top of the mountain (less than ¼ mile away), but found none. The South Kelsey Trail continues along the ridge to the left rather than dropping into the basin.

Little Bear Valley is among the more perfectly formed, if small, glacial cirques I've seen. A semi-circle of vertical, white cliffs looks down onto a 6 or 7 acre, aqua lake surrounded by meadow. One of less than a half dozen scraggly, extremely remote California stands of Alaska cedar graces these cliffs.

Visible from the Bear Peak/Bear Valley area, by the way, are Bear Mountain, Pear Paw Mountain, Bear Basin Butte and Polar Bear Mountain. That should tell you something about the area, although I doubt you'll run into many Polar Bears.

You've been following the South Kelsey Trail, a once major military and trade route from Crescent City to Fort Jones. The Kelsey Trail into the Marble Mountains, described in another chapter, also follows this path.

46. SOUTH-KELSEY TRAIL
(Siskiyou Wilderness Area)

Length: 3 miles
Water: Everywhere
Access: Good, mostly paved roads
Season: Any
Difficulty: Easy
Elevation: 800 to 1100 feet
Use: Non-motorized only
Ownership: Six Rivers NF
Phone: (707) 457-3131

Directions: From Hwy 199, follow the South Fork Smith Road, 14 miles to road 15N01 (where a sign says "Big Flat—1 mile"). Bear right on 15N01 and proceed 3 1/2 miles to road 15N39, which takes off downhill left. It's 2 miles down 15N39 to the roomy trailhead. Roads are blacktopped to 15N39. 15N39 is wide and gravel surfaced.

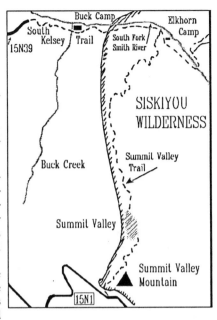

This National Recreation Trail follows an old military route which originally connected Fort Jones, then an actual fort, with Crescent City. Constructed in 1851 mostly by Chinese laborers, the original trail was nearly 200 miles long. Two other paths in this book, the Bear Lake Trail and the Kelsey Trail, also follow segments of this road, which remained in use until 1909.

Evidence of the trail's age and original purpose can be noted in spots. The moss covered stonework in fill areas is most obvious.

The South-Kelsey Trail is actually 16½ miles long and ends at the Bear Lake trailhead on Klamath National Forest. Its first 7 miles follows the South Fork of the Smith River, part of the National Wild and Scenic River system. The route then ascends the high Siskiyous.

The trail's first 3 miles, to the junction with Summit Valley Trail, just past Elkhorn Bar, offers a wonderful taste of the scenic river canyon. Try to imagine, as you walk, that you're part of an Army convoy, supplying a fort whose purpose was to maintain order among Scott Valley gold miners.

The trail's first ¼ mile is a connecting link dropping steeply from the trailhead to the actual military path. It then levels off, maintaining a contour 100 feet or so above the river. The canyon is steep and spectacular, with plentiful vistas.

Being on the north slope, the trail tends to be cool and dark, with lush vegetation. This makes well composed camera shots, despite long views down the canyon, difficult to come by. These middle elevation forests consist mostly of Douglas-fir, madrone, tanoak and canyon liveoak, with occasional Port Orford cedar groves and alder along the river. Moisture loving shrubs such as salal, thimbleberry and evergreen huckleberry, abound.

Groves of California laurel decorate the river and sheltered side creeks. Called Oregon myrtlewood in Oregon, the species' ecological niche changes as the state line is approached. Near San Francisco Bay, it is a common understory tree in Douglas-fir forests but also does well on open, brushy slopes, if rainfall is plentiful. In the Siskiyous, it's strictly an understory, creek bank tree. But it's equally beautiful and aromatic in both areas.

This is one of the world's rainiest places. A few years ago, nearby Gasquet Mountain, above the junction of Hwy 199 and South Fork Road, was deluged with over 400 inches of rain in one season, a world record.

Distance signs along the South-Kelsey Trail seemed a little goofy to me. The trailhead sign announced that it was 2 miles to Buck Shelter and 3 to Elkhorn Shelter. I reached Buck Creek in 30 minutes and Elkhorn in an hour.

A mile from the trailhead, the path rounds a rocky point and begins a slow ascent to the river, which it meets at Buck Creek. You'll find a lean-to shelter at Buck Creek, with a fire pit. The shelter occupies a beautiful flat near an excellent swimming hole.

Crossing Buck Creek may pose a problem as the trail seems to dead end at the creek. Accept on faith that it continues on the other side. A huge log, spanning the creek about 100 feet before the crossing, offers a shortcut.

Between Buck Creek and Elkhorn Bar, the trail follows at river level. Many excellent fishing access points dot this section, although the underbrush can be extremely dense and the ground soggy. All in all, it's a pleasant, level stretch, cooled in summer by the thick forest canopy.

Elkhorn Bar is similar to Buck Creek, also with a lean-to shelter. The surrounding flat is larger, however, with many side creek and picturesque little grottoes. Look for excellent views down a widened canyon as Elkhorn Bar is approached.

47. SUMMIT VALLEY
(Siskiyou Wilderness Area)

See map on chapter 46
Length: 2 miles
Water: Yes
Access: Blacktop and gravel roads
Season: May — October
Difficulty: Easy to moderate
Elevation: 4939 to 4076
Use: Non-motorized
Ownership: Six Rivers NF
Phone: (707) 457-3131

Directions: From Hwy 199, take the South Fork Smith Road (427), 14 miles to road 15N01, which takes off to the right at a sign reading "Big Flat—1 Mile." Proceed 15 miles to a saddle just past Summit Mountain. Look for a small sign on the other side of the guard rail. There's a turnout a little ways down the road.

I found myself playing word games with the mountain's name where this trail is located, while driving the long, beautiful road to the trailhead. All involved phrases like, "climbing to the summit of Summit summit." Or summit-thing like that.

Even more fascinating was the trail's oxymoron (self-contradicting) name. Not only is the name an oxymoron, however, the actual valley is also, as shall be explained.

The drive to the Summit Valley trailhead by itself, constitute a satisfying day's outing. Hwy 199, through the Smith River Canyon, ranks among Northern California's more scenic routes. The drive up the South Fork is equally scenic, as is road 15N01, following the ridge between the South Fork and the ocean.

The trail begins at a saddle just past Summit Mountain's main hump, in an elegant Brewer spruce grove. This is the heart of Brewer spruce country. These rare, lovely spires, with their dangling branches, thrive above 4500 feet here.

Summit Mountain is a serpentine outcropping nearly 5000 feet high. From the trailhead, the path shoots steeply up, cresting after ¼ mile. It misses the actual top, contouring immediately west of a narrow ridge. It similarly skirts at least two other peaks in the first mile.

For an impressive view of the main backbone of the western Siskiyous, scramble the short distance to the ridgetop. This is one of California's remotest, eeriest and most beautiful ranges.

You're standing at the edge of its most remote section. Sawtooth Mountain, composed of ancient, metamorphosed lava, is the vicinity's most impressive peak. On other nearby peaks, red outcroppings of weathered serpentine contrast markedly with the surrounding black jungle forests.

This is also the very heart of bigfoot country. Bluff and Blue Creeks, where more sightings have taken place than anywhere else, lie immediately south.

The views west are equally impressive, especially the mouth of the Klamath. Here and there, through notches in Rattlesnake Ridge, the last range to the west, the ocean appears.

Despite the trail's location on one of the wettest spots on Earth, views are outstanding because vegetation is stunted by the serpentine. The ridge is mostly landscaped with grass and shrubs, including pinemat manzanita, Sadler oak and ground juniper. Scattered, wind contorted trees include Brewer spruce, Jeffrey pine and western white pine.

Beyond Summit Mountain, the trail crosses to the east of the ridge and drops somewhat. Off the serpentine, the woods thicken, with Douglas-fir, grand fir and Shasta red fir taking over. The second mile, like the first, contains a few steep pitches but continues largely level. There are many grassy openings and side creeks.

As noted, Summit Valley lives up to its name. The huge, grassy expanse seems oddly perched on the ridgetop. Surrounded by forest on 3 sides, the valley's north end slopes down towards the canyon far below. The old shelter makes a wonderful picnic spot.

Beyond Summit Valley, it's another 6 miles to the junction with the South-Kelsey Trail. The elevation drop is tremendous. The canyons grow ever narrower and the views more and more constricted. If interested in this lower trail section, along the Smith's upper South Fork, drive around to the South-Kelsey trailhead, a few miles back down 15N01, at the end of road 15N39.

48. MIDDLE FORK APPLEGATE

Length: 2 miles
Water: Gallons
Access: Good gravel road
Season: All
Difficulty: Easy
Use: Any
Elevation: 2700 ft.
Ownership: Rogue River NF
Phone: (503) 899-1812

Directions: Take Hwy 238 from Jacksonville or south Grants Pass to the town of Ruch. At Ruch, turn up the Applegate River Road towards Applegate Lake. Past the state line, where the pavement ends, turn right onto Road 1040. Follow it five miles to where the road curves sharply uphill left. Proceed straight, not left, to just before the road curves uphill right. The trailhead is well marked near the river, with parking for 5 or 6 cars.

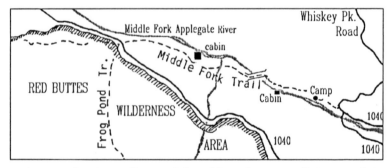

Among devotees of peaceful ambles along gurgling mountain streams, the Middle Fork of the Applegate River is a favorite. So much so that it has been included in the National Recreational

Trail system.

If you've never driven through upper Applegate area, you're in for a treat. Look for occasional glimpses of the orange, double humped Red Buttes as you approach Applegate Lake. Above the lake, in California, the rock outcroppings and deep pools offer some of the best swimming anywhere.

The Middle Fork Trail ultimately ties in with ½ dozen other trails, including the Frog Pond, Sweaty Gap, Azalea Lake, Butte Fork and Boundary Trails. We'll stick to the first 2 miles.

The path begins as a wide gravel road at the river's edge. After about ¼ mile, the road bumps into the river while a small path heads up the bank, following the river through a majestic forest of old growth Douglas-fir, white fir, sugar pine and ponderosa pine. Soon after, you'll be able to look across to one of the cabins and, if you care to, descend a little footpath and take a dip in the swimming hole. After a mile, the trail again meets the river at a log bridge crossing.

From the bridge on, amid ferns and mosses, the area begins to feel like a rain forest out of the Olympic Peninsula. The old growth stand is a spotted owl management area.

After a mile on the south side of the river, you'll come to a second log cabin, a perfect place for a picnic lunch and a good doubling back point. It's another mile to the road and the Frog Pond/Sweaty Gap Trail.

49. FROG POND TRAIL
(Red Buttes Wilderness Area)

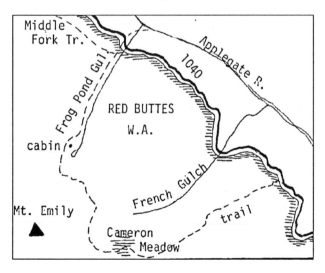

Length: 3 miles one way or 7 mile loop
Water: Lots
Access: Long, gravel road
Season: May—November
Difficulty: Difficult
Elevation: 3500 to 5300 ft.
Use: Non-motorized only
Ownership: Rogue River NF
Phone: (503) 899-1812

Directions: *From Grants Pass or Medford, Oregon, take Hwy (238 the Jacksonville or Williams Hwy), to the town of Ruch. From there, follow the Applegate Lake Road past the lake to the state line, turning right onto the Middle Fork Applegate Road (1040). Swing left where 1040 makes a hard turn uphill and road 1035 continues straight. The first trailhead is located 11 miles from the state line. The second, on the same road, lies 13 miles from the state line and is marked as the Middle Fork Trail leading to the Sweaty Gap Trail.*

This exquisite, little known path, with its floral meadows, looming cliffs, botanical oddities and stunning vistas of the Red Buttes, boasts all the trappings of a nearly perfect day-hike. Before elaborating its wonders, however, I should warn of a couple less-than-sublime aspects and suggest ways to minimize them.

The Frog Pond Trail may be reached from two trailheads, two miles apart on the same road. Although the actual path is only five miles, it is necessary to walk seven to complete the loop, including two miles along the road. From either trailhead, it's a fairly arduous two miles to the journey's "guts," the mile between McCloy Cabin and Cameron Meadows.

Unless you park a car at each trailhead, I recommend starting at the second trailhead, hiking three miles to Cameron Meadows, then doubling back. This not only reduces the trek by a mile, it avoids the first trailhead—and one of the most annoying trail sections I've ever encountered.

Although both entry points offer a stiff cardiovascular workout, the route from the first trailhead is much steeper and far less scenic. Follow it only if you enjoy beating through a jungle of insects, vegetation and spider webs. Higher up, this path repeatedly disappears across a series of meadows and life becomes a constant search for rock piles, blazes or (ha!) signs. At one point, only a three-inch square flasher marks the route—tacked to a tree 500 feet beyond where the path peters out.

If you employ this portion of the trail at all, make it the downhill leg. Under no circumstances should one attempt to hike in from the first trailhead.

The second trailhead offers a less steep ascent up a dry, wooded hillside, initially through a forest of Douglas-fir and white fir. Farther up, white pine, Shasta fir and the rare and elegant Brewer spruce shade the route.

This far trailhead is not signed as the Frog Pond Trail. It is actually the far end of the Middle Fork Trail up the Applegate (see the previous chapter). It eventually leads to the Sweaty Gap Trail to Azalea Lake. For the Frog Pond Trail, head uphill less than ¼ mile, then take the first left.

After 1½ miles, past some outcroppings and an old mine, the pitch eases as the trail negotiates an opening overgrown with the most beargrass I've ever seen. In May or June, when this spectacular lily species blooms, the display must be staggering.

Soon after, the landscape opens out to the emerald expanse of Frog Pond Meadow. The adjacent cabin, built in the 1930's by a gold miner named John Calvin Knox McCloy, incorporates seven live cedar trees into its frame. The large, lily pad choked pond, with it's convoluted shoreline, provides an exquisite centerpiece to the meadow, whose upper end is guarded by the soaring cliffs of Mt. Emily.

Above the cabin, the path winds along the meadow's edge, then disappears into a sea of wildflowers. I identified, among others, tiger lilies, spirea, corn lilies, Indian paintbrush, daisies, monkshood, pentstemon and cinquefoil.

Although the trail vanishes for a hundred feet or so here, the route is obvious. The huge, black-on-white "X" where the path resumes, would be difficult to miss.

As the path leaves the Frog Pond area, it passes a smaller meadow at the base of an immense outcropping. The droopy looking trees nearby comprise an extremely rare stand of Alaska cedar. Common to the northern Cascades, the species is confined in the Siskiyous to four or five tiny, stunted, widely scattered clumps.

Beyond the Alaska cedars, the trail climbs several hundred feet to a boulder strewn ridgetop. This mile segment, largely in the open, offers marvelous panoramas of the region's heights. Look for Whiskey Peak (opposite), Pyramid Peak (to the rear), and the immense, double humped Red Butte (dead ahead).

The path eventually drops into the Cameron Meadows basin. Higher, tamer and less lush—but no less impressive—than that containing Frog Pond Meadows, the surrounding rock faces are broken by patches of wildflowers, grass and picturesque conifer clusters. I suggest spending your time exploring—or perhaps scaling the ridgetop—instead of trying to sleuth out the trail, which disappears at the meadow's edge.

In fact, I wouldn't venture too far past Cameron Meadows even if you do locate the continuing path. Beyond a charming little pond ⅛ mile down, the scenery quickly deteriorates.

50. AZALEA LAKE
(Red Buttes Wilderness)

Length: 6 miles
Water: OK
Access: Long gravel and dirt roads
Season: June — October
Difficulty: Easy to moderate
Elevation: 4500 to 5900
Use: Non-motorized only
Owner: Rogue River NF
Phone: (503) 899-1812

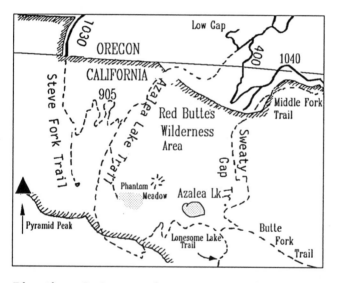

Directions: *In Oregon, take Hwy 238 out of Jacksonville or Grants Pass to the town of Applegate. Follow Thompson Creek Road to the gravel Steves Fork Road (1030). Turn left off 1030 near mile 5, over a bridge, onto a wide, steep dirt road. Take the first right past the summit. The roomy Azalea Lake trailhead lies a mile up this poor quality dirt road.*

For the alternate Steves Fork Trail, continue on 1030 to its end for the roomy trailhead.

The Azalea Lake Trail may be the most scenic pathway into the

Red Buttes Wilderness and perhaps in the entire Siskiyou Mountains. While fairly lengthy at 6 miles, and while it traverses extremely steep terrain, the miles disappear quickly on this surprisingly level path.

Both the Azalea Lake Trail and the Steves Fork Trail (plus a couple others), end at Azalea Lake. Since both begin in Oregon, reaching them requires a lengthy incursion into that state. The Steves Fork Trailhead strides the state line while the Azalea Lake Trail enters the golden State after ¼ mile.

The Steves Fork Trail is easiest to find. From the trailhead, the path follows an old logging road at first but soon crosses a footbridge and begins a gentle ascent through Douglas-fir, hemlock, white fir, Shasta fir and sugar pine. The path merges with the Azalea lake Trail after 3 miles. The junction is also 3 miles from the start of the Azalea lake Trail.

Steves Fork features outstanding views of the looming rock face of Pyramid Peak across a small cirque basin. The vista compensates for the route's steepness compared to the Azalea Lake Trail.

From the Azalea Lake Trailhead, it's an easy, 1½ mile walk to Fir Glade, a vast meadow with an old cabin and a profusion of wildflowers. The path, which had been following an old road, cuts sharply left just before Fir Glade, at an easily missed turnoff. The Steves Fork junction lies 1½ miles beyond.

The 3 miles past Fir Glade are remarkably level. The route crosses patches of dense forest, areas of more open woods and shrubs, and countless meadows and small springs. Wildflowers (Indian paintbrush, pentstemon, monkshood, etc.) abound.

The route steepens considerably at a pass between the Middle Fork of the Applegate and the Klamath River. Look for views of Whiskey Peak back towards the trailhead; the vertical, gray rock face of Buck Peak above Phantom Meadows; and towering Preston Peak in the distance to the west. Brewer spruce adorns the pass, along with some of the highest elevation knobcone and sugar pine in the Siskiyous.

After a mile, the trail reaches a second, higher pass, then descends sharply for one last mile, to the lake. Coming into view at the second pass, the lake nests inside a small glacial cirque at the foot of Figurehead Mountain's sheer cliffs. The view down the Butte Fork to the aptly named Red Buttes is memorable.

The lake itself, one of the few in the Siskiyous, is both beautiful and botanically interesting. True to its name, azalea bushes line its banks. It is surrounded by lodgepole pine. While the tree abounds in the Cascades and Marbles, this is the only stand I've seen in the Siskiyous.

The lake boasts a firm, gravel bottom (which becomes a little silty in the center), and clear, shallow, warm water. Swimming is excellent but fishing, they say, is only so so.

51. RED BUTTES
(Red Buttes Wilderness Area)

Length: 4 miles
Water: Amazingly little
Access: Poor poor dirt roads
Season: June—October
Difficulty: Moderate
Elevation: 4700 to 5900
Use: Non-motorized
Ownership: Klamath NF
Phone: (916)
465-2241

Directions: From Oregon, take Hwy 238 from Jacksonville or South Grants Pass, to the town of Ruch. From there, follow the road up the Applegate River, past Applegate Lake, to where the pavement ends at the state line. Immediately

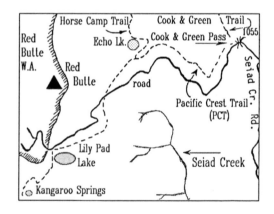

beyond, turn left onto Elliott Creek Road (1050), then right onto the steep Cook andGreen Pass Road (1055). Follow it to the pass. From California, take Hwy 96 (the Klamath River Road), to Seiad Valley. Follow Seiad Creek Road (48N20) to Cook and Green Pass. Park at the pass and head up the PCT to the right (west). The road to the right will take you three miles, to the base of the Red Buttes. It contains some extremely steep, rocky pitches and requires either 4x4 or a fair amount of nerve and skill.

The Red Buttes pop up every now and then from many back roads in the Rogue/Klamath country, although usually just for a second. Their double-humped camelback outline is an instant giveaway. Now that the battle for the Red Buttes Wilderness is over and the Pacific Crest Trail (PCT) is complete, access is fairly easy to this compact area of great beauty.

The best road view of the 6738 foot Red Buttes, is from Seiad

Creek. The creek itself is worth a visit, particularly a spot about 4 miles up. Look for where the road crosses the creek and takes off uphill. If you have four wheel drive, take the side road left to another little bridge. Proceed uphill, bearing right where the road forks. You will end up at an abandoned chrome mine amid a large Baker cypress grove.

Trails converge everywhere at Cook and Green Pass. I suggest taking the PCT to the Red Buttes, although one can also walk or drive up the road. The latter once ranked among the worst I've ever driven. As of 1991, however, they'd improved it somewhat. But it still contains some extremely steep, bumpy shots.

The PCT was rather ruthlessly gouged into the mountain above the road, breaking the hillside's clean, majestic sweep and marring the area's beauty. Nevertheless, it has several advantages over the road, which parallels a couple hundred feet down the hill. The vegetation is a little more varied and less disturbed. You'll see white pine, Jeffrey pine, incense cedar and manzanita on both but the trail also reveals Brewer spruce, sadler oak and abundant wildflowers. It also visits ridgetop areas of stunted pines.

Most important, the PCT skirts the rim of the Echo Lake cirque, one of the area's highlights.

It's 3 miles from Cook and Green Pass to where the PCT crosses the road, at the base of the Red Buttes. If you've come up the road, follow the PCT uphill right for ½ mile, for a look at Echo Lake. When you get back, follow it to the left, downhill, for another ½ mile, into the Lily Pad Lake cirque.

The trail's only potentially potable water is found flowing out a hose, just below where the PCT heads downhill from the road. I'd be leery of it, however, since the area is full of cows.

Lily Pad Lake isn't much but the setting is exquisite. It sits on one of at least six glacial cirque basins in the immediate vicinity. The trail around and above the lake affords a peek into the Hello Canyon cirque. Hello Lake cannot be seen. The road also visits Lily Pad Lake, plus an old chrome mine at the head of Hello Canyon.

The huge Kangaroo Springs cirque basin, below the 6894 foot summit of Kangaroo Mountain, about a mile past Lily Pad Lake, also merits a look. Distances are difficult to estimate since the trail winds all over the place. Beyond Lily Pad Lake, the PCT crosses the ridge between the East and West Forks of Seiad Creek. There, the Devils Peaks (Upper and Middle), come into view for the first time (see next chapter).

When I visited the Devils Peaks, I only hiked to the lower peak. So on my 1991 Red Buttes excursion, I decided it would be fun to sneak in Upper Devil's Peak. It turned out to be 6 gruelling miles from Cook and Green Pass to the Upper Devil. It would have been far easier just to hike the extra mile from Lower Devil's Peak.

Back at Kangaroo Springs, its cirque basin, like much of the area (including the aptly named Red Buttes), is composed of orange weathered serpentine. A band of white marble cuts across the formation, forming a major outcropping just below Red Butte.

The same band plays across the Kangaroo Springs basin. So the cirque contains several snowy white outcroppings, in gorgeous contrast to the orange cliffs, the green meadows and the profusion of multicolored flowers (pentstemon, Indian paintbrush, several kinds of yellow, white and blue daisies and a large, white lily, to name just a few).

The basin presently contain no lakes, only a couple ponds, on a terrace far below the trail. Since it's an older cirque whose carving glacier is long gone, the original lake is in the later stages of evolution—completely silted in and forming a marshy meadow with a creek meandering through.

From the far end of Kangaroo Springs, it's ½ mile to the junction with the Boundary Trail, which follows the rim of the Siskiyous to Azalea Lake, Pyramid Peak and Tannen Mountain.

I suggest returning to your car via the road, mainly for variety. It's slightly longer but avoids the long uphill trek back to Echo Lake. By now, you've probably had your fill of uphill treks.

Pacific Crest Trail at Red Buttes. (Chapter 51)

52. DEVILS PEAKS

Length: 5 to 6 miles
Water: Very little
Access: Paved hwy
Season: Any
Difficulty: Very, very steep
Elevation: 1371 to 5000 ft
(lower peak), 6041 (upper peak)
Use: Non-motorized only
Ownership: Klamath NF
Phone: (916) 465-2241

Directions: From I-5, north of Yreka, follow Hwy 96 down the Klamath River to Seiad Valley (about 40 miles). The easily missed trailhead is located 7/10 mile from the west end of the Seiad Creek Bridge. It is marked by a wide spot on the road's south (river) shoulder and a small sign on the north side saying "Trail." A gravel driveway enters the highway at the same spot.

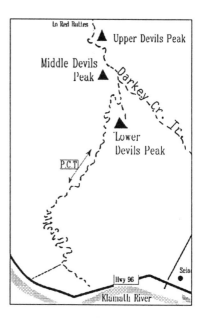

I've often wondered why so many beautiful places are named after the Devil. Old Scratch certainly had no hand in creating the Devils Peaks. Granted, they lie at the end (or start) of one of the Pacific Crest Trail's more Devilishly steep segments. But the towering spires are far better described as heavenly.

This chapter offers an excuse to mention a favorite auto excursion, the 60 mile Klamath River drive, from I-5 to the town of Happy Camp. While following northern California's second longest waterway (after the Sacramento), the road travels from a semi-desert rainshadow of manzanita and juniper, to Douglas-fir dominated coastal rain forest.

The trail is often passable during dry winters (at least to the Lower Peak), as it climbs a steep, exposed south slope. Above the 4000 foot level, you may find yourself slogging over snowy patches. During hard winters or following storms, you may not reach the top. I climbed it on Dec. 17th.

While the path didn't seem terribly steep, I was shocked on looking down from the summit. The mountain sweeps almost vertically down to the Klamath River, 3700 feet below. I couldn't imagine where a 5 mile trail might be squeezed in.

Lower Devils Peak is frequently visible along the trail and never appears very far away. Around every bend, the little beige blockhouse on its summit beckons, seemingly just a few feet away.

It's a lot farther than it looks.

From the trailhead, the route climbs steeply for ¼ mile, until joining the main PCT coming up from the Klamath. That's the first indication that you're on the right path. Turn right onto the PCT and follow its winding switchbacks through the woods for a mile, until reaching a little spring with a pipe dribbling water into a trough. This is the only water for many miles.

Past the initial junction, the trail levels slightly as it winds through low and middle elevation woods of oak, madrone, ponderosa pine and Douglas-fir. Majestic sugar pines begin to sprinkle the hillsides after a mile or two. Canyon liveoak, along the trail's lower half, attest to steepness and shallow soils.

The path jumps back and forth between the east slope, with views of Seiad Creek and the Klamath, and the west slope, with views of Rattlesnake Mountain and Thompson ridge. Thompson Ridge, riddled with logging roads, rises above the town of Happy Camp. The high summits beyond Happy Camp are Bear Mountain and Preston Peak.

The unfolding vistas should hold your attention while negotiating the steeper pitches. After 2 miles, the trail reaches a secondary summit, then starts uphill again, hitting 2 or 3 more false summits.

Some 4 miles from the trailhead, with the aforementioned blockhouse apparently so close you can touch it, the trail swings around to the peak's west face, grows extremely steep, and finally emerges from the woods into the rocky crags. In summer, this exposed region can be hot and dusty. In winter, the sheltered lower slopes yield to the crest's howling winds. Bundle up in winter no matter how warm the weather apears.

The trail crosses the main crest at a low spot between Lower and Middle Devils Peak, amid a small knobcone pine grove. This is the first glimpse of the Middle and Upper peaks. The Middle Peak, an inverted ice cream cone, is barren and uninspiring. The more impressive Upper peak, at 6041 feet, boasts jagged side peaks and occasionally forested pockets.

From the divide, the PCT continues north. After skirting the Middle Peak's east face, it crosses the ridge again to ascend the Upper Peak. It's a little over a mile, up an exposed, rocky trail climbing 1000 feet, from Lower Devil to Upper Devil. If you can't make it, don't worry. Lower Devil is sufficiently rewarding.

Beyond Upper Devil, the PCT continues to the Red Buttes, Mt. Ashland, Crater Lake and points north.

I hiked to Upper Devil's Peak from the Red Buttes, a gruelling six mile jaunt I ended up regretting (see previous chapter). It would have been easier to just hike the extra mile from the Lower peak. The path misses the Upper Devil summit by about 500 feet and it's a 10 minute off-trail scramble to the very top.

Where the path crosses the divide between the Middle and Lower Peak, look for a short way trail south. It leads along a saw-toothed ridge and up some boulders to the Lower Peak's summit.

The blockhouse is disappointing as there's nothing in it. But the panorama...

Aside from the landmarks described earlier, the ever present Mt. Shasta stands out. Goosenest Mountain, immediately north of Shasta, is recognized by the volcanic crater in its top. The Marble Mountains, south of the Klamath, may also be seen. Unfortunately, Lower Devils Peak isn't high enough to peer into the the Marbles' core. Only the lower peaks around Grider Creek are visible.

The view north, into the Red Buttes, provides the real blockbuster. At 6739 feet, Red Butte isn't much high than Upper Devils Peak. But it's colors are stunning. Its brilliant orange serpentine, and that of neighboring Condrey Mountain, contrasts with verdant alpine forests and meadows. In comparison, the Devils Peaks tend to be dominated by grays, tans, olives and other muted tones.

Remnant of 1987 fire on PCT. Upper Devils Peak. (ch.52)

On PCT, Lower and Middle Devils Peak,Above Klamath.(ch.52)

Approaching Upper Devils Peak from Red Buttes on PCT.(ch.52)

53. KELSEY TRAIL
(Marble Mountain Wilderness Area)

Length: 4 miles
Water: Not a problem.
Access: Narrow blacktop. Last mile is dirt
Season: Any
Difficulty: Moderately easy
Elevation: 2400 to 4300
Use: Non-motorized only
Ownership: Klamath NF
Phone: (916) 468-5351

Directions: Take I-5 to south Yreka and follow Hwy 3 to Fort Jones, turning right onto the Scott River Road. Past Spring Flat and just before Bridge Flat, the blacktop road crosses the Scott River. Turn right immediately over the bridge. Do not cross a second bridge, ½ mile up the dirt side road, but continue straight, past the house, to the roomy trailhead. The last few hundred feet are not as bad as they look.

The trail can also be reached from the Bridge Flat Campground. Hike up an unmarked skid road across the road and look for a small sign pointing left. Add a mile to the length if you begin here.

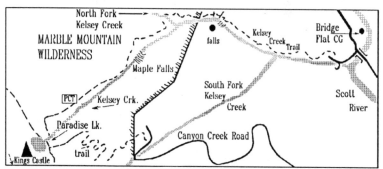

The Scott River Ranger District's Recreation Officer, Chuck Smith, pestered me for 2 years to check out this trail. A pet project, he's devoted much energy to its restoration. Unfortunately, paths following creeks tend to be boring, without highlights and low on my priority list.

I herewith apologize to Chuck. The Kelsey Trail turned out to be one of the most unusual, spectacular and varied I've seen.

For starters, it's 130 years old and was built by the Army. Fort Jones was an actual fort 130 years ago, and the area was gripped in a gold rush. The route served as a supply line to Crescent City until the turn of the century. The Bear Lake and South Kelsey Trails (Ch.45 and 46), also follow segments of this thoroughfare.

While the engineering is excellent, as indicated by the meticulous stone fill, I'd hate to depend on this trail for contact with civilization. Snowed over 7 months a year, two 6000 foot passes are crossed before it emerges on the Smith River's South Fork. What the path lacks in military convenience, it makes up in splendor. Far from wandering along a quiet creek, its only constant is the deafening crash of surging whitewater.

Occasionally, the trail indeed briefly traverses gentle woods. Sometimes, however, it drops down to the creek to peek at narrow canyons, waterfalls or maple flats. Often, it climbs hundreds of feet up, skirting cliffs and gravel slopes and crossing spectacular rock points.

In the 4 miles to Maple Falls, I counted at least 8 side creeks. Some charged down black gorges which never see the light of day. Some were wide, airy and boulder strewn. Some fanned out over glistening black rock faces while others dropped in stair-step pools and ledges. At least one entailed walking through knee deep water (in December). A couple streams on the opposite side plunged 1000 feet before meeting the creek.

From the well marked, oak shaded trailhead, the path takes off up a switchback to the right of the bulletin board. Despite gaining 500 feet per mile, this is a reasonably easy route. Upgrades tend to be concentrated into short switchback areas followed by long, level stretches. The surrounding forest consists of Douglas-fir, black oak, madrone, ponderosa pine and grand fir. Abundant canyon liveoak indicates thin soils and steep slopes.

The path soon rises to 100 feet above the creek, where it follows an aqueduct ditch for 1/8 mile. The ditch ends at an immense rock face, high above a beautiful, alder covered flat. Rusted metal half-pipes, which once carried water from the flat to the ditch, are stacked alongside the trail.

Beyond, the walkway climbs through pine-woods. At one point, a large area of mine tailings tumble down the opposite hillside. It was probably a gold mine, although serpentine formations nearby also suggests chrome or nickel. Look for white quartz veins as you walk. Area miners quested after this gold bearing mineral.

Two miles up, the path crosses a steep side stream, drops near the creek, ascends a couple switchbacks and makes a large "U" across a second creek. The Wilderness boundary lies 1/2 mile beyond.

Where the trail drops near the creek, a 30 foot waterfall surges through a 10 foot wide, black chasm. A short way trail leads to the falls and adjacent Fish Camp. Look for a few wooden benches and be very careful on the mossy rocks above the gorge.

At the North Fork, Kelsey Creek cuts south at the foot of a towering rock outcropping. The trail continues up the North Fork for ¼ mile, opposite the outcropping's sheer, north wall. Heretofore, the path has followed a sunny south slope. This 200 foot stretch, 3½ miles from the trailhead, follows a north face. Since snow lingers on north slopes, especially in dark canyons, this segment may be impassible in winter.

Presuming you make it past the North Fork, the path veers south. From there, Maple Falls beckons ½ mile ahead. Look for the trail to steepen and cut inland, several hundred feet above the creek. The 50 foot falls slowly emerge just beyond. A way trail leads down to a little maple flat and camp site atop the falls.

We suggest Maple Falls as a turn-a-round spot, although the North Fork provides an admirable objective in winter. A mile above Maple Falls, the canyon opens out to a wide, beautiful meadowned valley rising in a series of tiers to Kings Castle and Paradise Lake. Not visible heretofore, Kings Castle, a bread loaf shaped, 7400 foot marble outcropping, and the high crags of the Marbles, tower overhead.

Charming Paradise Lake nestles at the foot of Kings Castle, at an elevation of 6200 feet, 7 miles from the trailhead. The last ½ mile to the lake is extremely steep. The equally difficult Paradise Lake Trail, to the same spot, is described in the next chapter.

54. PARADISE LAKE
(Marble Mountain Wilderness Area)

See map, chapter 53
Length: 2 miles
Water: OK
Access: Very long, mostly good, dirt road
Season: June — October
Difficulty: Difficult
Elevation: 5100 to 6200
Use: Non-motorized only
Ownership: Klamath NF
Phone: (916) 468-5351

Directions: *Take I-5 to the south Yreka (Hwy 3) exit. Proceed to Fort Jones. Turn right onto the Scott River Road and follow it to the Indian Scotty Bridge. Cross the bridge and follow Canyon Creek Road (44N45), past the Lovers Camp turnoff to the Paradise Lake trailhead. The route is well signed.*

While not the highest peak in the Marble Mountains, Kings Castle, at 7400 feet, is among the most significant. It used to be called Marble Mountain and the Wilderness was named for it. The name was later changed to avoid confusion with the Marble Rim and Black Marble Mountain. Kings Castle is an appropriate name for an exquisite slice of scenery.

In 1970, the shortest route to Paradise Lake was the 7 mile Kelsey Trail. Logging roads have since pushed to within 2 miles of the lake. These roads are highly scenic, offering peeks into the Marble Valley area and close-up looks at Kings Castle. A brief view of Kings Castle also appears from the Scott River Road (near Chuck Smith's house). Look for a white outcropping resembling a giant loaf of bread, perched atop a green mountain.

Canyon Creek Road is wide and well groomed. For the last few miles to the trailhead, follow a spur which is much narrower and a little rougher. A quarter-mile before the trailhead, the road fords the South Fork of Kelsey Creek. You may wish to park there if water is high.

The steep trail can be negotiated in an hour or so. Very popular, it's not for questers of solitude in mid-summer. But you won't be disappointed. After winding breathlessly and seemingly endlessly back and forth up a densely wooded slope, the route breaks into a brushy ridge surrounded by giant cliffs. Canyon Creek, the Marble Rim and the Scott River Canyon can be seen in the distance.

Immediately after, the trail enters a little meadowed-basin decorated with clumps of Shasta fir and mountain hemlock. The shallow, 5 acre lake adorns its center. The lake has one deep spot, where it nestles against a low rock face below a vast green slope. The Kings Castle outcropping crowns the top of the slope. Another outcropping, to the left, is much larger but not as pretty.

The Paradise Lake Trail joins the Pacific Crest Trail at the entrance to the basin, just before the lake. A left turn on the PCT lands you in the Marble Valley after 4 or 5 miles. The Kelsey Trail to Maple Falls, described in the previous chapter, leaves the PCT at the lake.

55. MARBLE VALLEY
(Marble Mountain Wilderness Area)

Length: 5 miles
Water: OK
Access: Long, winding, gravel road
Season: June — October
Difficulty: Moderate
Elevation: 4300 to 6000 feet

Use: Non-motorized
Ownership: Klamath NF
Phone: (916) 468-5351

Directions: *Leave I-5 at the Hwy 3 exit (south Yreka). Follow Hwy 3 to Fort Jones and turn right onto the blacktopped Scott River Road. Proceed to the Indian Scotty Bridge. Cross the bridge onto the wide dirt road and follow the signs to Lovers Camp.*

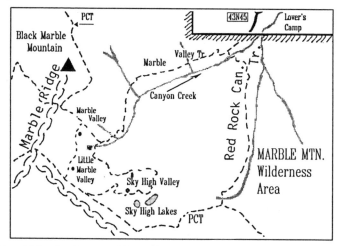

Point blank: The Marble Valley may be the most beautiful place I've ever been. I consider it the ultimate journey into the glacial valleys of the Klamath Mountains system. A word of caution, though. This is an extremely popular trail. If you visit on a July afternoon, be prepared for an endless procession of horses, pack animals, Boy Scouts, etc. They can raise much dust.

I suggest a September or October visit. It's cooler and there are fewer people—or mosquitoes. But check the weather forecast and know what time it gets dark.

From the huge Lovers Camp trailhead, with its horse corral, the trail strikes out along Canyon Creek for 3 or 4 miles. While there are some steep spots and the trend is uphill, the going is not too difficult. Canyon Creek flows through a wide valley with the trail high up the hillside. Many side creeks and open meadows alternate with woods of Shasta fir, western white pine and mountain hemlock.

Finally, the Marble Valley unfolds in front of you. It may take a while to soak in its exquisite beauty. Side trails abound so bring a map and do some exploring. The Sky High Lakes Trail takes off left at the valley entrance. Shortly after, the Marble Valley Trail merges with the Pacific Crest Trail, coming in on the right.

The actual valley is nothing more than a little wooded flat. Immediately west, however, rises a 1000 foot thick band of snowy white marble, called the Marble Rim or simply Marble Mountain. Kings Castle Mountain, 3 miles north (see Ch. 54), is also sometimes called Marble Mountain. The outcropping of black schist capping the Marble Rim's north end is incorrectly named Black Marble Mountain.

The Marble Valley side of the Marble Rim is a gently sloping expanse. The other side has been deeply gouged into a series of steep walled glacial cirques above Rainey Lake and Elk Creek. Try to get a look at both sides.

Little Marble Valley, down the PCT to the left, is even prettier than Marble Valley. It's floor and two sides are made of white marble. Wildflowers sprout between cracks in the tile of the valley floor. Geologically, this is a karst area with sink holes where hollowed out marble has collapsed.

You might wish to continue beyond the Little Marble Valley to the ridge at the valley's south end. From there, both sides of the rim, the major peaks of the Marbles and Trinity Alps, and Mt. Shasta may be viewed.

The National Speleological Society's Portland Grotto has mapped over 50 caves within the Marble Rim, all containing stalactites and other flowstone formations. One cave is considerably larger than that in Oregon Caves National Monument. It was only discovered in 1976.

Most of the cave openings are marked by vertical drops and are very dangerous. Also, dripstone formations inside are extremely fragile and take hundreds of thousands of years to form. The Forest Service and Speleological Society ask that only serious cavers visit these sites. For more information, contact the Portland Grotto.

After the Marble Valley, the Sky-High Valley may sound anticlimactic. It isn't. Of the hundreds of glacial cirque lakes in the Marbles and Trinity Alps, these tiny gems rank among the prettiest. Nestled at the foot of a soaring headwall and surrounded by meadow, the phrase "emerald necklace" comes to mind in describing the chain of two main lakes and several ponds. It's 1½ miles to Sky-High from Marble Valley. Lots of trout await catching in the 6 and 12 acre lakes but many anglers vie for them.

To return to your car, either double back or continue ahead to the PCT. Take a left there and another left onto the Red Rock Valley Trail, which also emerges near Lovers Camp. It's 5 miles back via that route. Red Rock Valley is a serpentine-type formation with orange cliffs rising above an open, meadow lined creek.

56. WRIGHT LAKES
(Marble Mountain Wilderness Area)

Length: 4 miles
Water: OK
Access: Wide, gravel road
Season: June — October
Difficulty: Extremely steep
Elevation: 3800 to 7400 feet
Use: Non-motorized only
Ownership: Klamath NF
Phone: (916) 468-5351

*Directions: Take the south Yreka exit (Hwy 3) from I-5. Proceed to
the town of Fort Jones and turn right, onto the Scott River Road. Take a left over the Indian Scotty Bridge, up Canyon Creek Road, and another left at the sign to the Boulder Creek Trail. This last spur, while steep and winding, is wide and surprisingly well maintained. The trailhead is roomy and well marked.*

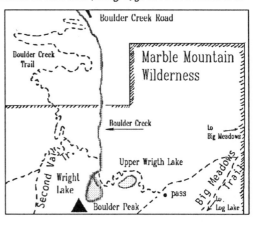

There is much to recommend the Wright Lakes/Boulder Peak
area. Boulder Peak, for instance, happens to be the highest summit in the Marble Mountains, at 8299 feet. Upper Wright Lake is
the loftiest among the Wilderness Area's 79 lakes, at 7400 feet.
Aside from abundant superlatives and beauty, the site is also botanically unusual.

In an earlier book, I recommended the 3½ mile Big Meadows
Trail as the best access to the area. With a trailhead elevation of
5800 feet, it's not only ½ mile shorter, it starts 2000 feet higher
than does the Boulder Creek Trail. In that book I barely mentioned the Boulder Creek Trail.

The Big Meadows Trail, unfortunately, is virtually impossible to find. While the turnoff from Scott Valley is well marked, the road soon deteriorates into an incomprehensible maze. Much of it crosses private land and the trailhead has been moved several times.

Boulder Creek is now the recommended route, despite its reputation as one of Northern California's more demanding trails. The trailhead is easily located and the hike is easier than one might expect. Several long, level pitches and many outstanding vistas, take one's mind off the drudgery.

The path begins in a middle elevation Douglas-fir forest, mixed with black oak and madrone. The first mile is pretty much straight up, with a couple level stretches. It then breaks out onto an old road for a mile, with rather easy going. So easy, in fact, one wonders why they closed it to autos.

The third mile, back on the trail, is by far the worst. But much of the rise is concentrated into a few very steep upgrades which don't last long. It, too, has a few flat sections, plus a fantastic view of Kings Castle and the Marble Rim.

Things level off again where the trail divides. The path right leads to Second Valley and Sky High Lakes. Stay left for Lower and Upper Wright Lakes.

A quarter-mile beyond the junction, the way breaks out onto a magnificent meadowed basin with cliffs and waterfalls, wildflowers and towering peaks. Things continue rather steeply but the worst is over.

The 26 acre Lower Wright Lake occupies a vast, open glacial cirque, two cirques above the one near the junction. Its brilliant aqua water nestles against a black headwall which soars 1000 feet to Boulder Peak.

Picturesque clumps of whitebark and foxtail pines decorate the huge meadow. The former is a gnarled, treeline species. Foxtail pine is also a treeline species, native mainly to the east side of the southern Sierra. After a gap of 600 miles in its range, it turns up in a few widely scattered sites in the Marbles and Trinity Alps.

Wildflowers include a profusion of red and purple Indian paintbrush, arnica, aster, monkshood, fireweed, corn lily, monkey flower, pentstemon, delphinium, sedum, gentian and many others. Many occupy a seep area on the trail above the lower lake.

The 12 acre upper lake isn't as spectacular as its neighbor. Its basin is smaller and more confined, with a steeper shore and much denser surrounding forest cover. I liked the sawtoothed ridge, overhead to the left above the upper lake.

The real payoff comes ¼ mile beyond the upper lake, at the high ridge. There, the world falls away and a stunning panorama of Scott Valley unfolds, with its patchwork ranchlands. Shasta pokes its inevitable head in the distance. The other glacier to the south is Mt. Thompson, highest in the Trinity Alps.

A faint trail right, from the ridgetop, climbs Boulder Peak.

57. TAYLOR LAKE
(Russian Wilderness)

Length: 1 mile
Water: OK
Access: Very poor, dirt road
Season: June — October
Difficulty: Easy
Elevation: 6500 ft.
Use: Non-motorized only
Ownership: Klamath NF
Phone: (916) 468-5351

Directions: Leave I-5 at the Scott Valley (Hwy 3) exit, just south of Yreka. Follow Hwy 3, 24 miles to Etna. Proceed west up Main Street towards Sawyers Bar and the Salmon River Country. At the first switchback beyond the pass, a low quality, two mile road takes off left to the Taylor Lake trailhead. The route is well signed.

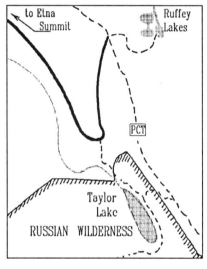

While the Taylor Lake Trail extends barely a mile, possibly less, it provides an excuse to explore Etna Summit, one of California's grander and lesser known scenic experiences. From the tiny Scott Valley town of Etna, a gravel road queues through woods and over rushing, boulder lined creeks, straining interminably upward.

I lived in Etna in 1970 and '71. My address was #1 Main Street. Working for the California Fish and Game Department, I negotiated Etna Summit Road almost daily, gathering Salmon River fishing data. Some job. A couple surprise blizzards introduced me to the fine points of driving in deep snow on steep, unpaved, back country roads. It's a useful skill.

At the road's crest, gateway to Never Never Land, the world falls away in an endless black expanse of forest. Thousands of feet below, the North Fork of the Salmon River can be seen. White granite parapets of the Marble and Russian Mountains frame the vista to the north and south.

The drive to Etna Summit is rewarding even if you never leave your car. From there, one can continue down to the Salmon to check out the canyon, embark on long trails into the south side of the Marbles, or visit the charming hamlets of Sawyers Bar, Forks of Salmon and Somesbar.

The Pacific Crest Trail spans Etna Summit. To the north, it offers a poor route into the Marbles. To the south, however, the PCT leads quickly to Ruffey, Meeks and Smith Lake, all tiny pools below a narrow ridgetop. It also leads to the ridge above Taylor Lake after 2½ miles.

Beyond Etna Summit, the main road swings left, then right as it makes its way down to the river. The Taylor Lake Road takes off at the swing right. This last, 2 mile route is extremely narrow and in poor condition, with very steep upgrades. We had to take a second pass at a couple of hills, partly because our car wasn't very powerful and partly because we kept having to stop half-way up to let cars pass. This is a very popular road. It's also very scenic, weaving in and out of high elevation, Shasta fir forests, open fields and meadows, razor peaks and sudden drop-offs to the river. The trail is well marked, with parking for about 10 cars. From there, the road switches sharply uphill, ending at the PCT above Ruffey Lakes.

The Taylor Lake Trail follows a bubbling creek through open meadows and over exposed rock surfaces. It's lovely and level but watch out for cows.

The 12 acre, teardrop shaped lake fills a flat, open plateau with jagged peaks to the south and west. A glacial valley cuts the far end of the lake. A poorly marked trail traverses the valley, leading the adventurous over the ridge to Twin Lakes and Hogan Lake. Taylor Lake has a level, roomy shore well suited for camping. Brook Trout fishing is supposed to be excellent.

58. PAYNES LAKE
(Russian Wilderness Area)

Length: 3 miles
Water: None
Access: Long, fair dirt road
Season: June — October
Difficulty: Difficult
Elevation: 4400 to 6500 ft.
Use: Non-motorized only
Ownership: Klamath NF
Phone: (916) 468-5351

Directions: *Get off I-5 at the south Yreka (Hwy 3) exit. Follow Hwy 3 past Etna to French Creek Road. Proceed to the end of the road, noting where it joins Sugar Creek Road so you won't get lost on the way back. Turn right at the "T" junction with the sign pointing to Paynes Lake. Follow the narrow, rather rough dirt road to the roomy, well marked trailhead.*

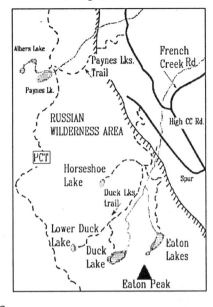

The prettiest of northern California's alpine glacial lakes all lie within areas of white granite. Unlike other rock types, granite tends to erode into rounded domes and has a soft-edged beauty all its own. It's the reason for the great popularity of the Trinity Alps and Sierra Nevada.

One of the northernmost granite-set glacial lakes is Paynes Lake. Expatriate Californians living in Oregon are particularly attracted to Paynes and nearby Duck Lakes because they remind one of the Sierra's granite peaks and domes.

Paynes Lake lies within the new Russian Wilderness Area in an extremely rugged little range between the Marbles and Trinity Alps. Before the creation of the Wilderness, it was known mostly to local fishermen.

The Russian Mountains are noted for their botanical diversity as well as their beauty. This is described in detail in the Duck Lake Chapter (Ch.59). Look for Brewer spruce, Shasta fir, white fir, western white pine, mountain hemlock, lodgepole pine, Sadler oak, rhododendron, evergreen chinkapin and scrub tanoak. Like I said, it's diverse.

The trail follows a thinly soiled, sparsely wooded granite ridge between two deep valleys. The first 1½ miles of steep switchbacks seems interminable. You know you're halfway there when you come to an all-too-brief level spot in a little shaded cove. The path then becomes steep again, and more open as it enters the Paynes Lake cirque. The 16 acre lake is quite deep and fishing and camping are excellent.

While Duck Lake is larger and possibly prettier, it looks smaller because the basin around Paynes Lake is larger. Much level, gently shaded, not too brushy land surrounds the lake.

Sparkling white granite domes thrust up on two sides and a vast meadow adorns the hillside immediately north of the main rock headwall.

The Pacific Crest Trail crosses the Paynes Lake Trail just below the lake. For the energetic, it's 7 miles along the PCT to Etna summit. The Paynes Lake Trail continues past the lake, shooting steeply up the meadow and nearby rock faces, to Lower and Upper Albers Lakes. It's only ¼ mile and both these tiny, exquisite pools are stocked with trout.

59. DUCK LAKE
(Russian Wilderness Area)

See Map, chapter 58.
Length: 3 miles
Water: OK
Access: Long, fair dirt road
Season: June — October
Difficulty: Moderate
Elevation: 4800 to 6700 ft.
Use: Non-motorized only
Ownership: Klamath NF
Phone: (916) 468-5351

Directions: *Follow the directions to Paynes Lake but turn left at the sign at the "T" junction instead of right. A mile or so past the sign, look for a turnoff doubling back uphill to the right. This last spur may be gated. It's a couple more miles to the trailhead, over a fair (with rough spots), dirt road.*

The mountains containing Duck and Paynes Lake are a small but formidable cluster between the Marbles and Trinity Alps. The range has a different name on every map. Rising between California's Salmon and Scott Rivers, they had been most commonly called the Salmon-Scott Mountains. A new Wilderness Area, however, named for the group's highest peak (8196 feet), suggests as good a name as any. I'm pleased to call them the Russian Mountains.

In 1970, the Russian Mountains were little known and seldom visited, except by local fishermen. Back then, there were few trailhead markings. I located Duck Lake Trail by driving a maze of logging roads, parking at a washout at Duck Lake Creek, and searching up and down the road.

The upper ends of these roads are now closed off and inside the Wilderness. Personally, while I love hiking, I also enjoy pleasure driving and sightseeing. So I find it a little aggravating to have to hike up a perfectly driveable road.

The path up from the well marked trailhead is rather steep, especially at first. It soon turns onto a road, which it follows up some very steep logging spurs. Then it takes off sharply uphill, through the woods again before emerging onto a high road. Turn left here, following the signs. After a level ¼ mile hike along this road, the old trailhead is finally reached, 1½ miles past the new trailhead.

The old trailhead is actually two trailheads 100 feet apart. The Eaton Lakes Trail comes in first, then the Duck Lake Trail. If you continue up the road, you'll end up at Horseshoe Lake after a mile.

Above the high trailhead, the Duck Lake Trail contains a few steep pitches, especially near the beginning. It isn't nearly as bad as the Paynes Lake Trail, however.

Duck Lake, at 26 acres, is among the range's largest, although the surrounding basin is rather small. The trail climbs through woods of Shasta red fir, western white pine, mountain hemlock and Brewer spruce, with lodgepole pine at the lake. A ½ mile side trail to Little Duck Lake breaks off ¼ mile below Duck Lake.

The last pitch to the lake winds through a maze of giant, white boulders, remarkable for their smooth roundness. It's a lovely area. The surrounding peaks aren't as impressive as those at Paynes Lake but the gentle granite domes and white rock shore makes the lake appear like a giant swimming pool. The woods are denser than at Paynes Lake and the banks are steeper. All lakes offer excellent brook trout angling.

The two Eaton Lakes grace the end of the well marked, ¾ mile side trail noted earlier. The path is steep, rocky and faint in places. Eaton Lake occupies 13 acres, with the much smaller upper lake immediately beyond.

Paynes, Duck, Eaton and Horseshoe Lakes are all included in a proposed Forest Service Botanical Area. It will protect prime examples of what botanists call "glacial relics," or remnant populations of plants whose natural ranges became distorted during the last ice age.

You won't see them all from the trail but there are 17 conifer species in the vicinity, including the rare Brewer spruce and Pacific silver fir. Except for this area, the latter is not found south of Crater Lake.

Also hidden around are groves of foxtail pine, a treeline species found in the southern Sierra, and a few widely scattered locations in the Marbles and Russians. A keen observer might also ferret out the only California populations of subalpine fir and Engelmann spruce.

60. WHITNEY FALLS
(Mt. Shasta Wilderness)

Length: 1½ miles
Water: None
Access: Fair dirt road
Season: June — October
Difficulty: Easy
Elevation: 5600 to 6200
Use: Non-motorized
Ownership: Shasta-Trinity NF
Phone: (916) 926—4511

Directions: Take I-5 to the Weed/Klamath Falls (Hwy 97) exit. Head towards Klamath Falls for 1 3/4 miles. Past the Haystack Butte gravel pit, take the first dirt road to the right. The major intersection leading back to Grenada (A-2), means you've gone too far. Follow the dirt access road 4 miles, past the railroad tracks, to the Bolam trailhead. The road of compacted volcanic gravel is driveable but very narrow. Stay off it during storms.

Heading south on I-5 towards Mt. Shasta's magnificent mass, one might notice two immense white gashes on the peak's flank. They're well up the mountain rise—maybe⅓ of the way—but in the trees just below where the really steep slopes zoom to the summit. The gashes are two mighty river gorges cut through loose ash. The one on the right, class, is the objective of this hike.

This is one of only 2 or 3 trails into the new Mount Shasta Wilderness from the north. This particular entry is dramatic, not far from the highway, and a short, easy hike. The looming views of Shasta, obviously, enhance the appeal.

Shasta-Trinity National Forest wishes hikers to be aware that at present, routes are unmarked. Much of the trail follows old logging roads, most of which don't really go anywhere. The Forest Service has plans for long range improvements.

The trailhead boasts a huge bulletin board and plenty of turn-around room. Nevertheless, it took me several minutes to find the trail, located on the right, across the creek bed which is likely to be dry.

The trail's first mile follows an old road along the canyon of Bolam Creek. Where it wanders away from the usually dry creek bed, the terrain becomes brushy and choked with manzanita. A few lonesome pines and white firs poke up here and there. The brushfield used to be a vast forest whose trees were all hauled away over the road you're walking on.

The path eventually rejoins Bolam Creek, then curves sharply uphill to the right.

Bolam Creek is named for Bolam Glacier, a huge ice fall on Shasta's main peak, immediately left of Whitney Glacier. Whitney Glacier occupies the valley between Shasta and Shastina. Resembling an inverted flower pot, Shastina is Shasta's main subpeak.

A quarter-mile after leaving Bolam Creek, the road/trail appears to head for a small draw but veers left before entering it. A sharp eye will notice a faint trail up the draw. I built a stone cairn (or "rock duck") to mark the turnoff. The road continues another mile or two, then peters out.

This ¼ mile side trail is the actual Whitney Falls Trail while the old road is the Bolam Creek Trail. The road's upper end is used by scramble hikers to access Whitney and Bolam Glaciers.

The Whitney Falls Trail winds briefly through some woods and across a grassy flat. At the flat's far end, the world suddenly falls away and you find yourself peering down into an awesome canyon with walls of loose, sandy ash.

The walls form an immense "V", sloping down to Whitney Creek at 45 degree angles on both sides. Almost entirely lacking in vegetation, the slopes undercut the rim at the top. Several large trees with exposed roots will soon be sucked into the chasm.

Far below, the boulder strewn river makes a broad meander, then disappears downhill. Upstream, the canyon head is blocked by a sheer rock face, 200 feet high, over which the falls tumble.

One slight problem: Both falls and creek are likely to be dry, except in spring. But that in no way diminishes the grandeur of the scene. The trail skirts the canyon rim towards the falls but never quite gets there.

Whitney Glacier is only two miles from the falls, over apparently passable terrain. I wonder if it would be feasible to someday extend the trail to the Glacier's snout?

A final word: Shasta not only can create its own weather, it can do so in a hurry. The October day I visited Whitney Falls was sunny and in the high 60's. On the way back to my car, within minutes, it clouded over around the peak, the temperature dropped 20 degrees and a howling wind came up. I was sweaty, in short sleeves and without a jacket—a perfect formula for hypothermia. It could just as suddenly have snowed.

61. CLEAR CREEK TRAIL
(Mt. Shasta Wilderness)

Length: 2½ miles
Water: Lots but, not drinkable
Access: Very long, sometimes rough dirt roads.
Season: June -- October
Difficulty: Difficult
Elevation: 6400 to 8000 Ft.
Use: Non-motorized only
Ownership: Shasta-Trinity NF
Phone: (916) 964-2184

Directions: Take I-5 to the McCloud Exit and head west on Hwy 89 towards McCloud. At Snowmans Hill, turn up the Shasta Ski Park Road (88). Head right at the junction with Road 31 and continue about 10 miles to Road 41N61, which is a four way intersection. You'll see a Clear Creek Trail sign.

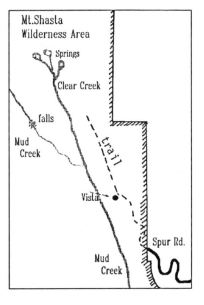

It's 4 winding miles up 41N61 to the trailhead. Some of the many turns are clearly signed, some are marked only by little yellow cards and at some, you simply follow the most used fork. The last couple miles are rutted, cut by water bars and obviously muddy certain times of the year. I made it easily in a two wheel drive, although some driving skill was required. The trailhead is quite roomy at the upper end of a clearcut.

I hate to report this, but Mt. Shasta, one of the world's most spectacular peaks, is rapidly being torn apart and carried away in large chunks. This is not apparent from the three sides visible from paved highways. From the north, west and south, the mountain appears just what it is—a huge, relatively young, momentarily dormant volcano.

The seldom seen east side, however, accessible only over a 35 miles of dirt road between Hwy 97 out of Weed and Hwy 89 out of Mt. Shasta City, reveals a very different situation. That side of the peak looks not like a fresh young upstart but like a glaciated crag out of the Swiss Alps.

Vast canyons, some over 1000 feet deep, extend nearly to the summit. Massive sheets of glacial ice gouge into the peak, excavating ton upon ton of boulders, ash and silt, which are then carried away down rushing creeks and over waterfalls, to the valleys below.

If this keeps up, in a few million years, there will be nothing left of Shasta but the centermost lava plug, much like Pilot Rock, a few miles north.

The main culprit in all this is the aptly named Mud Creek, which, along with adjacent Clear Creek, is visited by the Clear Creek Trail.

Before describing this trail, however, I should throw in a few words about the roads east of Shasta. Most notable is Military Pass Road (Road 19), which leaves Hwy 97 a couple miles beyond the Whitney Falls road. I found Military Pass a big disappointment. The wide, rather washboarded dirt route, reaches the top of a gentle rise in 4 or 5 miles, then levels off for several miles before dropping slightly. One would hardly call this a "pass."

The road offers only occassional glimpses of Shasta, through a forest of lodgepole pine (contrasted to the ponderosa pine/white fir forest at Whitney Falls and the Shasta fir/white pine/mountain hemlock forest along the Clear Creek Trail).

Eventually, the road becomes wide and gravelled. It dead-ends at Road 13, which winds slowly back to the town of McCloud. Road 31, intersecting the Military Pass Road shortly before the Road 13 junction, ends up near Mt. Shasta City. It, too, is long, winding and mostly boring but wide and easily driveable. It offers even fewer views of Shasta than does Military Pass.

Road 31 contains a potentially dangerous booby trap (which is why I suggest starting from Hwy 89 for the Clear Creek Trailhead). I discovered it while barreling along at 35 miles per hour. On coming over a small rise, I found myself 10 feet away from a very wide creek flowing across the road. In a split second, I decided: A) there wasn't time to stop, B) the creek bottom was driveable and C) I had a 50-50 chance of making it though the 1½ foot deep water.

Instead of slamming on the brake, I punched the accelerator and barely made it across. My hands shook for the next few minutes.

As noted, the road from 31 to the trailhead is sometimes steep, rutted in spots and a little hard to follow. It's hard to believe, approaching the trailhead, that you're at 6400 feet or that you've climbed 1000 feet since Road 31.

The path begins as a rather steep amble through a fine looking woods. The only problem is that while Mud Creek Canyon's 1000 foot deep cut is obviously only a couple hundred feet to the left, the path keeps veering right. It's frustrating.

After a mile, however, the trail hits an opening on the rim and the full magnitude of Mud Creek, Clear Creek and the Wintun, Konwakiton and Mud Creek Glaciers are revealed. It's easily one of the most mind boggling vistas I've ever witnessed.

Note especially Mud Creek Falls and the back side of Thumb Rock. The latter is a main landmark on the popular Avalanche Gulch summit climb.

For the next 1½ miles, the path shoots straight up a long, narrow, gravelly opening with forest on both sides. Vistas into the canyon, a couple hundred feet to the left, are obscured by trees. This last trek contains no level spots and nothing to break the monotony as it rises 1200 feet to an 8000 foot ridge.

I found myself walking in six-inch baby steps near the end.

The trail peters out at the base of a 1000 foot rocky hump near the snout of the Wintun Glacier. From the trail end, the wide, barren valley around the head of Clear Creek spreads out below, while Mud Creek Canyon veers off south. A series of springs feeds the Clear Creek headwaters.

The walk down is much, much easier.

62. MT SHASTA/HORSE CAMP
(Mt. Shasta Wilderness Area)

Length: 2 miles (Horse Camp), 6 miles (Summit)
Water: Very little
Access: Winding, paved road
Season: June—October
Difficulty: Moderate (Horse Camp)
Extremely difficult (Summit)
Elevation: 7100/14,161
Use: Non-motorized only
Ownership:Shasta-Trinity NF
Phone: (916) 926-4511

Directions: Take I-5 to the central Mt. Shasta City exit. Proceed through town to Mt. Shasta Boulevard, turn left, then right on Alma Street, following signs to Everitt Memorial Hwy. The Bunny Flat trailhead is at mile 11 of this paved, somewhat curvy road.

Anyone who can't find northern California's Mt. Shasta isn't looking very hard. It pops into view on I-5 somewhere around Corning, 110 miles south of the summit. On an exceptionally

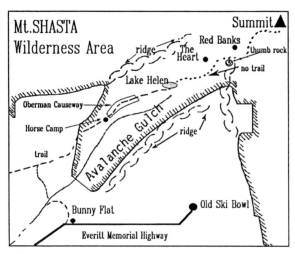

Mt.SHASTA
Wilderness Area

Summit ▲

ridge — The Heart — Red Banks
thumb rock
no trail

Lake Helen

Oberman Causeway

Horse Camp

trail

Avalanche Gulch

ridge

Bunny Flat

Old Ski Bowl

Everitt Memorial Highway

clear day, the mountain can even be seen from the top of Mt. Diablo, near San Francisco. I once saw it from an airplane near the Utah/Nevada line.

Although it's a 9 hour, 6 mile hike to the top, we've included Shasta because of its prominence as a scenic landmark. To make a day-hike out of it, which many people do, you'd have to hit the trail by flashlight at 3 or 4 in the morning. Most climbers camp out at Horse Camp or Lake Helen, however.

Even if you only manage the first 2 miles, to Horse Camp, the path ranks among the region's 2 or 3 most beautiful trails.

The Horse Camp Trail is fairly easy. We suggest the Bunny Flat trailhead to get there. The Sand Flat trailhead, a mile away, is a little longer and requires a 1 mile drive through the woods on a dirt road. It offers better camping and a little more seclusion than Bunny Flat, although there are no actual campground facilities.

From Bunny Flat, hike up the trail, bearing left over the rise, for a mile to the old rain gauge tower. It's ¼ mile from the tower to the junction with the Sand Flat Trail and another 1¼ miles through the woods to the stone shelter at Horse Camp. The woods, not surprisingly, consist almost entirely of Shasta red fir, a local variety of California red fir.

The Sierra Club, which maintains Horse Camp, prefers you spend the night inside only in an emergency. The stone patio out back offers an incredible view of Avalanche Gulch and one of the most delicious springs you'll ever drink from.

The path beyond Horse Camp is not only beautiful, as it approaches treeline, it's one of the oddest trails I've ever been on. At the turn of the century, a local enthusiast named Oberman decided to build a trail to the summit by lining up huge boulders, each with a flat side. He dislodged them with a crowbar and dragged them into place with a mule.

His "causeway" extends for about a mile, amid whitebark pine, narrow little heather lined canyons, and scree fields. It peters out, as do many hikers, where the summit route takes off sharply up-hill, over a rock face, towards Lake Helen.

While there's no maintained trail beyond the causeway, the route is well established. Thousands of hikers have worn an eas-ily followed pathway (several pathways, actually, which braid in and out of one another). They are revealed each summer as the snowpack recedes. You'll cross snow no matter what season you go.

Atop the rocks at the end of the causeway, the trees make their last stand in the form of stunted, contorted whitebark pines. From here on, up the steep, loose scree fields, things become pretty bleak. The only life consists of a few tenuous belly flowers. The banks of nearby Avalanche Creek, however, offer a brilliant green ribbon of life (red heather and monkey flower, mostly), amid the desolation.

As delicious as it looks, it's best not to drink the creek water, which flows from Lake Helen. Being the most popular camping spot on the mountain, sanitary conditions at Lake Helen are highly questionable.

About 45 minutes from Horse Camp, the whitebark pine grove makes a good turn-around spot. Note a couple of things as you look around here. First, the causeway and the trail to Horse Camp, which seemed fairly steep, look perfectly level from this vantage point. Second, Shasta is impossible to photograph. The higher you climb, the greater and more awesome is its vastness. The best a camera can do is isolate tiny patches of its overwhelm-ing beauty.

For those contemplating proceeding to Lake Helen, or attempt-ing the summit, consider this: Distancewise, Horse Camp is ⅓ of the way to the summit and Lake Helen is ⅔'s. By measured ele-vation, however, Lake Helen is ½ way while timewise, it's only ⅓ of the way. It's an hour to Horse Camp, 3 hours to Lake Helen and 9 hours to the top.

The arduous climb up America's most beautiful peak can be accomplished with minimal technical gear or expertise. Stamina, patience, planning and common sense is required. Hiking through snow is easier than over loose, gravely scree. It is best accomplished on crampons (which can be rented in Mt. Shasta City), and in early morning when the crust is firmer.

Beyond the high whitebark pine grove, the route negotiates a series of ever steepening glacial moraines of loose rock and ash. They continue for well over a mile, to an altitude of 10,500 feet.

Halfway up Avalanche Gulch, 3500 feet above Bunny Flat, above the moraines, you'll come to Lake Helen, a large depression filled with snow and climbers. The lake rarely contains water. From there, head right, up the steep snow fields (or scree fields), towards Thumb Rock and the Red Banks, staying to the right of a prominent island in the snow called "The Heart." This is the most strenuous part of the ascent, gaining 2000 feet elevation at a 35% grade.

The Red Banks, a brilliant escarpment just below the summit, make up one of the more noticeable formations. In mid-summer, they're easily visible from the freeway. Experts recommend ascending via Thumb Rock, which projects from the ridge at the beginning of the Red Banks, and making your way over the top of the banks. The climb is difficult, especially at that altitude, but safer than the route along the base of the banks. The latter is prone to falling rock and avalanches.

If you turn back at the whitebark grove or Lake Helen, you might amuse yourself by looking for pieces of the Red Banks among the multi-hued cobbles and boulders strewing the area.

The top of the Red Banks is slow going but easier than below. Unfortunately, this portion of the trek ends at Misery Hill, which is as steep, if not steeper, than the approach to Thumb Rock. Misery Hill isn't very high but it takes you to the 14,000 foot level.

If you're among the more tenacious 50% of climbers, you'll soon reach the 14,000 foot summit plateau, a fascinating little flat marked by a sulfurous hot spring. While the fumerole's warmth once saved John Muir's life during a blizzard, the fumes can irritate your skin and corrode metal. Keep cameras away.

The actual summit lies atop a large plug dome above the summit plateau. It's a quick (relatively) scramble up loose rock to the top of the world. Weather cooperating, you're in for the view of your life. You should be able to peer into not only the Shasta and Klamath basins but the Sacramento Valley and (sometimes, if you have sharp eyes), the ocean. Look for Lassen, Castle Crags, Mts. Eddy and McLoughlin, the Trinity Alps and so on.

Alternative to the Bunny Flat route is the steeper but shorter Ski Bowl route, entirely above treeline. From the now abandoned ski area at the road end, it follows the old lift tower, past Green Butte to the Thumb Rock ridge, then contours around to Lake Helen where it picks up the route from Horse Camp.

There are dozens of dos and don'ts associated with the Shasta climb, most of which haven't been a factor on other hikes described here:

Do climb with someone who's done it before and knows the route. Bring an ice axe and crampons and know how to use them. Know something about altitude sickness and hypothermia. Bring at least 2 quarts of water. Watch for falling rocks, avalanches and hidden crevices. Spend a month working out before attempting the climb. Bring proper clothing and avoid exposure. Be aware that the mountain creates its own weather and a calm, sunny day can turn into a blizzard within minutes.

Ponderosa pine at edge of Whitney Creek Canyon. (ch.60)

Shasta Avalanche Gulch from Horse Camp Cabin.(ch.62)

Bring moleskin, sun glasses, lip balm, lunch, first aid, etc. Do not bring carbonated beverages which may explode in the thin air. Read carefully Shasta-Trinity National Forest's "Mt. Shasta Climber's Guide." Register at the Ranger Station in town (there are signs), before starting out. Don't litter.

And finally, take your time, enjoy yourself and don't worry if you don't reach the summit. You can always try it another day.

63. BLACK BUTTE TRAIL

Length: 2½ miles
Water: Not a drop
Access: Bumpy but level dirt roads
Season: May — November.
Difficulty: Difficult
Elevation: 4400 to 6325 ft.
Use: Hikers only
Ownership: Shasta-Trinity NF
Phone: (916) 926-4511

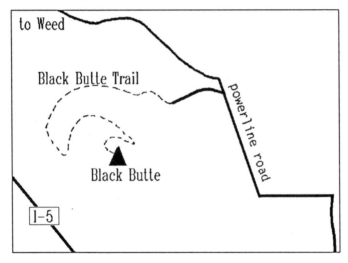

Directions: Leave I-5 at the Central Mt. Shasta City exit. Proceed through town to Mt. Shasta boulevard and turn left. Turn right after a couple blocks, onto Alma Street, then left on Everitt Memorial Highway (at the high school). About a mile up Everitt Hwy, you'll find a dirt road with a "Black Butte Trail" sign.

The dirt road makes a hard right just off the highway and a 90 degree left a mile later. It swings right again just before the powerline (not at the powerline) and left, about a mile later (at a logging landing), onto the final trailhead spur. The last two trailhead signs, at the powerline and spur roads, are down. Look for the posts where they used to be. Parking is limited at the trailhead.

The grim, barren visage of Black Butte attracts almost as much attention to I-5 travelers in the Mt. Shasta area as does Shasta itself. In fact, on days when the more famous mountain is fogged in and not visible, tourists can sometimes be seen photographing Black Butte, which rises straight up from the freeway, thinking it to be Shasta.

Black Butte is a giant cone anchoring Shasta's west flank. It was formed when ash, pasty lava and pyroclastic material (pyroclastic means "hot rocks"), shot out of a crack in the unstable volcanic ground. Other, smaller cones may be seen along the same fissure radiating from Shasta. Black Butte's seemingly treeless slopes rise 2000 feet, at almost a 45 degree angle, between the towns of Mt. Shasta and Weed.

The trailhead is easy to find, over rather dusty dirt roads. When I first hiked this path in 1970, there were no signs anywhere. I simply followed roads from the south end of Weed which seemed to lead to the back of Black Butte. I ended up on the powerline road and located the trailhead access soon after.

You could drive a ways up the peak then, with four wheel drive and a little nerve. These days, a newer, much better dirt road parallels the old powerline road, access is much improved and so is the trail. The developed trailhead area is lovely.

The path offers few surprises as virtually the entire route can be seen from I-5. Uniformly steep and precarious, with loose rock everywhere, the peak always reminded me of the evil Mt. Doom, in the last chapters of "Lord of the Rings." The route is very exposed so carry lots of water if it's hot out.

Once on the trail, there are more trees than one might expect, mostly white fir and western white pine, with a little ponderosa pine at the bottom and Shasta red fir and lodgepole pine at the top. There are also more breaks in the peak's upward sweep than one might expect, with several subpeaks and cinder cones atop the main cone.

While the trail's rise is nowhere killingly steep, the grade rarely lets up and portions of the path are extremely rocky, especially a half-mile segment through a canyon, right after the first switchback, about a mile up. The final half-mile to the top, while gorgeous, is one of those infuriating places where you keep thinking you're almost there but the path seems to go on and on and on.

The summit, capped with the base of an old lookout, offers a view that will knock your socks off. Look for Mt. Shasta, obviously, and Mt. Eddy, the Shasta Valley, Castle Crags, Weed, Mt. McLoughlin...and tourists, far below, taking your picture.

Note: When I re-hiked this trail in 1991, my nine year old daughter, Anna, accompanied me. Although she isn't very athletic, and the trail, rising 2000 feet in 2½ miles, ranks among the more challenging, and her cheap sneakers rubbed her heel raw, she hung in and made it to the top. I was impressed.

Anna's favorite part of the hike occurred about ⅔ of the way down, when we rounded a bend and the Weed McDonald's popped into view, far below. We ate dinner there, of course.

64. CALDWELL LAKES

Length: 1½ miles
Water: Lots
Access: Good gravel road
Season: June — October
Difficulty: Moderate
Elevation: 6000 to 7100 ft.
Use: Any
Ownership: Shasta-Trinity NF
Phone: (916) 926-4511

Directions: Leave I-5 at the Edgewood exit, just north of Weed near the airport. Turn west, then north, then west again, ending up on Parks Creek Road heading towards Stewart Springs. At Stewart Springs, turn right, over the bridge, following the blacktop

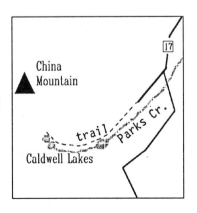

road (17) towards Deadfall Lakes. A sign on the right, 5½ miles from the bridge, notes the turnoff up a logging spurs to the Caldwell Lakes trailhead.

These three small lakes, in the Trinity Divide Range west of Mt. Shasta, are shallower and more intimate than many of the area's other lakes. The two acre pools offer solitude, superb vistas and fine brook trout fishing.

From the roomy trailhead in a wooded flat, the rhododendron and Sadler oak lined trail makes its way up to a little meadow containing the lower lake. Look behind you en route, for an outstanding view of Shasta, framed in a steep walled, orange serpentine rock gorge. One of the best photos I ever took was from this spot. Unfortunately, it's long since disappeared into the vast maw which consumes old photos left lying around.

All three lakes are shallow and full of logs. The two upper pools lie immediately adjacent to one another, ½ mile beyond the lower lake. They're more accurately a single, hour glass shaped lake. The upper lakes occupy a marshy flat in open woods.

I don't believe the setting is a glacial cirque, although a sheer, white rock face rises immediately northwest. The granite monolith looks to me like simply the flank of China Mountain. China Mountain is the second highest peak in the Trinity Divide after Mt. Eddy, and higher than any peak in the Marble, Russian or Siskiyou Wilderness areas. Its 8542 foot summit, a mile from the lake, isn't nearly as obvious from a distance as Mount Eddy. China Mountain is set back, rather gentle, and timbered all the way to the top. It looks like just another foothill.

65. DEADFALL LAKES/MT. EDDY

Length: 2½ miles (lakes),4 (Eddy)
Water: OK
Access: Good blacktop road
Season: June — October
Difficulty: Easy (lakes), difficult (Eddy)
Elevation: 6400to9025 ft.
Use: Non-motorized
Owner: Shasta-Trinity
Phone: (916) 926-4511

Directions: Take I-5 to the Edgewood exit, north of Weed. Turn west, then north, ending up on the Parks Creek/Stewart Springs road. Follow Parks Creek to Stewart Springs and turn right, over the bridge. Continue up the long, blacktopped road (17), to the Pacific Crest Trail trailhead at the summit, or to the Deadfall Lakes trailhead shortly after.

At 9025 feet, Mt. Eddy is the highest peak in the vast Klamath system, which includes the Marbles, Trinity Alps and Siskiyous. The handsome chain containing Mt. Eddy has been dubbed, variously, the Trinity Mountains, the Trinity Divide or the Eddy Range, between the Trinity and Upper Sacramento Rivers.

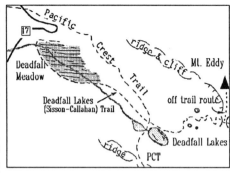

Eddy has much to recommend it besides altitude. The summit is reasonably accessible, if not a hop, skip and a jump. Its west flank is home to a string of 5 of the most beautiful alpine lakes ever. One wonders how this fabulous area escaped Wilderness designation.

The Trinity Divide's cluster of snowcapped peaks, looming above I-5, would attract far more attention were they not dwarfed by Shasta's 14,000 foot presence.

This easy walk may be my very favorite. My wife and I make an annual pilgrimage to the spot, with children and friends. The route visits 5 lakes and offers a challenging climb, an unrivaled profusion of wildflowers and a botanical oddity.

Two trails, a mile apart, lead to Deadfall Lakes. At the summit of Parks Creek Road, at a spacious parking area, the Pacific Crest Trail begins its jaunt into the area. Beyond the summit, the road switches down to Deadfall Meadows. The Deadfall Lakes trailhead, from the meadows, is actually the start of the Sisson-Callahan National Recreation Trail.

The PCT reaches Deadfall Lake in 2½ miles. The way is mostly level, mostly wooded and gouged into a steep mountainside. Sisson-Callahan is shorter but moderately steep, traversing meadow, marsh and occasional wooded patches. You'll find more wildflowers per square foot along this lower route than any place I can think of in California.

However you go, the two trails eventually cross. To reach the main lake, continue on the PCT or turn right onto it. For Mt. Eddy and the upper lakes, continue on Sisson-Callahan or turn left onto it.

Sisson-Callahan ultimately ends after 9 miles near Lake Siskiyou. Aside from its brief flirtation with Deadfall Lake and Mt. Eddy, most of the trail parallels the North Fork of the Sacramento. The PCT, of course, continues to Toad Lake, Castle Crags and Mexico.

It's a few hundred yards from the trail junction to Lower Dead-fall and Deadfall proper. The lower lake is a short scramble right while the main lake lies a short scramble left.

At 25 acres, Deadfall Lake is second in size in the Trinity Divide after Castle Lake. It occupies a large basin with steep, grassy slopes and few trees, except for a few pines and scattered Shasta red fir. Level campsites adorn the outlet and inlet. Brook trout fishing is supposed to be pretty good. The lake bottom is solid, if a little rocky. But at 7300 feet elevation, the water tends to be bone chilling.

If the main lake bores you, which it won't, take Sisson- Callahan to the upper lakes. The route is moderately steep, through open, grassy woods surrounded by cliffs of orange serpentine. Between the main and upper lake, it passes a tiny lake with no name. A nearby fifth lake can be seen from Mt. Eddy, but not from the trail.

Of all the natural lakes I've visited, Upper Deadfall looks the most like a swimming pool. It's a small, shallow tarn with clear water and a sandy bottom. Tarns are depressions created by melting blocks of glacial ice. The shore is brush free and gently shaded by park-like woods. Swimming is fabulous and the water warmer than that of the main lake.

Above the upper lake, the trail passes a marshy area at the base of yet another cirque. This lakeless cirque's headwall rises 1000 feet to the Eddy summit. Beyond this last, colorful bowl, the path switches back and forth to the ridge. This is a fairly short segment, but with grades approaching 30%.

Between bowl and ridge, look for stunted little trees with short (½ inch), stubby needles in closed bundles of five. These are foxtail pines, mainly native to high elevation areas of the eastern slope of the southern Sierra, 800 miles south. A few widely scattered patches have been recorded in the upper reaches of the Trinity Divide and Marbles.

To climb Eddy, simply follow the ridge left from the trail crest. On a slope corrected map, it's only ½ mile to the summit. But with almost a 1000 foot rise, much of it at a 45 degree angle over loose scree at 9000 feet, this can be a workout.

An old trail to the Mt. Eddy summit begins about 80 feet beyond the crest of the Sisson-Callahan Trail, on the Sacramento River side. It offers no particular advantage over the route just described. The faint path is in remarkably good condition, considering it hasn't been maintained since 1910.

The summit offers an old lookout cabin and the best view of Shasta ever, which is saying a lot. Look also for the glaciers of Mt. Thompson in the Trinity Alps to the west, the towns of Weed and Mt. Shasta and the valleys of the Sacramento, Shasta, Scott and Trinity Rivers.

Immediately west, the peak drops over the aforementioned 1000 foot headwall above the 5 Deadfall Lakes. Its east face swoops down an immense, barren avalanche basin. Far below, two glacial cirques cut sharply into the basin's base. Dobkins and Durney Lakes may be seen hiding inside the cirques. To visit them see Ch. 66.

66. DOBKINS/DURNEY LAKE
(Shasta-Trinity National Forest)

Length: 2 miles
Water: Gobs
Access: Poor 4WD road
Season: June—October
Difficulty: Moderate
Elevation: 5600 to 7000 ft
Use: Any
Ownership: Shasta-Trinity NF
Phone: (916) 926-4511

Directions: Leave I-5 between Weed and Mt. Shasta City, at the Abrams Lake Exit. Turn west, then bear right onto Old Stage Road, heading back towards Weed. Follow Old Stage Road to Sugar Pine Road. Turn left on this gravel route, which becomes Dale Creek Road. A 4WD road takes off left, along upper Dale Creek, just before Dale Creek Road fords the creek. Follow this jeep road as far as you dare, hopefully to a small grassy flat about 3 miles up, park and walk.

A major reason for living in our area is the knowledge that places like Dobkins and Durney Lake await those adventurous enough to seek them out. This little known brace of alpine glacial jewels, in the shadow of Mt. Shasta and Mt. Eddy, ranks high on my list of the most beautiful spots imaginable.

Unrelated but adjacent to Shasta, and the Cascade Mountains to which Shasta belongs, is the vast Klamath Mountains geological system of northwest California and southwest Oregon. The Cascades are made of relatively young volcanic peaks while the Klamaths contain some of the oldest and most rugged granite formations anywhere.

The high point in the entire Klamath system is 9025 foot Mt. Eddy. While dwarfed by Shasta's 14,161 foot heights, immediately east, few other peaks in the region match Eddy's dramatic splendor and botanical diversity.

Dobkins Lake lies in a dramatic glacial basin, at the foot of a series of sheer headwalls rising 2000 feet to the Eddy crest.

While the Dobkins Lake "trail" isn't particularly strenuous, reaching it can be. It was supposed to be a 1½ mile jeep road, from Dale Creek Road to the trailhead. It turned out to be over 3 miles, of which I walked 2¾'s.

The jeep road is extremely steep and rocky, although wide and fairly stable. It's one of the few roads in this book my little Toyota couldn't handle. High ground clearance is essential.

Still, the upper Dale Creek jeep road offers some of the most impressive views anywhere of Mt. Shasta and the Shasta Valley. It peers almost straight down on Black Butte, the prominent, 6200 foot cinder cone beside the freeway (see Ch. 63). Once on the trail, which veers south along Dobkins Creek rather than the west trending Dale Creek, Shasta disappears from view.

The trail, such as it is, officially begins just past a small grassy flat, 3 bone jarring miles from where the jeep road leaves Dale Creek Road. A side spur crosses the creek at the far end of the grassy flat while the main jeep road swings left and uphill soon after. Where the road swings left, a fork takes off very steeply upward, paralleling the creek.

The road away from Dale Creek accesses Little Crater Lake, a 20 acre water body perched on a mountaintop, 2200 feet overhead (see next chapter). This is a killer trek on a difficult to find trail. While Dobkins/Durney and Little Crater Lake can be done in the same day, I recommend either making two trips out of it or spending the night.

Back at the "trailhead" above the grassy flat, where the jeep road swings away from Dale creek and a steep fork parallels it, follow the fork for about ¾ mile, along the east bank of Dale Creek and, soon after, Dobkins Creek. You're unlikely to notice the transition from one creek to the other. The road eventually fords Dobkins Creek and disappears up the opposite hillside.

From that point on, there is no road or trail that I could see, although several are indicated on the map (differently on different maps). Best is to simply follow the creek or the valley bottom, since the creek tends to braid. I suggest walking on the far side (west—opposite where the roads were). Otherwise, you'll end up at Durney Lake (Dobkins to Durney is easier than Durney to Dobkins).

This is an open, serpentine soil area with towering cliffs, green meadows, wildflowers, insect eating cobra plants, plus scattered clumps of Western white pine, Shasta red fir and mountain hemlock. The going can be rigorous—and brushy in spots—but it is very interesting and difficult to get lost.

Eventually, a mysterious road appears out of nowhere, which may be followed the last ½ mile to Dobkins Lake. The latter, a brilliant, 3 acre, turquoise inlay, is flanked on three sides by cliffs of orange serpentine, soaring to the Eddy summit and it's associated ridges.

Conversely, the lakes are visible from the top of Mt. Eddy. The latter is best scaled via the beautiful Deadfall Lakes Trail (see Ch.65). The view up from Dobkins Lake gives more of a sense of Eddy's barren immensity then does the view down from the summit. My advice is to sample both.

At the lower end of Dobkins Lake, look for a short, steep, very faint trail to the adjacent ridgetop. While the path soon disappears, it's an easy, ½ mile hike along the ridge to Durney Lake. About the same size as Dobkins but 250 feet higher, Durney occupies a larger basin with a broad, grassy flat just below the lake. It's a fabulous camping spot, with Durney Creek meandering through the middle.

To get home, simply follow the creek downhill.

67. LITTLE CRATER LAKE
(Shasta-Trinity National Forest)

Length: 1½ miles
Water: Depends on
route—expect none
Access: Poor 4WD road
Season: June—October
Difficulty: Arduous
Elevation: 5600 to 7800
Use: Any
Ownership: Shasta-Trinity NF
Phone: (916) 926-4511

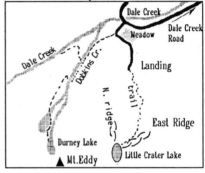

Directions: *Leave I-5 between Weed and Mt. Shasta City, at the Abrams Lake Exit. Turn west, then bear right onto Old Stage Road, heading back towards Weed. Follow Old Stage Road to Sugar Pine Road. Turn left on this gravel route, which becomes Dale Creek Road.*

A 4WD road takes off left, just before Dale Creek Road fords Dale Creek. Follow this rough, steep jeep road about 3 miles to where it swings uphill and away from Dale Creek, just beyond a grassy flat. It's ¾ mile farther to a logging landing where a skid road doubles back uphill. Park at the landing.

This is the only chapter where I won't tell you how to reach the main destination. I'll describe only how I got there, relating a few mishaps along the way. Either follow my route or create your own adventure. While the actual trail can be elusive, finding Little Crater Lake isn't that difficult.

Is Little Crater Lake worth subjecting yourself to a possible off-trail trek rising 2200 feet in 1½ miles? It was to me. At 20 acres and 7600 feet in elevation, the lake occupies a spectacular bowl just below 9025 foot Mt. Eddy. Like its namesake, Little Crater Lake has no outlet. The encircling rim ranges from 200 feet to 1500 feet above the water.

It took my friend Brian Boothby and I three attempts to reach this place. We finally succeeded but never did locate the trail the Forest Service wishes people to use. On our first effort, we had to settle for Dobkins and Durney Lakes, reached via the same roads (see previous chapter). Fortunately, they more than compensated.

A year later, we tried again. Approaching on a sunny, mid-June day, we noticed a tiny cloud atop Mt. Eddy. By the time we reached Dale Creek, it was pouring rain. In the two hours before we went home, the rain let up only make room for hail and snow.

Two months later, with a 4WD pickup, we ventured forth once more. The vehicle had no problem with the Dale Creek jeep road, although we averaged between one and 10 MPH over its steep boulder fields.

About 3 miles up, shortly beyond the grassy flat marking the Dobkins/Durney trailhead, the main road swung left and uphill while a steep side road took off parallel to Dale Creek. Our trail allegedly began ¾ mile farther up the main road, where it dead ends at a logging landing.

Per Forest Service instructions, we parked at the landing and hiked up a steep skid road. The trail was supposed to take off after 1000 feet. We passed a side road to the right after 500 feet and stayed left, on the main track. A quarter-mile later, we came to another fork. This time we opted for the right hand prong. Nowhere did we see a trail.

Each time the route split after that, we followed the uphill fork. Finally, we emerged at a tremendous rock fall (of white granodiorite), which shot up 1000 feet at slopes approaching 100 percent. On the skid road along its base, we found a small rock monument, which we took as a trail marker.

We later decided the monument was erected by a hiker who, like us, couldn't find the trail and didn't want to get lost on the way back.

The rockfall requires putting your body into 4WD. After an eternity of boulder hopping, panting and trying to figure the way, we hit the ridge, expecting the lake to unfold before us. We were greeted instead by a dizzying dropoff to the Dobkins Creek basin, with Mt. Eddy towering in one direction, Mt. Shasta in the other, and vistas everywhere.

A few hundred feet south, the white boulders ended and the ridge became smooth and level. It led to an obvious bowl, with a headwall rising above the far end. Apart from the summit we'd just climbed, the area was all orange rock, typical of weathered serpentine.

After 10 minutes easy walking, amid grass, rocks, profuse wildflowers (paintbrush, yellow lupine and red heather), and scattered Western white and whitebark pine, mountain hemlock, Shasta red fir and mountain mahogany, we reached the crater rim.

Before climbing down to the lake, we stoppped to examine the lake's former outlet, a rocky notch spilling from the bowl to the Dobkins Creek basin, over a 1000 foot cliff. The lake surface is presently 200 feet below the notch.

Unlike big Crater Lake, this crater is not a volcanic formation. Shasta may be a dormant volcano but the Mt. Eddy area is completely unrelated. Like every other lake basin in the region, this was carved by a glacier. It is ringed on two sides by cliffs and on two others by moraine deposits.

The lake itself is vast, aqua blue, clear and gorgeous. Having little shoreline vegetation and only sparse forests above, the bottom is smooth and uncluttered. Fishing is excellent, although the exact species populating the lake is debatable. They look like off-color brown trout, possibly crossed with rainbow.

Heading back, we encountered a pathway just below the north trending ridge we came in on. We were fairly certain it wasn't the Forest Service trail because that supposedly swings wide to the east, along a different ridge, before zig-zagging back down to the logging landing.

Our trail shot almost straight down for a mile, becoming very faint in spots. For the final ½ mile, it grew even steeper. I can't imagine climbing it and would sooner stick to the rocks. Eventually, it skirted a series of meadowed slopes, veering downhill at each without crossing it. At one, we spotted faint tire tracks on the far end and decided to investigate, even though the trail didn't go that way.

A couple hundred feet later, we found ourselves 1000 feet up the skid road from where we'd parked, breathing a sigh of relief.

For readers wishing to hike up this way, follow the skid road from the logging landing. Turn uphill left at the first fork and look for a spot, soon after, where the way becomes impossibly steep and curves slightly right. You'll see a grassy opening on the left. Cross the field to the trail.

There are, it turns out, at least four "trails" to Little Crater Lake. Ours is called the Billy's Jeep Trail, although old Billy had to winch his rig up a couple of spots. Had we not spotted the faint cut-across, we'd have ended up at an old logging spur, 2 miles and 1200 feet below where we parked. Many people still use this lower trailhead, which also connects to the Forest Service trail.

Gnarled pines near Etna Summit-Russian Wilderness.(ch.57)

Lodgepole pines--Toad Lake, Trinity Mountains. (ch.68)

The Forest Service trail was built in 1972 to protect the fragile meadows cut by the path we took. Its head was marked with a 3 foot stone cairn, somewhere between where we came out from the Billy's Trail and the skid road's next uphill fork. Either we missed it, or it's been vandalized or bulldozed over. In any case, the Billy's Jeep Trail should have intersected it. Oh well.

Because of increased use, the Forest Service plans a complete remapping and survey of the area in the near future. In addition, road and trailhead signs are on order. It's anybody's guess when they'll be up, however.

68. TOAD/PORCUPINE LAKE

Length: 1½ miles
Water: Lots
Access: Long, gravel and dirt road
Season: June — October
Difficulty: Easy
Elevation: 6900 feet
Use: Any
Ownership: Shasta Trinity NF
Phone: (916) 926-4511

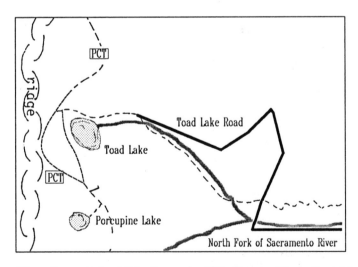

Directions: *Take I-5 to the central Mt. Shasta City exit and head west and south, past Lake Siskiyou, to road 26, up the South Fork of the Sacramento. Where 26 crosses to the river's north bank, 2½*

miles up, look for a turnoff right, with a Toad Lake sign. Take a hard left ¼ mile up, then follow the steep, winding, dirt and gravel route 10⅓ miles to its end, ½ mile from the lake.

In the April 16, 1978 edition of "California Living", I wrote the following:

"The chuckhole had been lurking behind a rock, waiting to pounce on the first intruder. Upon spotting my pickup, it leaped out, grabbed a front tire and chucked it in the air, as chuckholes do. Inside, I bumped my head on the ceiling and came down full weight on the accelerator. When I finally regained control, I was inches from a 5000 foot drop-off.

Four creek crossings, six washouts, two patches of axle deep mud, twenty acres of hardpacked snow and fifty rock slides later, I arrived at Toad Lake. It was early May and the 6900 foot lake was partially frozen over."

I admit to dramatic exaggeration but the quotation does convey an accurate sense of a May drive to Toad Lake. July poses much fewer hazards. The lake itself is a favorite 23 acre fishing spot, high in the crags of the Trinity Divide Range. Its shoreline is level and accessible with excellent camping spots. The road ends a short ½ mile away.

With such a short trail, this is actually more of an auto excursion than a hike. It qualifies for inclusion only because of a number of other trails nearby.

If you're determined to make a real hike out of it, look for a trail to the left, five miles before the road ends. This alternate trailhead lies ¼ mile past the road's crossing over the Middle Fork of the Sacramento. It's a two mile hike from there, up the Middle Fork, to Toad Lake. This scenic, if steep walk violates my personal rule about not hiking to a place where you can drive.

From Toad Lake, two trails lead to Porcupine Lake. Both are a mile long and climb steep, sparsely forested rock faces. The Pacific Crest Trail runs along the crest of the ridge immediately west of both lakes. A short spur connects from the near (north) end of Toad Lake. It's ½ mile south, along the PCT to another short spur, leading up to Porcupine Lake.

One can also reach Porcupine Lake by continuing on the Toad Lake Trail around the west side of the lake and up over the ridge to the south. It joins the PCT at the ridgetop.

The odd, 8 acre Porcupine Lake occupies a crater-like depression at the foot of a large headwall. To reach it, scramble down the surrounding jumble of boulders. Porcupine Lake has no outlet.

69. CASTLE LAKE/HEART LAKE
(Castle Crags Wilderness Area)

Length: 1½ miles
Water: OK
Access: Paved road
Season: May — October
Difficulty: Moderate
Elevation: 5400 to
6050 feet
Use: Non-motorized
Ownership: Shasta
Trinity NF and private
Phone: (916) 926-4511

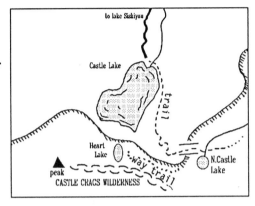

Directions: Leave I-5 at the Central Mt. Shasta City exit. Head west, then south, towards Lake Siskiyou. Turn left on the 7 mile paved road to Castle Lake. The Trail to Little Castle Lake begins along the lake's south shore.

Although Castle Lake is mainly a driving destination, small lakes in the vicinity offer opportunities to get out on the trail. You may even have time left to check out Gray Rock and Cliff Lakes, up the South Fork of the Sacramento (Road 26), beyond Lake Siskiyou.

At 42 acres, Castle Lake is the largest natural body of water in the Trinity Divide Range, between the Sacramento and Trinity Rivers. The range includes Mt. Eddy, highest in the Klamath Mountains system. Castle Lake offers easy road access,a nearby campground and superb fishing for brook and rainbow trout. It is set in a typical glacial cirque, with a sheer,gray rock headwall on the far side.

For many years, Castle Lake was the focus of fish stocking experiments conducted by the California Department of Fish and Game. They had a little booth where they measured every fish taken. The booth is no longer there but the University of California at Davis now conducts water quality studies at the lake, which have implications in the preservation of Lake Tahoe.

Although Castle Lake tends to be crowded, the problem is easily alleviated since few people stray far from the parking area. If you need to get away, the trail to the left, around the south shore, leads to Little Castle Lake and beyond.

Compared to it's neighbor, Little Castle Lake is a mere speck (and nearly dry in 1991), covering only 2 acres. Normally, its about 8 feet deep with, they say, pretty good fishing.

The ¾ mile walk up from Castle Lake, rises 400 feet to a rocky crest, through woods of Shasta red fir and western white pine. It's quite steep but blessedly short. Little Castle occupies an open, terrace-like bench framing a fine view of the upper Sacramento Valley. The trail continues another 4 miles, over (to me) relatively featureless ridges, to the Mt. Bradley Lookout. Be aware that Little Castle Lake sits on private timberland. While public access is permitted, visitors should show appropriate respect. The Forest Service is attempting to acquire the property.

Nearby Heart Lake is about the same size as Little Castle Lake. A gorgeous pothole in a rocky pocket above Big Castle Lake, it is well worth a look if you're a bit adventurous. From the saddle between Castle and Little Castle Lake, a faint way trail ends up at Heart Lake in about ¾ mile.

Actually, the area is riddled with way trails and false paths. The best way to locate the Heart Lake Trail is to scramble up the rocks to the right (west) of the saddle above Little Castle Lake. After 100 feet or so, you'll find yourself looking down on a grassy flat, where two trails can be seen. Take the more obvious path (on the left). And don't worry too much about getting lost in this open highland dotted with green fields and clumps of phlox, pussy feet, delphinium and sedum.

The Heart Lake Trail, like the Little Castle Lake Trail, is also rather steep but not very long. Pretty soon, you'll drop into the tiny Heart Lake cirque, with it's white headwall. The pool is tiny, clear and full of jumping fish. A large boulder juts into the middle of the lake from the shore, forming the heart shape. The view down from the stream outlet, 700 feet above Castle Lake, is breathtaking.

Both Heart and Little Castle Lakes lie within the Castle Crags Wilderness Area. Castle Lake, with its access road, obviously does not.

70. GRAY ROCK LAKES
(Castle Crags Wilderness Area)

Length: 1½ miles
Water: Lots
Access: Good oil-top roads to terrible jeep road
Season: June — October
Difficulty: Easy to slightly difficult
Elevation: 5600 to 6350

Use: Non-motorized in wilderness, any outside.
Ownership: Shasta-Trinity NF
Phone: (916) 926-4511

Directions: Leave I-5 at the central Mt. Shasta City exit. Head west and south, around Lake Siskiyou, to Road 26; a wide, paved route up the Sacramento South Fork. For Gray Rock Lakes, turn left over a wooden bridge 6 miles beyond Lake Siskiyou. Park just over the bridge or drive as far as possible up the extremely poor, 2 mile road to the cramped trailhead. A small sign marks the path.

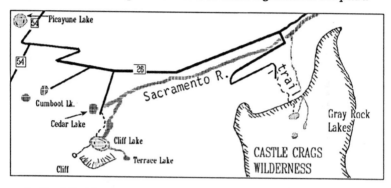

In the Mt. Shasta City Park, a little spring bubbles into a stone impound. This enchanted spot is supposed to be the source of the Sacramento River, California's longest. From there, the waters flow through Lake Shasta into the Sacramento Valley and finally, past San Francisco Bay into the ocean.

It's all very charming, except that it isn't the river's true source. The South Fork of the Sacramento, branching just south of Mt. Shasta City, continues another 13 miles into the high peaks between the Sacramento and Trinity Rivers.

The South Forks' source is the far less poetic Gumboot Lake, an excellent fishing spot at the end of an easy, paved or oil topped road. Gumboot isn't as pretty as some other lakes. It's shore is brushy and it occupies the middle of a sparsely wooded field below a ridge.

A Gumboot, by the way, is a boot made of India rubber "gum," an old fashioned material for boots and waders. The lake, presumably, has eaten a few of them.

Aside from Gumboot, several extremely lovely lakes may be reached from Road 26. The turnoff to Castle Lake, the largest natural lake in the Trinity Divide, is passed at Lake Siskiyou. Fifteen acre Cliff Lake lies between the Gray Rock Lakes and Gumboot Lake. At least one brochure claims Cliff Lake is the area's prettiest but I bestow that honor on Timber Lake, on the Gray Rock Lakes Trail.

Cliff, Timber and Gray Rock Lakes occupy glacial cirques in a dark schist outcropping called the Gray Rocks, at the northeast end of the new Castle Crags Wilderness. Easily seen on the left from Road 26, the Gray Rocks are unrelated to Castle Crags.

We'll begin with the Gray Rock Lakes since they offer the area's only real hiking.

Just over the bridge to the Gray Rock Lakes' access road, a sign says "Gray Rock Lakes—2½ miles." Those miles cost me a muffler, an exhaust pipe and almost a radiator. A 4x4 with good clearance and power would have no problems, however. The road is extremely steep and bumpy, switching back and forth several times before attaining the trailhead a mile later.

Either park at the bridge or drive as far as you can. Parking and turnaround room is available at all switchbacks. For those opting to walk to the trailhead, a very steep trail cuts across the road's switchbacks. The road is better for walking up while this cut across trail offers a quick route down.

From the tiny trailhead area, the narrow path heads into a huge, open glacial valley with a view of Shasta in the opposite direction and the Gray Rocks at the head. The path is moderately steep at first but it's only ½ mile to Lower Gray Rock Lake.

Lower Gray Rock Lake's 11 acre chunk of alpine splendor occupies a compact, wooded basin amid western white pine, Shasta red fir and lodgepole pine. Above, the main cirque trends uphill to the left, where Upper Gray Rock and Timber Lake hold sway. Both are smaller than Lower Gray Rock Lake but prettier, if possible. Especially Timber Lake, nestled against the main headwall near the summit. Both upper lakes lie a steep ½ mile above the lower pool.

To reach Cliff Lake, mentioned earlier, turn left up a barely noticeable logging road 8¾ miles from Lake Siskiyou, shortly past where Road 26 swings away from the river. When I visited, only a small Smokey Bear poster marked the turnoff. As with the Gray Rock Lakes, drive as far as possible, then park and walk. The rutted, muddy access road crosses a couple creeks and passes some ponds.

By foot or car, it's 1½ miles to Cliff Lake, with it's soaring headwall below a string of jagged peaks. The shore is brushy and the water is full of snags. Also, much of the lake is on private property. Only the eastern shore is open to the public.

71. CASTLE DOME
(Castle Crags State Park)

Length: 3 miles
Water: At Indian Springs
Access: Paved roads
Season: May — November
Difficulty: Very steep
Elevation: 2600 to 4800
Use: Hikers only. Horses on PCT
Ownership: Castle Crags State Park and private
Phone: (916) 235-2684

Directions: Leave I-5 at the Castella/Castle Crags exit, south of Dunsmuir. The park entrance is about 1/4 mile from the freeway. Day use fee is $5.00 in summer. Follow the signs to trailhead/Vista Point. Alternatively, leave I-5 one exit north, at Soda Creek, where the

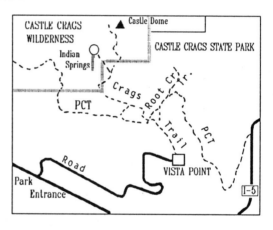

Pacific Crest Trail crosses the freeway. From the trailhead, head left and follow the PCT into the park.

While freeway travelers through the California far north expect to be awed by Mt. Shasta, neighboring Castle Crags catches most people off guard. Rising above the dull, forested hills, the crags resemble an immense upwelling of melted candles. Or perhaps upended driftwood boards eroded into grotesque spires. They are actually a small, fortress-like granite island whose glacially sculpted domes and minarets recall the southern Sierra.

I had more trouble obtaining reliable information on this unusual, challenging and exquisite path than any I've ever written about. I encountered signs pointing the wrong way, a park brochure with an off-scale map where a 2 inch line took me an hour to walk while a 3 inch line took 10 minutes, and a misleading statement in the brochure that the Crags Trail leads to "the base of Castle Dome." Since one side of the Dome's base sits at about 3000 feet and lies outside the Crags, while the other side is well inside the Crags at 4800 feet, correctly interpreting this statement is important.

I've been assured the signs have been corrected and a more accurate brochure is being prepared.

According to the original brochure's map, entering the park via the Soda Creek PCT trailhead adds an extra ½ mile to the Castle Dome hike, with an added elevation rise of 400 feet. The latter is correct but the added distance is more like 3 miles.

The PCT here is fairly level, following an old railroad bed. Use it only if you're absolutely unable to come up the the park's $5.00 day use fee or if hiking in from the south.

Both the PCT and the Crags Trail from the Vista Point trailhead, begin in middle elevation forests of Douglas-fir, pine, madrone and oak. The Crags Trail quickly climbs to higher elevation Shasta red fir and white fir forests. Jeffrey pine and incense cedar decorate the more open, upper slopes. Look for a few Brewer spruce near the end.

The Vista Point drive alone justifies the effort. The winding road ends at a spot on Kettlebelly Ridge with a commanding view of both Castle Dome, the Crags and, immediately north, Mt. Shasta. The brilliant green meadow between the Dome and the rest of the crags is the trail's destination. The meadow is covered mostly with manzanita, as it turns out, not grass.

The first 1½ miles from the Vista Point are a rigorous and boring climb up Kettlebelly Ridge. There are a few interesting views. Note the sparse underbrush here, one of many indicators of frequent forest fires in this dry country.

Approaching Indian Springs, the Crags' southeast wall suddenly pops into view. Indian Springs sits at its base, at 3600 feet. While a lovely spot and a 3 minute walk, save Indian Springs for the return trip. You'll find its cold, sweet water the most delicious you ever tasted.

Shortly after Indian Springs, the park boundary is passed, with the remainder of the trail on National Forest land. Soon after, the trail breaks out of the woods and starts climbing the actual Crags. This final mile, while quite steep, is so exquisite you won't think much about the exertion. I found myself smiling a lot.

On emerging from the woods, all you see at first is the Dome, plus a massive, gray wall you're somehow supposed to climb. After snaking around a series of zig-zags and spires and up seemingly impossible cliffs, the green meadow finally comes into view. If you look carefully, you can sometimes see climbers on the dome from here. If you listen carefully, you can hear them.

The trail ends at the far end of the meadow, under a huge pine tree. The route up the dome is fairly obvious. Take some time, however to explore the edges of the meadow. The gentle granite slopes immediately surrounding it plunge 1000 feet on the other side, in nearly vertical drops.

The real challenge, however, is the dome. While not very high, it's a long way down if you slip. You can feel perfectly secure one minute, then suddenly, the angle changes a few degrees...

From the trail end, a faint way trail leads past a small notch, near a tremendous drop-off, onto the dome. Make your way up, bearing slightly left, to a small outcropping. This is the hardest part. From there, a slight draw can be followed to the summit. It's rather unnerving but you should make it. (By "should," I mean if you don't chicken out, not if you don't fall. Good luck.)

72. TWIN LAKES

Length: 1 ½ miles
Water: No
Access: Very long, gravel road
Season: June — June
Difficulty: Easy
Elevation: 5700 to 5900 ft.
Use: Open to all
Ownership: Shasta Trinity NF
Phone: (916) 926-4511

Directions: Leave I-5 at the Castella/Castle Crags exit. Follow road 25 (Whalen Road), past Castle Crags State Park, 11 ¾ miles to the road summit. Bear left at the fork, 1 ¾ miles later.

Turn right 3 miles beyond, just before the second creek crossing. Roads are mostly wide, gravel

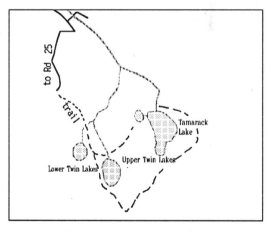

thoroughfares. The last mile to the trailhead is of lower quality but easily driveable.

Readers may be wondering why I've wasted so much time,
  Arranging line by tedious line, this chapter into rhyme.
Could it result, you might well ask, from not enough to say,
  About the Twin Lakes area in a more conventional way?
Rest assured, the lakes don't need such help from up above,
  My writing, on the other hand, could use a little shove.
So readers, put away your fears; there's no need to be frantic,
  I vow I never will again resort to such an antic.
Now for an easy, scenic side trip, near Castle Crags State Park,
  You'll find the Twin Lakes Trail to be an interesting lark.
The road up from the freeway, while full of zigs and zags,
  Presents the best views ever of the awesome Castle Crags.
The huge white domes of Castle Crags stand out bold and stark,
  And the vista's even better than the ones inside the park.
With high peaks soaring all around, road 25's divinity,
  It makes a wondrous shortcut from the freeway to the Trinity.
Up at Horse Heaven Meadows, the road reaches its crest,
  If this Heaven's just for horses, a human one's just west.
A wide side road, downhill left's the one you ought to take,
  And after 3 or 4 more miles, you're almost at the lake.
The last mile may be a little rough but no need to get jumpy,
  Take a wrong road here, however, and things really do get bumpy.
The trailhead is lovely, with lots of parking places,
  And rocky summits everywhere with smiling, happy faces.
On the left, a vast green meadow turns your heart to Jell-O,
  Although in late summer and in fall, the green turns into yellow.
Above the field rises up a ridge of serpentine,
  Although the rock is orange outside, inside it's blackish green.
Another thing to look for before heading out the trail,
  Can be found a short way to the right, inside a grassy dale.
A tiny sea of pitcher plants there lift their heads up high,
  In quest of wandering bugs to eat, especially a fly.
Beyond the tree lined meadow, the trail's short and level,
  It meets a lake in half a mile, where one can stop and revel.
Amid western white and lodgepole pine, white fir and Shasta red,
  Lower Twin Lake's 8 acre pool lays down a lovely bed.
Continue walking through the woods 1/4 mile or so,
  And you'll find that Lower Twin Lakes has another lake in tow.
It's called Upper Twin Lake, and I ask you, did you ever,
  Wonder why it's namer didn't try to be more clever?
At 12 acres, Upper Twin is larger than it's brother,
  Or its sister or its father or its cousin or its mother.

Upper Twin adorns the base of a rocky glacial headwall,
 As do most other Klamath lakes, including nearby Deadfall.
On up the path (or down it), lie two more pristine pools,
 Tucked neatly in a vast moraine like treasured, alpine jewels.
Big Tamarack's the largest, and its broad surface exceeds,
 21 acres, although beware, that some of it is weeds.
One last lake, Little Tamarack, tops off this fine quartet,
 Or bottoms it off, we should say, as it's the smallest yet.
At 2 acres, this little pond's primary claim to fame,
 Is that it's at the trail's end and very glad you came.
"Tamarack," I might point out, is a rare alternate name,
 For "western larch," as most call it in the tree labeling game.
The tamaracks nearest Tamarack Lake are found in alpine glades,
 400 miles to the north, in Oregon's Cascades.
The lakes were not, so it turns out, named for larch at all,
 But for the nearby lodgepole pines which grow so straight and tall.
In days of old, the pioneers called lodgepole "tamarack pine,"
 Although the trees are similar only to one consuming too much wine.
In closing, let me now throw in this final bit of dope:
 Though the lakes are shallow, fishing's great...
  at least that's what we hope!

73. NORDHEIMER CREEK

Length: 4 miles
Water: Very little
Access: Good gravel roads
Season: All (avoid in summer)
Difficulty: Easy
Elevation: 1400 to 2150 feet
Use: Any
Ownership: Klamath NF, some private
Phone: (916) 468-5351

Directions: The trailhead is off the lower Salmon River Road, between Somesbar and Forks of Salmon. Somesbar may be reached via Hwy 96, the Klamath River Road, from either I-5 or Hwy 299. Forks of Salmon may be reached either from Somesbar or via the North or South Fork Salmon Roads from Etna or Callahan, out of Yreka. The turnoff to the one mile, gravel spur to the trailhead is well marked.

This trail not only offers an easy path through pleasant, scenic surroundings but an excuse to visit the fabulous Salmon River country. Before describing its highlights, however, I should point out a couple low lights.

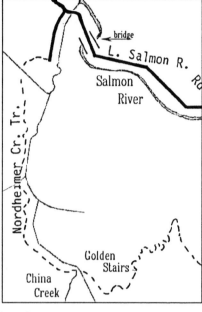

First, the narrow, low elevation canyon resembles a pizza oven in summer, which is also mosquito and gnat season. Also, it's lined from one end to the other with poison oak. The Forest Service—and yours truly—recommends avoiding this trail in very hot weather.

What, you might then ask, would lead someone to drive down the lower Salmon, in the dead of winter, looking for a trail up a side canyon to hike? Hunting grizzlies, perhaps?

Don't ask me. My job is only to describe.

The lower Salmon offers rewards in any season. Despite its remoteness and the effort required to visit, it ranks among the country's great scenic rivers. The partially paved road between Somesbar and Forks of Salmon peers into a narrow, gray slit of a rock gorge with churning whitewater at the bottom. At times, it's a vertical drop of a couple hundred feet from road to water. And in places, the road hugs a narrow ledge barely wide enough for a single car.

It's beauty is enhanced in winter by frequent low cloud ceilings. They make the gorge appear deeper and more mysterious and enrich the color in the surrounding lush forests. The Salmon also ranks among the nation's great steelhead streams (and salmon streams, obviously).

Presuming you're in the neighborhood, it's winter, you're tired of fishing the main river, and you don't mind walking 2½ miles before trail meets creek, here's the scoop on the Nordheimer Creek Trail:

As noted, the one mile side road to the trailhead is well marked from the Salmon River Road. Look for it 2 miles below Forks of Salmon, at Nordheimer Flat, just beyond bridges spanning first the river, then Nordheimer Creek. This level, gravel access road ends at a gate leading to private, creekside property. Parking is ample and the trail lies uphill to the right.

For its first mile, the trail inscribes a wide arc around the private land holding. After a steep ¼ mile, it picks up an old aqueduct ditch which it follows for the next 2 miles. The route is well shaded, although that doesn't seem to alleviate the intense summer heat. Or the intense summer insects buzzing around the side creeks.

Look for low elevation vegetation consisting of canyon liveoak, Oregon white oak, tanoak, madrone and tons of ceanothus and poison oak.

Douglas-fir and ponderosa pine also abound. California black oak seems strangely absent. The abundant bear scat, I presume, was not left by grizzlies.

Nothing makes a more level trail than an irrigation or mining ditch. One can saunter along observing the flora and fauna or taking in the grandeur of the creek canyon. Hillsides above and below are, for the most part, quite steep.

Section of the Salmon River near Nordheimer Creek. (Ch. 73)

After 2 miles, the trail appears to leave the ditch and drop down to the creek. While you may wish to eat lunch here or throw water on your face (don't drink from the creek), this short path is not the main trail. The path beyond was unmaintained when I visited (in 1988), from here on, slash and debris sometimes creats a problem. Stick to the ditch and you should eventually pick up the route again. The Forest Service plans further development.

The trail penetrates deeply into the unfolding chasm and grows ever more lovely. Highlights include gravel tailings from the Chinese gold diggings near China Creek, and the Golden Stairs. The latter is an immense, moss covered rock face which the trail somehow manages to climb. The Golden Stairs are 3½ miles from the trailhead and a good turning back point. The route beyond leaves the creek and climbs 1½ miles to a logging spur.

74. SALMON MOUNTAIN
(Trinity Alps Wilderness Area)

Length: 2½ miles
Water: OK
Access: Long, good gravel road
Season: June — October
Difficulty: Moderate
Elevation: 5600 to 6957
Use: Non-motorized only
Ownership: Klamath, Shasta Trinity, Six Rivers NF
Phone: (916) 468-5351

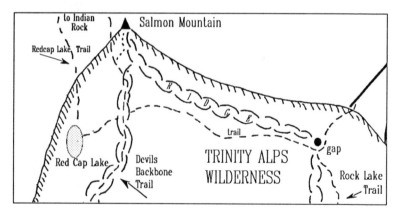

Directions: *Take Hwy 96, the Klamath River Road, from I-5 or Hwy 299, to the town of Somesbar. From there, follow the Salmon River Road to the town of Forks of Salmon (17 miles). There, turn up the South Fork Road towards Callahan. Just past Forks of Salmon, immediately over the bridge, road 10N04 takes off right (just before the bridge and left, if coming from Callahan). 14 miles up, where 10N07 runs into 10N04 a second time, turn right, onto 10N07 and follow it as far as you dare. It's about⅓ mile from this last junction to the unmarked trailhead.*

To understand the significance of Salmon Mountain, the Trinity Alps' western most peak, one must first understand why some consider the Trinity Alps as two ranges, even though it's a single chain. The best way to visualize it is to hike up the Caribou Lakes Trail, over 30 miles away on range's eastern end. From there, the system keeping such magnificent watch over California's vast Salmon River country is revealed in its entirety.

The Caribou Lakes Trail reveals the range's eastern end as higher and composed largely of white granite. West of Mt. Thompson, the Trinity Alps' highest peak, the granite fades out. The range's remainder is composed largely of greenstone and schist. These ancient, crumbly, gray/green or tan, metamorphosed rocks underlie the nearby Siskiyou and Marble Mountains as well as the western Trinity Alps.

Many maps call only the range's eastern, granite based portion the Trinity Alps. It's western side is usually labeled the Salmon Mountains. The Salmon Mountains' highest summit is... Salmon Mountain.

Salmon Mountain's 7000 foot crest drains into the Salmon, Trinity and Klamath Rivers and straddles 3 National Forests: the Klamath, Shasta Trinity and Six Rivers. It offers vistas in all directions of some the most "back" back country the Golden State offers.

The trailhead drive peers down on the Salmon River, Nordheimer and Knownothing Creeks. In 1970, it was a steep, 10 mile hike to nearby Knownothing Lake. Today, it's a ½ mile stroll from the upper end of road 10N04.

Road 10N04 winds steeply for a couple miles as it ascends High Point Ridge from Forks of Salmon. Then it levels off. For 8 miles or so, the wide, gravel route is fairly level, crossing vast burned (in 1987) and clearcut areas.

Road 10N04 meets road 10N07 after 14 miles. The latter is a poor quality fire break along the ridge top. Turn right at this junction, then left, for the trailhead. It lies ⅓ of a mile from 10N04, up a very steep, sandy road. Park where you feel comfortable. Salmon Mountain rises blatantly to the right.

The trailhead is unmarked. Where the road ends, look for a Wilderness Boundary sign on the left. The trail takes off from there, trending upward through the woods, ½ mile, to a small, grassy knob. This is a crucial spot, marked only by a signless post. Avoid the more obvious trail uphill and straight ahead. It ends up bearing left, towards Rock and Knownothing Lakes.

Instead, take a hard right at the knob and head downhill 50 feet or so, until you come to an old road. Follow it into Shasta Trinity National Forest, a mile, through wet alpine meadows of corn lily, yarrow, monkshood and arnica. Not to mention grass, willow and the sickening sweet smelling snow brush. There's a distinct lack of tree diversity along the trail, however, with only Shasta red and grand fir, plus a few incense cedars.

The path drops steeply to the muddy meadows, then climbs towards Devils Backbone. Shortly after re-entering the woods, you'll come to two trail junctions, for Devil's Backbone and Red Cap Lake. Stay right at both for Salmon Mountain, Indian Rocks, Orleans Mountain, Anaheim, Azusa and Cucamonga.

Beyond the Red Cap Lake turnoff, the route becomes quite steep for a mile, remaining mostly in the woods. You'll soon see Red Cap Lake far below, a tiny lily pond in a miniature glacial cirque. The steep trail down is hardly worth the effort, unless you're looking for a camp site.

The path breaks into the open just below the Salmon Mountain summit. A glance to the rear reveals the gray domes of Devils Backbone. One wonders why they're forested on the east and barren on the west, the opposite of what you'd expect. Ahead lies the narrow ridge between the Salmon and Klamath Rivers. Neither river is visible. You're now in Six Rivers National Forest.

At the trail's high point, scramble uphill to the right to climb the peak, up a barren slope of scree and manzanita brush. It's only a couple hundred feet to the lip of a small, lakeless glacial cirque. At your feet, a vertical rock face plunges a couple hundred feet to a lovely meadow.

The final summit lies a few hundred yards south, at a large rock cairn. Reaching it involves making your way up a series of steep, staircase outcrops. It's not particularly difficult.

The view from this centrally located aerie exceeds all expectations. Most impressive is the glacial horn of Mt. Thompson, highest point in the Trinity Alps, to the east. And no, you can't see the ocean.

75. TRAIL GULCH/LONG GULCH LAKES
(Trinity Alps Wilderness Area)

Length: 3½ miles (8 mi. loop)
Water: Lots
Access: Good paved and gravel roads
Season: June — October

Difficulty: Moderate
Elevation: 5400 to 6400 feet
Use: Non-motorized only
Ownership: Klamath NF
Phone: (916) 468-5351

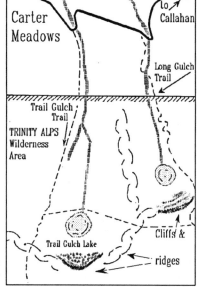

Directions: Take I-5 to the south Yreka (Hwy 3) exit. Turn right at the town of Callahan and follow the paved, two lane road towards Cecilville. Just beyond the summit, look for a gravel road on the left which runs along the flat below the main road. Follow it to the Long Gulch trailhead and, a mile later, the Trail Gulch trailhead.

I used to wonder how two such lovely bodies of water ended up with such unaesthetic names. Finally, I concluded that the names were meant to discourage the swarms of humanity who converge on places with more poetic names like Emerald and Sapphire Lake. The secret of Trail and Long Gulch Lakes' beauty is now out as both were recently included in the new Trinity Alps Wilderness Area.

The glacial cirque forming Trail Gulch is among the most noticeable in a cluster of extremely deep cirques viewable from the paved road near the Callahan/Cecilville summit. It's a beautiful drive over a fine highway offering an excellent geology lesson.

Trail Gulch Lake offers a 3½ mile hike from the roomy trailhead. The route contains some steep pitches but isn't too bad as it wanders from woods to meadows along the creek. A side trail left, three miles up, leads to the lake.

If you continue straight, it's less than ½ mile to the ridge top. There, one can peer into an area much like the Yosemite high country, with glacially polished granite domes. Look for the 9000 foot summit of Mt. Thompson nearby, the one with active glaciers. A short walk along the ridge affords a dizzying view down to Trail Gulch Lake.

The lake rests at the base of a sheer headwall. The aqua water is surrounded by woods on the downhill side but boasts a large corn lily meadow above the creek inlet just east of the headwall. For the best swimming, follow the trail through the meadow, past lingering snow fields, to the gap between the headwall and a little island.

It's a steep, 1½ miles up the rock face to the east, around the top of Long Gulch cirque and back down to Long Gulch Lake. The latter is virtually identical to Trail Gulch Lake but only 10 acres. The trail from the Long Gulch trailhead is shorter but steeper and rockier than the one up Trail Gulch. Given a choice, I'd use it as a way out, not in (or double back and not use it at all), although it's a perfectly good route. Both lakes are popular these days and offer good brook trout fishing.

76. HIDDEN LAKE
(Trinity Alps Wilderness Area)

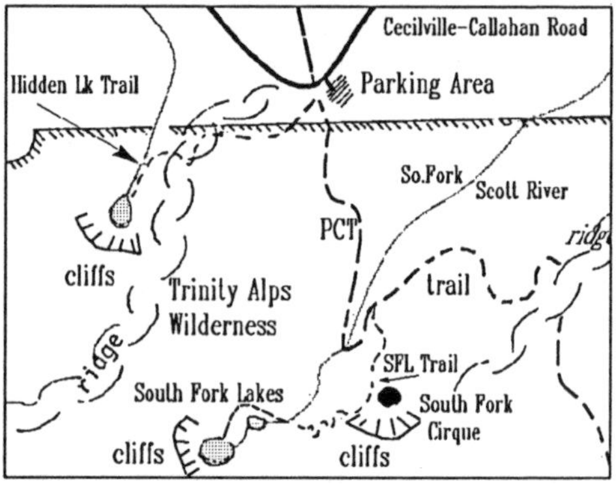

Length: 1½ miles
Water: OK
Access: Paved highway
Season: June —
October
Difficulty: Easy
Elevation: 6200 to
6700 ft
Use: Non-motorized
Ownership: Klamath NF
Phone: (916) 468-5351

Directions: Take the
south Yreka (Hwy 3) exit off I-5 and proceed 30 miles to Callahan. Turn right at Callahan onto the paved, two lane road to Cecilville. Park at the summit, on the left, in the parking area.

The objective of my very first hike in northern California was Hidden Lake. The memorable event occurred in 1970 with my wife, seven children (including one of ours), and a suitcase full of fried chicken. Everybody had a wonderful time swimming, fishing and chowing down.

It was a splendid introduction to my favorite real estate on Earth. The road is paved, the trail flat and short, the lake picturesque and the surrounding scenery breathtaking.

Approaching the pass between Callahan and Cecilville, a maze of rocky peaks, gouged by huge glacial cirques, appears on the left. The cluster lies within the Trinity Alps Wilderness but technically belongs to the Scott Mountains.

The cirques are extremely deep and there are dozens of them. From the trail, the South Fork cirque (which does not contain South Fork Lake), is most obvious. Less obvious, obviously, is the Hidden Lake cirque.

At the pass, you'll see a little hillock with a helipad on top. A short, dirt driveway to the left leads to a parking area. Trailheads, sign-in boxes and signs clutter the area. The main trailhead, for the Pacific Crest Trail, leads to South Fork Lake and points south. Only a tiny oak plaque, tacked to a tree, marks the Hidden Lake Trail. If you jump aboard the PCT too near the end of the parking area, you'll miss it.

The Hidden Lake Trail winds through high elevation woods of Shasta fir and mountain hemlock for a while, then comes out on a brushy ridge. The South Fork of the Scott River lies far below; with the Scott Mountains' steep, craggy flanks rising beyond. The orange rock is serpentine while the jagged gray stuff is schist.

It's an amazing vista. Don't be surprised to find yourself taking deep breaths and saying "wow" a lot.

Finally, the trail re-enters the woods and crosses a series of low, rolling glacial moraines. Then the 3 acre lake appears, gentle and shaded, with the usual cliff rising from the far end. The area near the outlet is relatively flat, with open woods and easy lake access. The lake has clear water, a solid bottom and little shoreline brush. It's a marvelous place to eat chicken out of a suitcase.

77. SOUTH FORK LAKES
(Trinity Alps wilderness Area)

See map, Chapter 76
Length: 3 miles
Water: Lots
Access: Good paved road
Season: June — October
Difficulty: Difficult
Elevation: 6200 to 6700
Use: Non-motorized only
Ownership: Klamath NF
Phone: (916) 468-5351

Directions: *Take I-5 to the south Yreka (Hwy 3) exit. Proceed to the Scott Valley town of Callahan and turn right on the road to Cecilville. The trailhead is at the summit of the paved, two lane road between Callahan and Cecilville, on the left.*

Both the South Fork Lakes Trail and the Hidden Lake Trail begin at the same trailhead and appear the same length on the map. Since the Hidden Lake Trail is fairly level and the elevations are similar for both routes, it's astonishing to find that the South Fork Lakes Trail is twice as long and infinitely more difficult. Unlike the Hidden Lake Trail, the South Fork Trail drops several hundred feet before ascending into the high cirque containing the lakes.

The cluster of deeply gouged glacial cirques seen from the highway near the Callahan/Cecilville summit, and from the Hidden Lake Trail, is described in other chapters. The South Fork Lakes Trail penetrates its deepest and most impressive cirque. Oddly enough, however, that's not where the lakes lie.

The first half of the trek follows the Pacific Crest Trail south from the parking area. The route descends gradually through a forest of Shasta fir, mountain hemlock and western white pine, to a crossing of the South Fork of the Scott River. It's a little muddy and mosquitoey at the crossing, an open area of moisture loving shrubs, willows and wildflowers. The turnoff to the lakes is just beyond, uphill to the right.

The path soon enters the immense, tan cirque seen from the highway. It is found to contain only a meadow, surrounded by thousand-foot cliffs. Admiration of the basin is tempered by the thought that your objective lies near the top of the headwall.

Red Buttes from the Pacific Crest Trail.

Now the fun begins. The really steep push, up rockfalls and cliffs, only lasts a mile but can be a challenge. I spoke with a man with his eight year old daughter before starting up. He warned me that the trail was so steep, he was forced to let his daughter rest once.

Amid vertical rock faces on all sides, the trail suddenly disappears over the top into a piney woods on a gentle plateau. The shallow, 3½ acre lower lake soon appears in the middle of a field.

A five minute stroll through the woods from the lower lake leads to the 4½ acre upper lake. You can't miss it, although one could miss the trail to it. The upper lake is nestled at the base of a low cliff, in a tiny cirque even more hidden than that containing Hidden Lake.

Fishing is outstanding, I hear, and the entire experience is worth the effort. Even if you are forced to rest once. Or even twice.

78. EAST BOULDER LAKES
(Trinity Alps Wilderness Area)

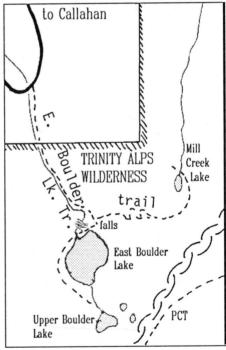

Length: 2 miles
Water: Do not drink!
Access: Good gravel and dirt roads
Season: June—October.
Difficulty: Easy
Elevation: 5850 to 6700 feet
Use: Non-motorized
Ownership: Klamath NF and private
Phone: (916) 468-5351

Directions: Take I-5 to the Hwy 3 south of Yreka. Follow Hwy 3 to Callahan. Turn right just past the Callahan Emporium (40N16, which becomes 40N17). Follow signs to the McKeen Divide and East Boulder Lake. It's 3 miles to the Divide, 3 more to the trailhead. Roads are well signed. A mile before the trailhead, bear left, uphill, at the fork, taking the road marked "Dead End." From there on, follow the main road to the roomy, well marked trailhead.

Hundreds of lakes adorn the vast Klamath Mountains of northwest California. And a superficial description of East Boulder Lake would differ only slightly from that of dozens of others. The lake, for the record, covers about 30 acres inside a glacial cirque, at an elevation of 6700 feet.

East Boulder Lake, however, is unique. The first time I visited, I was astonished to find it completely different from others in the region. Of course many lakes in the Marbles and Trinity Alps boast some special quality and can be considered unusual. But not quite this unusual.

At 6700 feet elevation in this region, one may encounter a variety of vegetation types. Western white pine and red fir grows just about everywhere while mountain hemlock and lodgepole pine tend to be a little more selective. Brewer spruce is rather rare and whitebark pine is rarer still. Foxtail pine turns up only on a few very widely scattered sites.

The last thing one would expect at this elevation, amid some of California's lushest forests, is a high desert plant community. Why this particular basin, and no other, abounds with desert sage and rabbit brush, one can only speculate.

It may have to do with the proximity to Scott Valley, 6 miles away and 3500 feet down. Such vegetation is common to the upper valley, a rainshadow where moisture is blocked by high mountains. Poor, porous soils and logged off, south slope sites, lend themselves to high desert invasion.

The desert brush may have been helped into the East Boulder basin by clearcut logging and cattle browsing. The entire cirque is open, grassy, seemingly barren of trees and full of cattle.

I highly recommend the East Boulder area, not only for it's botanical features but for it's equally unique beauty. The trail is fairly easy while the access road is wide and not overly long or steep, with fine vistas. Look especially, as you drive to the trailhead, for imposing rock faces below Craggy Peak and Bolivar Lookout.

The trailhead area occupies a beautiful, wooded ravine within sight of Craggy Mountain's granite cliffs. The trail takes off through woods of mostly white fir, Jeffrey pine, western white pine and incense cedar. A little steep at first, the path soon levels off as it passes a series of creekside, grassy openings.

Since the trail crosses private property, visitors should respect it accordingly. They should also respect public property, of course. Also, because of the cattle, I'd avoid drinking from the numerous creeks and springs along the trail.

After ascending gently through alternating woods and fields, the trail passes a sizeable waterfall on East Boulder Creek, ¼ mile below the lake. There the path shoots sharply but briefly upward and enters the lake basin.

From the grassy flat above the waterfall, the barren East Boulder cirque can be seen to the south while the forested Mill Creek cirque yawns atop the cliffs to the north. Mill Creek Lake is far smaller (3 acres), than East Boulder Lake (32 acres). The unsigned Mill Creek Lake Trail begins just above the waterfall. Walk north (left), across the field and follow the old road up the cliffs.

The East Boulder basin is underlain by serpentine, with nearby ridges and outcroppings weathered to a lovely cinnamon brown. It contrasts beautifully with the greens and yellows of the fields.

The surrounding peaks, by the way, between the Scott and Trinity Rivers, are called the Scott Mountains. This despite forming an unbroken chain with the Trinity Alps, to the west and south. It doesn't make much sense.

Despite the East Boulder basin's desolate appearance, it hosts a surprising variety of trees. In addition to those mentioned earlier, I noted Shasta red fir, lodgepole pine and a single whitebark pine. Brush species include sage and rabbit brush, manzanita and mountain mahogany.

East Boulder Lake's designer decorated it with brown, rocky shores, wide, flat banks, clear water, picturesque, widely scattered clumps of trees and a low cirque headwall rising in the distance. The lake sits in the basin's center, well away from the encircling black/brown ridge. I especially enjoyed the clear, unshaded, boulder lined creek between the lake and the waterfall.

Continuing along the trail, past East Boulder Lake, will land you at 7 acre Upper Boulder Lake and a pair of secluded 1 to 2 acre ponds. The trail peters out at Upper Boulder Lake, despite the Forest Service Map. To connect with the Pacific Crest Trail, take the side trail from East Boulder Lake towards Mavis Lake. Ten other lakes in the region all offer wonderful fishing, outstanding sightseeing and not a trace of sagebrush.

East Boulder Lake is nowhere near Boulder Lake, just south of Coffee Creek, although both lie within the Trinity Alps Wilderness. I guess any place with boulders is fair game for the name. Neither lake struck me, however, as particularly boulder strewn. In my experience, Duck Lake, in the Russian Wilderness, has the most boulders. I didn't see any ducks there, though. Go figure.

79. TANGLE BLUE LAKE
(Trinity Alps Wilderness Area)

Length: 3 miles
Water: Lots,
probably not good
Access: Fair dirt road
Season:
June—October
Difficulty: Moderate
to easy
Elevation: 4500 to
5700
Use: Non-motorized
Ownership:
Shasta/Trinity
Phone: (916)
623-2121

TRINITY ALPS WILDERNESS AREA

39N20
Gate

mine road

trail

Cabin

Tangle Blue Lake

Directions: From I-5 at Yreka, follow Hwy 3 through Scott Valley. Past Callahan, turn right (staying on Hwy 3), towards Trinity Center and Weaverville. Take the first turnoff right, beyond Scott Mountain Summit, where the sign says "Tangle Blue Lake" and "39N20." From the turnoff, it's about 3½ miles, past two major side roads, to the trailhead. Look for a bulletin board and a trail marker. The trail follows the gated road. Parking is ample.

The miners and trappers who first explored most of northern California, were by and large a pragmatic bunch, not given to poetic musing. Thus, place names in the region tend to be utilitarian and descriptive rather than fanciful.

The area's lakes, for example, no matter how beautiful, were usually named for a person (Mavis Lake, Stoddard Lake, Wright Lake), a prominent feature (Long Gulch Lake, Cliff Lake or the oxymoronic Granite Lake), something which impressed the namer (Fish Lake, Big Bear Lake), or simply its location (South Fork Lake, Kidder Creek Lake).

Occasionally, to be sure, the pioneer mountain folk would lapse into humor (Gumboot Lake, Knownothing Lake, Maneaten Lake). And some of their names are inexplicable (Kangaroo Lake). But hardly ever was a namer moved to poetry. And even then, the result tended to be a little hackneyed (Emerald Lake, Sapphire Lake).

Tangle Blue Lake alone, among the emerald and sapphire pools of the vast Trinity and Marble country, sports a moniker worthy of Whitman and Longfellow.

Given that it bears the region's prettiest name, the question remains: Do the trail and lake match it in beauty? The answer is decidedly affirmative. Furthermore, among the Trinity Alps' hundred or so glacial cirque lakes, Tangle Blue boasts possibly the shortest and easiest access road and trail.

Which brings up another question: Why couldn't I find the trailhead when I attempted to visit in 1988? In 1991, I encountered no difficulty whatsoever.

The Forest Service, it turns out, has installed several road signs since my earlier visit, partly in response to my negative feedback. The sign at the turnoff, the numbers marking the side roads, and the trailhead bulletin board, are all new. The last side road before the trailhead looks like the main road. Without the identifying sign, I was faced, in 1988, with having to follow out every possible turnoff in this maze of logging roads. With the new markers in place, finding the trailhead is simple, although the markers tend to get knocked over and vandalized.

Another 1988 problem was a plague of inaccurate maps. That, alas, remains the case. The Trinity Alps Wilderness map shows the trail incorrectly and includes almost none of the present road system. The Shasta-Trinity National Forest map, on which Tangle Blue Lake appears twice (once on each side), is only a little better. The light green version has only a sketchy depiction of the area. The dark green side shows the roads accurately but not the trail.

The only map correctly tracing both the access roads and the trail, oddly enough, is the Klamath National Forest map, where it overlaps Shasta-Trinity National Forest. If anything, it gives too much detail and is difficult to figure out.

For its first half, the path follows old mining roads. There is, in fact, no actual trail from the parking area, just a gate across the road. Walk past the gate, down to the creek and over the bridge. Beyond, the route climbs steeply uphill, then swings right and meets the creek again soon after. Where a road takes off left, up the hill, about ½ mile up, continue straight, along the creek.

After a mile or so, beyond a second gate and the Wilderness Boundary sign, the scenery opens onto a large flat with some of the biggest incense cedars I've ever seen. The early miners might have named this place Cedar Flat.

Uphill from the cedar (and Douglas-fir) flat, several wet, grassy meadows blanket the steep slope. A keen observer will spot patches of fly-eating darlingtonia plants scattered in the grass. These are rare "hanging bogs." Generally, bogs and swampy areas, where darlingtonia grow, occur in depressions or low lying sites. A hillside seep such as this, usually does not provide enough water, consistently and over a wide area, to support a bog community.

While water abounds along the trail, I wouldn't drink it. Between hikers (the trail is quite popular), horses, habitation sites, old roads and (no doubt), grazing cattle, the risks are prohibitively high.

Despite the route's 1200 foot elevation rise, vegetation changes are minimal. At the trailhead, look for incense cedar, Douglas-fir, ponderosa pine, western white pine and white fir. Near the lake, the Douglas-fir and ponderosa pine fade out, while white pine and white fir become the dominant species. A few Shasta red firs sneak in as the lake is approached. By and large, however, the site isn't high enough to support a full compliment of upper elevation species.

In fact, it's hard to believe the trail rises 1200 feet. Much of it is perfectly level and few of the upgrades seem particularly steep or long.

Beyond the cedar flat, the trail bumps into the creek, continuing on the opposite bank. This crossing, to the creek's north side, is not reflected on the Trinity Alps or Shasta-Trinity map, even though the south bank is quite steep and probably never held a trail. The shallow creek is easily forded without getting wet.

Soon after the crossing, the path disappears in a maze of rock strewn gullies and side streams. The easiest way through is to follow the orange flagging. After crossing the main side creek, take a hard left back towards Tangle Blue Creek to rejoin the trail.

A couple miles from the trailhead, the route climbs to the edge of a large, grassy flat. It skirts it a ways, then drops back to the creek and crosses it a second time, at the ruins of Messner Cabin. From the cabin, it's a straight, fairly steep, ½ mile shot through the woods to the lake.

As you hike this last, south trending leg, the rocky spires capping the cirque headwall begin to emerge in the distance. Then, while gray cliffs unfold beneath the spires, sunlight appears through the trees, hinting at an impending large opening. Finally, the path breaks out onto a large meadow, with the lake at the far end.

Tangle Blue, as noted, holds its own in beauty among the Trinity Alps' many alpine glacial lakes. Being at a somewhat lower elevation than most, however, the glacier which formed it melted away earlier. Thus, the 12 acre pool has progressed further in its evolution than other, higher lakes. The silting-in process is well along and the lake is shallow and choked with logs and branches fallen from the tree lined shore. Since the bottom is extremely mushy, I wouldn't try swimming.

Take particular note of the inlet, near the base of the headwall. Like the Mississippi's mouth, a large delta, created by erosion, is pushing into and gradually filling the lake. A lovely meadow decorates the formation.

The word Tangle, in the lake's name, correctly suggests abundant decaying vegetation in its waters. Since the water is therefore cloudy and algae laden, the Blue part of the name turns out to be merely wishful thinking. Maybe it was blue 100 years ago but it's greenish-brown now.

Don't worry, however. It's still well worth a visit— especially if you're a fisherman. Brook and rainbow trout by the dozens heralded our visit by leaping out of the water in a choreographed salute. Several stayed for dinner.

80. BIG BEAR LAKE
(Trinity Alps Wilderness Area)

Length: 3 miles
Water: Lots
Access: Level gravel road
Season: May — November.
Difficulty: Moderate
Elevation: 3000 to 5800 feet
Use: Non-motorized only
Ownership: Shasta Trinity NF
Phone: (916) 623-2121

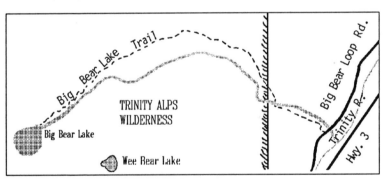

Directions: Take Hwy 3 from Weaverville or south Yreka, to the north end of Bear Creek Loop, north of Coffee Creek. The extremely roomy, well marked trailhead lies 2 miles up this wide, level, gravel road. It's 1 mile up from the loop's south end.

If I had to pick a single trail capturing the Trinity Alps's essence without involving a 10 to 20 mile hike, this would be it. The lake is the most beautiful of the Alps' outer lakes and the trailhead may be the most easily reached in the entire Wilderness.

As lovely as Big Bear and the other outer lakes are, however, few lakes in the world compare in beauty and grandeur to those at the Trinity Alps' core, in the Mt. Thompson area. So don't expect perfection from Bear Lake, just near perfection. On the other hand, trails to the core are all 10 to 20 miles long.

My only problem with the Bear Lake Trail was that some things didn't quite "compute." Its length, for example, is listed as anywhere from 4½ to 6 miles. I reached the lake in 1 hour and 45 minutes and estimated the distance at 3½ miles. The Weaverville Ranger District recently re-measured the route at 3.09 miles.

With a 2800 foot elevation rise, a 3 mile trail should be horrendously steep. Although described as "arduous" in several references, I didn't find the going that difficult.

Something is out of whack. Either the trail is longer than it seemed, steeper than it seemed, the listed elevations are wrong, or I passed through some mysterious time/space warp the day I visited.

Suffice to say, I found the excursion lovely throughout, highly varied and not unbearably strenuous. Granted, there are steep spots and the uphill trend rarely slacks off. But I disagree with the "arduous" designation and with allegations that the path is unbearably hot in summer due to its many exposed, brushy sections.

Hiking on an overcast October day, my perception may have been "clouded." Still, the path struck me as a nearly ideal balance between open and shaded areas.

Beginning in a dense, middle elevation forest above the canyon of Bear Creek, the trail hugs the stream for its entire length. Rising rather steeply at first, things level off near the bridge over Bear Creek. The crossing, an enchanted little deep woods spot, is not nearly as scenic as that to come. Beyond the bridge, the trail steepens, then levels off for a considerable distance.

For the first couple miles, the forest consists mostly of Douglas-fir and black oak. Scattered tanoak suggests a fair amount of rainfall. Diminutive but exquisitely flowered Pacific dogwoods add to the beauty, especially in spring. Occasional stands of knobcone pine indicate past fires or logging clearcuts, as do patches of manzanita brush.

This fairly level middle section reveals excellent views of the granite peaks on the south side of the creek. High up near their tops, a glacial cirque has been gouged into the rock, with an outlet crashing sharply into Bear Creek. I believe this cirque houses Little and Wee Bear Lakes, which may be reached by hiking cross country to the southeast from the main lake.

Bear Creek Canyon eventually narrows, curves south and white granite walls close in on either side. While the path steepens again here, the interplay of woods, open areas, side creeks and stone ramparts is appealing. Upper elevation mountain hemlock, white fir, Shasta red fir and western white pine populate the forested areas. Look for alder along the creek and ferns, willow, grass and coffeeberry lining the seeps and side creeks.

The last mile or so follows much closer to the creek. This section is steep, a little muddy and quite brushy, but the unfolding cirque ahead urges one on.

Immediately below the lake, the trail passes a couple of small, wooded glades with masses of azalea lining the path. Azaleas bloom in spring and occasionally in fall but not in summer.

Just beyond the azalea glades, the trail climbs up a rock face, passes more azaleas, and, at last, finds the lake. This last rock face is a gently rounded, glacially polished terrace. The creek fans out over it before forming a small waterfall.

All one can really say about the deep, 28 acre lake, is that it makes a fitting climax to a beautiful hike. White, billowing granite slopes encircle 80% of the cirque, leading up to a crown of jagged spires and minarets. Fishing is excellent and there's plenty of room to camp near the outlet.

81. STODDARD LAKE
(Trinity Alps Wilderness Area)

Length: 2 miles
Water: OK
Access: Long, good dirt road
Season: June — October.
Difficulty: Moderate
Elevation: 5100 to 6400 feet
Use: Non-motorized only
Ownership: Shasta-Trinity NF
Phone: (916) 623-2121

Directions: Take Hwy 3 from Weaverville or Scott Valley. North of Trinity Lake and Coffee Creek, turn west onto Eagle Creek Loop (north end). Proceed 2 miles to the Horse Flat Campground and follow the signs 7 miles, to the well marked trailhead. Park on the shoulder.

As one of a number of large, beautiful lakes adorning the periphery of the Trinity Alps Wilderness, Stoddard Lake makes an ideal day-hike. While trails to the Alps' core average 10 to 20 miles, most of these outer lakes offer a delectable taste of the region with far less effort.

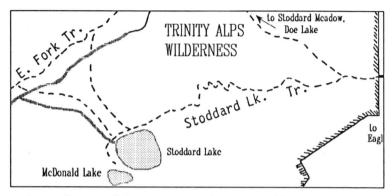

An ambitious fishermen or sightseer could camp at Trinity Lake and visit Stoddard, Boulder, Granite, Tangle Blue and Big Bear Lakes in two or three days. A relaxing afternoon in a boat on Trinity Lake and dinner in a restaurant might top off their efforts.

The Stoddard Lake Trail is only 2 miles long. At 25 acres, just 5 lakes in the Wilderness exceed Stoddard's size. While the 9 mile dirt road from Hwy 3 to the trailhead is steep, winding and very dusty in summer, the road is wide, well graded and scenic. Views of the white peaks of the Big Bear Lake area, across Eagle Creek, dominate.

The cramped trailhead lacks turnaround space in the immediate vicinity. After parking along the road shoulder, head up the moderately steep, brush lined trail.

Stoddard Lake, and the entire trail, lie within a serpentine rock formation. The jagged, brown and black peaks contrast markedly with the rounded, white upthrusts of the granite summits across Eagle Creek. Serpentine adapted vegetation abounds.

The trail's first ½ mile is choked with an astonishing variety of shrubs. Sadler oak, evergreen chinkapin and scrub tanoak all thrive on serpentine. Look also for scrub liveoak, plus rhododendron, manzanita and other heath species.

After ¾ mile, a side trail breaks away amid a grassy flat. Both paths lead to Stoddard Lake. It's a mile farther to the lake via the Doe Lake Trail and Stoddard Meadow. Although this longer, right-hand route isn't as steep, I suggest the path to the left. A 5 mile trail up the East fork of Coffee Creek also leads to Stoddard Lake.

Beyond the junction, to the left, the trail winds rather steeply uphill. But it's fairly short and quite interesting. Between wooded patches of Jeffrey pine, western white pine, white fir and incense cedar, you'll discover numerous seeps, meadows and side creeks.

I noted at least two darlingtonia bogs, with masses of pitcher plants (Darlingtonia californica) rearing their cobra heads in quest of hapless insects. Such bogs, along with Jeffrey pine, are a sure indicator of serpentine. You'll also find a variety of yellow and blue daisy species, Indian paintbrush, Indian pink, Etc. Visiting in October, I observed only a remnant of the floral display.

Finally, the path crosses the ridge and drops 600 feet into Stoddards' deep basin. Tortured serpentine crags, rearing above two sides of the cirque, dominate the steep descent to the lake.

The vast emerald expanse's shores are densely wooded with lodgepole pine and the tree species noted above. The north bank, where the trail emerges, is steep and rocky while the opposite side is more level with colorful, open meadows. The best campsites can be found along the forested ledge near the outlet.

The lake's large size and the steep, towering headwall blasting from the water, suggests considerable depth and fertile fish production. The 84 foot deep lake thus offers a popular, easily reached fishing and camping spot. Go in peace.

82. CARIBOU LAKES TRAIL
(Trinity Alps Wilderness Area)

Length: 10 miles
Water: Surprisingly little
Access: Good gravel roads
Season: June — October
Difficulty: Moderately steep but very long
Elevation: 5000 to 7000
Use: Non-motorized only
Ownership: Klamath NF
Phone: (916) 468-5351

Directions: Take Hwy 3 from I-5 south of Yreka, via Scott Valley, or from Weaverville. Turn west on Coffee Creek Road and follow it 17 miles to Big Flat Campground. Hwy 3 is a paved, two lane road. Coffee Creek Road is wide, level and gravel surfaced. The campground/trailhead is roomy and well developed. Obtain a free Wilderness Permit at the Coffee Creek Ranger Station.

There's a good reason for including this 10 mile route, even though no other path herein exceeds 6 miles. It ranks among the four "ultimate" northwest California trails, so outstanding that people visit (or should), from all over the country. The others are the Marble Valley Trail, the trek up Mt. Shasta and the King Crest Trail.

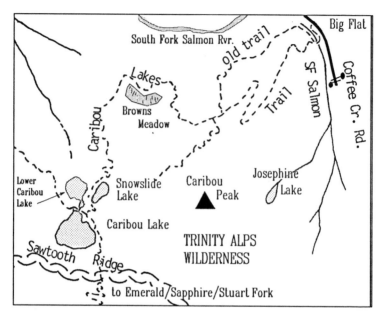

Of the four, only the Caribou Lakes Trail does not qualify as a day-hike. Nevertheless, it's omission from this book would not be reasonable. It would be like discussing California highways without mentioning 101. Or it's mountains without bringing up Whitney.

The Caribou Lakes Trail penetrates the core of the Trinity Alps, one of America's loveliest mountain clusters. This jumbled maze of sawtoothed ridges shows outstanding evidence of past glaciation. Its beauty is capped by at least 50 lakes set in cirque bowls of polished white granite. The highest peak, Mt. Thompson, tops out at only 9002 feet but contains the only active glaciers west of the Sierra/Cascade chain and south of the Washington Olympics.

The Caribou Lakes Trail does not afford the closest possible access to Mt. Thompson and its glaciers. That honor goes to another pathway, the Grizzly Lake Trail, out of Cecilville. Grizzly Lake occupies an exquisite 42 acres at the glacier's snout.

The Caribou Lakes Trail, coming in from the Trinity River side, ends a couple valleys east of Grizzly Lake. It is shorter, (10 miles versus 19), less steep, more varied and every bit as beautiful as the Grizzly Lake Trail. The view of Mt. Thompson from the Caribou Lakes Trail is breathtaking. Caribou Lake, at 72 acres, checks in as the Alps' largest. A hike from the Caribou Basin to Grizzly Lake, while possible, requires some daring as there is no trail.

The Caribou Lakes Trail begins at Big Flat Campground near the end of Coffee Creek Road. A sign at Big Flat directs hikers left, down an old road across a grassy ravine. The trail crosses a wide creek, then starts uphill, switching steeply back and forth for the next 3 miles.

The main item of scenic interest, in this first 3 miles, is the view of the immense valley below, surrounded by glacially cut peaks and ridges. Big Flat and the trailhead area can be seen at one end of the valley. A sharp eye will pick out Coffee Creek Road, as it continues beyond Big Flat past a closed gate.

Now Coffee Creek flows into the Trinity River and the road apparently crosses no ridges or divides. It is reasonable to assume, therefore, that the creek running alongside upper Coffee Creek Road, the same creek forded near the trailhead, also flows into the Trinity and is probably Coffee Creek. Therein lies a tale.

Surprisingly, that stream is actually the South Fork of the Salmon River. It ultimately drains west into the Klamath instead of east into the Trinity. At some point, as I understand it, the upper Salmon eroded its way onto Big Flat and actually stole this valley from Coffee Creek.

The county and National Forest boundaries were defined, at the time, by the Trinity/Klamath divide. So when the divide changed, so did the boundaries. Thus, the valley jumped from Trinity County and Trinity National Forest, to Siskiyou County and Klamath National Forest.

The designers of the Caribou Lakes Trail must have felt it would be overwhelming to blast hikers with the region's full beauty all at once. So it's doled out a little at a time, building to a crescendo.

First, there's the view of the aforementioned Coffee Creek/South Fork Salmon valley. Then, you approach, but never quite reach, a beautiful granite rock face. After 3 miles, past a grassy flat by a trail junction, the trail picks its way over a huge outcropping of glacially polished granite. At mile 5, it crosses Brown's Meadow.

The trail's only drinkable water (don't quote me), trickles out a pipe a few hundred yards past the meadow. A mile beyond, Mt. Thompson comes into view. 1½ miles later, the lakes finally appear, in a cirque across a tremendous glacial valley.

The world-class vistas begin where the trail comes around a bend and the Mt. Thompson cluster appears. The afternoon sun glistens blindingly off permanent snowfields and polished white rock. Sparkling, jagged dikes, radiating from the summit, look like a giant, diamond tiara. Immense glacial ravines assault the mountain's northern flank. Caribou Creek, 2000 feet beneath your feet, rushes through a "U" shaped chasm with hanging side valleys. By the time melt water from the Thompson glacier arrives at Cecilville, 20 miles distant, it has dropped 7000 feet.

For the next couple miles, the route continues climbing, at one point inching its way around a huge white cliff resembling a wall of icicles. You don't know until you get there, how the trail plans to cross the expanse.

Occasional patches of western white pine, lodgepole pine, mountain hemlock and Shasta red fir line the trail. I also noted a single Brewer spruce, about ½ mile above Snowslide Lake.

Eventually, Caribou Lake emerges in the distance, inside a giant, steep walled cirque left of Mt. Thompson. Then Lower Caribou Lake appears, in a granite bowl, under a waterfall emerging from the main lake.

Granite carved by glacial ice has a softly rounded, pillowy look. Thus, Lower Caribou Lake, half the main lake and nearby Snowslide Lake, all appear set into a giant, rather rumpled, down comforter of white satin.

At one point on the trail, both the main (upper) and the lower lake can be seen, beneath an immense granite slope rising up to a razor ridge on the left. It's impossible to imagine where Snowslide Lake, immediately left of Lower Caribou Lake, might fit in. But a third cirque magically emerges from the granite wall. Between miles 7½ and 9, the trail drops 500 feet, to a narrow, pillow ridge between Snowslide and Lower Caribou Lakes.

My wife nominates Snowslide as the prettiest of the three Caribou Basin lakes. The main Caribou Lake's beauty is slightly diminished because its cirque cuts a band of boring, crumbly schist on one side.

At 10 acres, Snowslide Lake is the smallest of the trio. It's surface, at 6700 feet, lies 200 feet above the 22 acre Lower Caribou Lake and 150 feet below Caribou Lake. White slopes shoot up 1000 feet from Snowslide's eastern shore, culminating in a row of stone spires that resemble a giant marimba.

Expect a continuous stream of hikers and horses on this extremely popular route. The campground at Snowslide Lake, on a rocky hump separating Snowslide from Lower Caribou Lake, tends to be busy and crowded. The upper lake also attracts many campers but offers more room to spread out.

The trail up from Snowslide to the much larger Caribou lake, winds through a maze of marshmallow granite to Caribou's eastern shore. Again, sawtoothed ridges careen down to a series of gentle meadows and glacially rounded granite outcroppings. Brook and rainbow trout fishing is superb in all three lakes.

For a glimpse of the two most beautiful lakes you're ever likely to experience, continue up the trail an 11th mile, to the pass 700 feet above Caribou Lake. It's steep, of course, but not very long. The views of the Caribou Basin and Mt. Thompson should keep your mind off the panting and perspiration.

From atop the narrow, high ridge, the trail plunges into the valley of the Stuart Fork (of the Trinity). The astonishingly deep, "U" shaped glacial valley reminded me of a Swiss travel poster.

On the map, it appears about ¾ of a mile from the ridge to the Stuart Fork Trail. In that span, however, the trail drops 3000 feet. I contented myself with merely peering down. Which was fine since it was possibly the most beautiful scene I've ever witnessed.

The Stuart Fork Trail culminates at the deep cirque shared by Emerald and Sapphire Lakes. To see them, scramble west along the ridge for ¼ mile, around the base of yet another row of saw-toothed marimbas. The most exquisite lakes on Earth soon appear, 3000 feet straight down from the south face of Mt. Thompson. Sapphire lake, higher of the pair, covers 43 acres and reaches a depth of over 200 feet. It is the Alps' deepest by 130 feet.

Except for Mt. Thompson, the high peaks surrounding the Emerald/Sapphire cirque are not visible from the Caribou Lakes Trail. Offering a bedlam of mirror maze reflections of Mt. Thompson, it's hard to believe that so many peaks, so close together, can be so beautiful.

The steep walled, round bottomed cirque in their midst looks as though hewn with a giant ice cream scoop. Emerald and Sapphire Lakes occupy the cirque's barren, rocky bottom, beneath their very own, if small, hanging glacier. I could have stayed there forever. In many ways, I did.

83. BOULDER LAKES
(Trinity Alps Wilderness Area)

Length: 1½ miles
Water: No
Access: Long dirt road
Season: June—October
Difficulty: Easy. Uphill
Elevation: 5350 to 6100 feet
Use: Non-motorized only
Ownership: Shasta-Trinity NF
Phone: (916) 623-2121

Directions: *Take Hwy 3, from Weaverville or Yreka, to a well marked turnoff west, just south of Coffee Creek. It's 11 miles to the very roomy trailhead. The last 3/4 mile of the dirt access road is a little rough and narrow.*

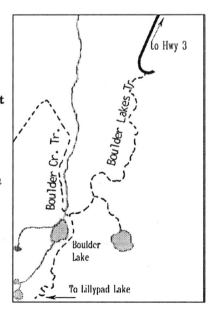

This is an ideal trail for those wishing to experience the Trinity Alps' high lakes with a minimum of hiking. Both Boulder and Little Boulder Lakes compare favorably to many in the Wilderness (although nothing compares favorably to Emerald, Sapphire, Caribou, Grizzly, Big Bear or Papoose Lakes).

Of the many logging roads nibbling at the Trinity Alps from Hwy 3, the well graded dirt road to the Boulder Lakes trailhead may be the most scenic. It winds steeply upward for 11 slow miles, crossing creeks and logging operations while peering out across the Trinity River and neighboring Billy Peak's white upthrust.

Approaching the trailhead, several near peaks are revealed, in a maze of granite outcroppings. The craggy ridge cut by the Boulder Lake cirque is seen from the road as blending from white granite on one end, to red serpentine on the other.

While logging operations may slow you down slightly, bear in mind that this paid for the road. A decade ago, visiting Boulder Lake required a steep, 7 mile hike from Coffee Creek. The stacks of slash and hardwood logs are called YUM piles. The initials stand for "yarded unmerchantable material." Dragging such debris to the landing reduces fire and insect danger and gives planted seedlings a leg up against undesirable competition.

The last ¾ mile to the trailhead, though driveable, is steep, narrow and rough. The trailhead area, by contrast, brings to mind a supermarket parking lot.

Although the trail climbs steadily to a ridgetop for ¾ of a mile, the distance is short and the grade gentle and well shaded. The woods are composed of western white and lodgepole pine, plus Shasta and white fir. Sadler oak dominates the understory.

I noted a single mountain hemlock, ¼ mile above Little Boulder Lake. Common in the Siskiyous and Marbles, the species begins to fade out south of the Russian Mountains. It occurs sporatically in the Trinity Alps, abounding around Callahan Summit but absent in many areas to the south.

After ¾ mile, the path crosses a gentle ridge and begins to circle into the Boulder Lake cirque. This down side is a little steeper and shorter than the up side. It's also far more scenic, revealing a series of massive granite domes at the cirque's head. A steeply terraced canyon cuts between the domes.

The path above Boulder Lake heads up into the canyon, past a couple smaller, well hidden lakes.

The shore of the 8 acre main lake is densely wooded. Pond lilies decorate much of the lake's shallow water. The trail emerges near the lake's outlet, on a beautiful wooded flat. There it joins the trail from Coffee Creek, which heads up the cirque, through the aforementioned canyon and over the ridge, to Lilypad Lake and points south.

On the way back to your car, a one mile (or less), side trail breaks off at the ridge top towards Little Boulder Lake. It's a steep drop into the tiny bowl, over open, rocky outcroppings.

The 4 acre pond at the bottom is a hidden gem, with a wooded, rocky shore choked with azaleas. A polished, snow white granite slope, several hundred feet high, rises out of the water on one side. Like it's sister, Little Boulder Lake's shallow water supports a community of pond lilies. Both lakes offer outstanding fishing and picnicking.

84. GRANITE LAKE
(Trinity Alps Wilderness Area)

Length: 4¾ miles
Water: Much
Access: Good gravel road
Season: June — October
Difficulty: Moderate
Elevation: 4000 to 6000 feet
Use: Non-motorized only
Ownership: Shasta Trinity NF
Phone: (916) 623-2121

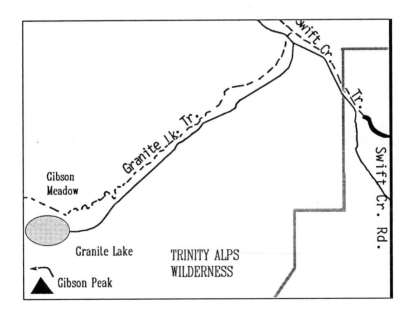

Directions: *Take Hwy 3 from Weaverville or south Yreka to the Swift Creek turnoff at Trinity Center. Follow the good quality gravel road 6 miles to the roomy trailhead. The trail begins at the lower parking lot beyond the horse trailer area.*

Granite, that gleaming white, smoothly rounded rock from the earth's core, abounds in the Trinity Alps and contributes greatly to the region's beauty. Thus, the word "granite" turns up frequently in local place names.

While Granite Lake may not boast the most original name, it ranks among the wilderness area's prettiest bodies of water. The trail offers much variety and many points of interest.

From the trailhead, the path scoots sharply down to Swift Creek, which it follows for ¾ of a mile. The wide, rushing, boulder strewn stream lives up to its name and I was sorry to have to turn away from it.

Swift Creek flows through a serpentine area of white and Jeffrey pine. Side creeks along the trail are home to azalea fringed bogs where fly eating darlingtonia's rear their cobra-like heads. At one point, the creek cuts an immense, steep sided gorge. From the trail along the top, one hears crashing water and can almost make out a huge waterfall.

The Granite Lake Trail leaves Swift Creek over an elaborate metal bridge. I'm told that of several such bridges the Forest Service constructed a few years ago, this is the only one still standing. Once over the bridge, the path makes a right turn up Granite Creek.

The next 2 miles are a little frustrating as the trail punches rather steeply through a dense Shasta fir forest.

Glance ahead for evidence of the Granite Lake cirque or 8400 foot Gibson Peak, it seems continually frustrating. The only highlights here are a sizeable waterfall on the main creek and a couple maidenhair fern grottoes.

Eventually, the scene opens out to a series of lovely, if narrow, meadow areas alternating with small forest clumps. To the right rises a naked, grassy ridge culminating in cinnamon colored, weathered serpentine.

The ridge must be quite unstable since it has littered the canyon with huge boulders. Hundreds of smashed trees lie jack-strawed on the ground. Long, level terraces in this section alternate with steep rock faces. The beautiful creek, fringed with alder, willow, grass and wildflowers, cascades through the open country in a progression of low falls. At last, the sawtoothed spires above Granite Lake emerge in the distance.

A mile from the lake, the trail inscribes a series of switchbacks up a narrow spot in the canyon. At the top, the lush, pond dotted expanse of Gibson Meadow unfolds. It's a little less than a mile across the meadow and up a couple more terraces to the lake cirque.

Granite Lake rests in a sprawling basin ringed in granite minarets. Gibson Peak's white frosting dominates the scene. The 18 acre lake, while beautiful, was a little disappointing, however. The side of the lake away from the cliff is extremely brushy. Only one small spot on the shore is easily reached and that has a very steep bank. Campsites are all well away from the water.

From the lake, the trail can be seen climbing 1600 feet in 1½ miles to an inviting looking pass leading to the heart of the wilderness. From there, exceptionally long, difficult paths lead to Summit Lake, Sapphire Lake and any place else you might desire to go.

85. GRANITE PEAK TRAIL
(Trinity Alps Wilderness)

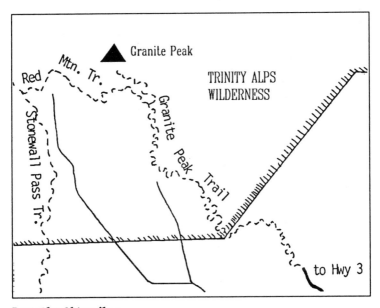

Length: 4½ miles.
Water: A little
Access: Good dirt road
Difficulty: Very difficult

Elevation: 4100 to 8091
Season: June — October
Use: Non-motorized only
Ownership: Shasta-Trinity NF
Phone: (916) 623-2121

Directions: Take California Hwy 3 from the third Yreka exit off I-5, through Scott Valley and over the Scott Mountains, following signs to Trinity Center, Trinity Lake and Weaverville. Past Trinity Center and the Estrelita Marina, look for a turnoff on the right to the Granite Peak Trail. Follow this dirt road 3 miles to a huge parking area on an old logging landing.

On the Forest Service map of the Trinity Alps Wilderness, this trailhead is mislabeled Stonewall Pass. Do not accidentally take the real Stonewall Pass road.

The Granite Peak Trail, in California's Trinity Alps Wilderness, is simply too beautiful for words and impossible to describe without feeling tongue-tied. As a reporter, however, it's my duty to try. If the news that the mountain is "real pretty—with a terrific view," somehow falls flat (pun intended), blame it on the inadequacy of our language.

I could evade the issue by bowling readers over with statistics and superlatives. To seekers of physical challenge, for example, this path, soaring 4000 feet in 4 miles, ranks as a genuine killer. It left me sore and limping for three days.

Still, Granite Peak is not the highest mountain or the steepest trail I've ever been on (Highest: Mt. Whitney in the southern Sierra at 14,495 feet. Steepest: The Buck Creek Trail in the King Range south of Eureka, rising 3200 feet in two miles.)

Nor does it compare, for example, to Mt. Shasta, where scrambling up loose scree and rocks at high elevations is required.

On the other hand, this pathway may hold the record for most switchbacks in the shortest distance. On the map, it resembles a seismograph readout after an earthquake. I lost count after the 50 switchbacks and several pitches with grades in excess of 80%.

Fortunately, the area's magnificence pretty much keeps your mind off your aching calves. Every time you decide the scenery couldn't possibly get better, you come around a bend and discover a whole new world, spread out like Shangri-La.

Despite this beauty, Granite peak, rising above Trinity Lake in the Shasta-Trinity Whiskeytown National Recreation Area, is only an outer sentinel. The inner Trinity Alps, not visible from any road and accessible only over rugged trails 10 to 20 miles long, contain some of America's most breathtaking scenery.

Trails from Hwy 3 to the outer Alps' summits and high lakes (including the Granite Peak Trail), though much shorter, afford only a tantalizing preview of the inner range's spectacle. In fact, Granite Peak's greatest reward is it's glimpse into the inner Alps, 10 miles to the northwest.

The trail's first mile inauspiciously follows an old road up a series of foothills. A middle elevation forest of Douglas-fir, incense cedar, sugar pine and black oak shades the area. One by one, these species fade away as the elevation relentlessly soars.

After a mile, the route mutates into actual trail. For the next 1½ miles, it works its way around to the peak's south face, up a slope pocked with giant boulders and airy stands of pine and cedar. Trinity Lake soon comes into view far below and remains to the summit.

At 2½ miles, the path suddenly hits an immense avalanche gully, with a picturesque stream running down the middle. Far above, the emerald meadows and blocky granite facets of the summit beckon like the Gardens of Babylon. (It's not really the summit but it's comforting to pretend).

The trail spends ½ mile zig-zaging up this fascinating, brush choked, nearly vertical ravine, bouncing off the Shasta fir/white pine forests on either side. The ravine contains every high elevation brush species imaginable—squawcarpet, bittercherry, manzanita, oceanspray, snowbrush, evergreen chinkapin, azalea, etc. Masses of wildflowers, changing colors from season to season as different species pass in and out of bloom, choke the thinner-soiled sites.

Beyond the ravine, 3½ miles from the trailhead, the path reaches a false summit. This enchanted spot, with its precarious rock formations and open meadows, offers the first glimpse of the true summit's jagged skyline, 1500 feet overhead.

Continuing relentlessly upward from the false summit, this time out in the open, the path traverses a nearly perpendicular white granite slope, interspersed with wildflowers, brush and an occasional stunted red fir.

Finally, rounding a ridgetop, a view of the inner Alps unfolds that will turn even the most cynical observer to maple syrup. Immediately north and west, the bleak, orange expanse of Red Mountain is revealed. The green splotch of Red Mountain Meadow, below Stonewall Pass' rocky lip, stands out like an oasis on the lifeless serpentine upwelling.

Beyond Red Mountain, the round bottomed, glacially carved valley of the Trinity River's Stuart Fork recalls the final scene of The Sound of Music.

North of Red Mountain, at the Stuart Fork's source, rise the brooding inner Alps—notably Thompson Peak and Sawtooth Mountain. Although only a little higher than the outer Alps, their glistening slopes and radiating mazes of jagged spires—liked a huge, jeweled crown—place them among the most majestic peaks anywhere.

Dozens of the world's most beautiful lakes decorate the inner Alps' alpine basins. Aside from being larger and deeper than similar basins in the outer Alps, active glaciers continue to sculpt their upper slopes—the only glaciers in California (or Oregon) west of the Sierra/Cascade system.

It's ¾ of a mile from the false summit to the junction with the trail to Stonewall Pass, Stony Ridge and the inner Alps. The summit lies another panting ¼ mile to the right.

After reaching the lookout base on the summit ridge's southern end, scan the horizon for Shasta and Lassen, the Sacramento Valley, the Sierra Nevada and Weaverville.

Closer at hand, a couple of stunted foxtail pines nestle among the crest's spires and crags, along with oceanspray, fireweed and tasteful clusters of mountain hemlock and Shasta red fir. Foxtail pine is native mainly to subalpine areas of the southern Sierra. After a 600 mile gap in its range, it turns up again in a few widely scattered sites in the Trinity Alps and Marble Mountains.

Hikers often spend the night atop Granite Peak before venturing home or into the Alps. I'm told that on exceptionally clear nights, moving headlights along I-5 in the Sacramento Valley can be seen far the the distance. All in all, it's not a bad payoff.

86. NORTH YOLLA BOLLY TRAIL
(Yolla Bolly Middle Eel Wilderness Area)

Length: 2 to 4 miles
Water: OK
Access: Excellent, mostly paved roads
Season: June —October
Difficulty: Moderate
Elevation: 5500 to 7863
Use: Non-motorized only
Ownership: Shasta Trinity NF
Phone: (916) 352-4211

Directions: Take Hwy 36 from Red Bluff (off I-5), or from Fortuna, south of Eureka (off 101). West of Wildwood and the Hayfork Creek bridge, turn south onto road 30, the Wildwood-Mad River Road. Do not take the Stuart Gap Road (11), from the Harrison Gulch Ranger Station. Follow road 30 for 10 miles to Pine Root Saddle. Turn left at the saddle to road 35 and continue 11 miles to

Stuart Gap. All intersections are well signed. The pavement ends at Stuart Gap. Turn right at the gap, onto the gravel road, and proceed 2 miles to the trailhead.

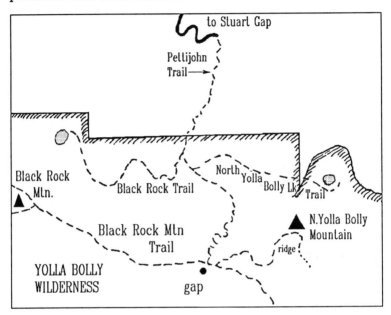

This compact cluster of trails explores a small range in the Yolla Bolly Middle Eel Wilderness, one of California's more underrated areas. Covering far fewer acres than the nearby Trinity Alps Wilderness, with not nearly as many lakes or high peaks, people think of the Yolla Bolly as miniscule and insignificant. At 148,000 acres, however, it deserves far more than to be considered the Rhode Island of California Wildernesses. The Wyoming or Nebraska would be more accurate.

The North and South Yolla Bolly Mountains are very different from the Trinity Alps or Marbles, with a beauty and importance all their own. They are also very different from each other, as we shall see. The Wilderness' north side offers the easiest road access and shortest trails.

The drive to the trailhead is scenic enough by itself to justify leaving home. Between Platina and the turnoff to road 30, beyond Wildwood, the previously curvy highway straightens somewhat as it leaves the grassy foothills and enters the forest. Middle elevations woods here consist mostly of pines and are much less dense than those to the north and west.

The 20 mile forest road from the 36-30 turnoff to the trailhead is virtually all blacktopped. After following a lovely canyon of red serpentine rock, the road climbs to Pine Root Saddle and cuts east through still more pine forest.

Near Stuart Gap, the rock faces of the North Yolla Bollys come into view. The pavement ends at Stuart Gap, two miles from the trailhead. The forest here (5500 feet), consist mostly of white and grand fir, plus Shasta red fir, western white pine and incense cedar.

The Stuart Gap trailhead lies in a huge field of bull thistle. There's plenty of parking, with campsites ¼ mile back.

It's a highly scenic, 2 mile walk from the trailhead to the high ridge, passing at least 5 side trails. The main path climbs through woods for a mile. Moderately steep at first, it soon levels off. Look for views of Black Rock Mountain immediately west. The 7755 foot peak, capped by a lookout tower, has a black north face which tumbles vertically into the Black Rock Lake glacial cirque.

Past a meadow, and side trails to Black Rock and North Yolla Bolly Lakes, the steep, well shaded route ascends to the ridgetop. North Yolla Bolly Mountain eventually comes into view. The gray outcropping is as severe as Black Rock Mountain and the summit is 100 feet higher. Black Rock stands off by itself, however, while North Yolla Bolly is more integrated with the line of peaks. That's probably why they put the lookout on Black Rock.

The North Yolla Bollys are composed of a crumbly gray/green rock called greenstone. A very old, metamorphosed lava, greenstone is a major component of the Siskiyous, Marbles and western Trinity Alps.

The North Yolla Bollys are, in fact, the southernmost range of the Klamath Mountain system, which includes the Siskiyous, Marbles and Trinity Alps. The unrelated South Yolla Bollys are much younger, belonging to the California Coast Range (Franciscan) province. Like the rest of the Franciscan formation, they're constructed of a wacky gray sandstone called graywacke.

The trail from Stuart Gap crests at 7000 feet, in a magnificent grassy prairie dotted with rock outcroppings and windswept whitebark pines. From here, one can follow the 1½ mile trail to the Black Rock Mountain lookout, on the right, or continue towards the Middle Eel and South Yolla Bollys.

From the ridge crossing, a trail left ascends North Yolla Bolly, second highest peak in the Wilderness (after the South Yolla Bollys' Mt. Linn, 200 feet higher at 8092 feet). After descending ⅓ of a mile through the woods, across a very steep slope, the North Yolla Bolly Trail enters a charming little cirque. There's no lake but it's a marvelous camping spot, with water and a meadow.

The path climbs very steeply out of the cirque, becoming increasingly difficult to follow. Just before rejoining the ridge, I lost it altogether. On the map, it continues for a considerable distance.

After marking the spot where I lost the trail, I scrambled perhaps 200 feet to the ridge crest. From there, I headed left (east), along the ridge towards its highest point. This last ¼ mile involved picking my way over loose scree and jagged rock but I finally reached the summit. The views of Shasta, Lassen, the Sacramento Valley and the South Yolla Bollys, were exquisite.

The 1½ mile Black Rock Lake Trail merits exploration. It holds a fairly even contour at first, swinging past a lovely creek which turns out to be the the South Fork of the Trinity. It then climbs like mad before dropping into a rocky cirque. Black Rock Lake is the Wilderness's largest at about 10 acres (probably less).

The North Yolla Bolly Lake trail is steeper but only a mile long. The lake isn't much—3 or 4 acres perhaps—but the setting is lovely. The trail crests after ¾ of a mile, then circles into a tiny but very deeply gouged glacial cirque. The last ¼ mile down to the lake is extremely steep. I especially liked the contrast between the lake and its surrounding rock walls, framing the Sacramento Valley in the distance.

87. IDES COVE TRAIL
(Yolla Bolly Middle Eel Wilderness Area)

Length: 4½ miles (10 mile loop)
Water: Lots
Access: Very long, dirt road
Season: June—October
Difficulty: Easy
Elevation: 6800 to 7500 feet
Use: Non-motorized only
Ownership: Mendocino NF
Phone: (916) 824-5196

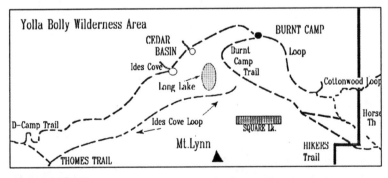

Directions: *Leave I-5 at Corning and take road A-9 west to Paskenta. At Paskenta, go straight (onto road M-2), where A-9 swings left across a bridge. Follow M-2 to the Cold Springs Guard*

Station. The pavement ends 19 miles after Paskenta. The last 6 miles to Cold Springs are a little rough, with gravel and broken blacktop.

At Cold Springs, turn right on road M-22 at the signed junction. Follow M-22's dirt surface 8 miles, to a signed turnoff left. Continue 1 mile to another signed turnoff, to the right, indicating the backpacker's trailhead. M-22 contains a few torn up spots at logging landings. The last 1 mile spur to the trailhead contains a very steep, very tight switchback but then levels off. The trailhead area is quite roomy.

This National Recreation Trail explores the South Yolla Bolly Mountains, highest in the Yolla Bolly Middle Eel Wilderness. Unlike the North Yolla Bollys, however, no trail ascends the highest peak, 8092 foot Mt. Linn. The path skirts its upper flank while the best view of the summit is back on the road.

Still, it's a beautiful, mostly level trail which the Forest Service has laid out as a 10 mile loop. If that's too long, highlights at mile 1½, 3 and 4½ make natural turnaround spots while the Burnt Camp cutoff slices the loop in half.

This is one of three trails herein reached by driving west from the Sacramento Valley. Others are the North Yolla Bolly/Stuart Gap Trail out of Red Bluff and the Snow Mountain/Summit Springs Trail out of Willows. Of the three, roads to this trailhead best explore the California Coast Ranges' eastern foothills.

Take particular note, passing Paskenta, of a long, grassy, hogback ridge topped with brown outcroppings. Called, appropriately, Rocky Ridge, it is the southernmost tail of the vast Klamath Mountains system, which includes the Siskiyous, Marbles, Trinity Alps and North Yolla Bollys.

Above Paskenta, the road climbs from grasslands, with cottonwood along the creeks, through a zone of scraggly digger pines and oak pockets, into open stands of ponderosa pine and Douglas-fir. Vistas of the Sacramento Valley are long and spectacular.

Roads in this highly convoluted region can be painfully slow, however, so allow plenty of driving time. Five or six miles past Cold Springs, look for a magnificent view of Mt. Linn. ¾ of a mile before the trailhead, a steep curve took my little Toyota two runs to surmount. You'll find the trailhead atop a large, grassy, park-like knob, dotted with pines.

The trail climbs ever so slightly for its first 3 miles, with occasional steep (but short) ups and downs. After ½ mile, the far end of the loop trail comes in on the right. It's about a mile along the main, high trail from this junction to Square Lake.

The route here, despite being relatively level, cuts across very steep slopes of loose scree. Forests are less dense than in the North Yolla Bollys, with middle elevation trees persisting to higher elevations. Ponderosa and Jeffrey pine predominate, even at 7000 feet, joined by an occasional Shasta red fir and western white pine.

The North Yolla Bollys are easily observed from the trail. It's hard to believe they're 15 miles away since they seem much closer. Black Rock Mountain, with it's lookout tower, particularly stands out. Mt. Shasta also looms in the distance, along with Mt. Thompson, highest peak in the Trinity Alps.

The South Yolla Bollys are geologically unrelated to the North Yolla Bollys. The latter are made of greenstone schist, like much of the Trinity Alps, Marbles and Siskiyous. The South Yolla Bollys are constructed of a fine grained, beige sandstone called graywacke. A thickly bedded beach sediment, graywacke comprises the major bedrock of the northern California Coast Ranges, called the Franciscan Formation.

Square Lake isn't much, in terms of size. It's shallow and covers only an acre or two. But it occupies a fairly large glacial cirque immediately below Mt. Linn's main summit. Barren cliffs and rocky slopes charge upward from the lake to well above treeline. Stunted whitebark and foxtail pines decorate the high ridges overhead.

Square Lake is surrounded by a vast meadow which tumbles from the heights. Between lake, meadow, Mt. Linn and vistas of North Yolla Bolly, it's a great destination and picnic spot.

Should you continue on, Long Lake lies a mile down the path, amid similar terrain. Its cirque is smaller, however, and the trail passes well above the lake. Look for a stand of foxtail pine in the vicinity.

Between Square and Long Lake, the Burnt Camp Trail comes in on the right and offers a shortcut down to the return side of the Ides Cove Loop. Follow it for a 5 mile instead of a 10 mile outing.

Three miles from the trailhead, the route reaches its high point of 7500 feet, barely 700 feet higher than the trailhead. There, it crosses the main ridge coming down from Mt. Linn, with vistas to the south for the first time. The trail drops 500 feet in the next ½ mile and continues along the ridge for another 1½ miles beyond that.

Four miles from the trailhead, the Thomes Trail takes off south along Thomes Pocket Ridge. A half mile further, the return loop of the Ides Cove Trail makes a hard switchback to the right while the D Camp Trail continues ahead.

The D Camp and Ides Cove Trails meet on the southwest flank of 7300 foot Harvey Peak. To climb Harvey, continue up the D Camp Trail to its highest point, then scramble uphill to the right. The Ides Cove Trail's return segment is a little longer, lower and more wooded than its outward portion, with fewer highlights and vistas. It passes a couple pleasant springs and meadows, especially at Cedar Basin and Burnt Camp.

Beyond the junction with the South Fork Cottonwood Trail, the path begins a steep, one mile to climb past the horse trail, which breaks off to the left. It rejoins the upper trail ½ mile from the trailhead.

88. SOLOMON PEAK
(Yolla Bolly Wilderness Area)

Length: 3¾ miles (or 8 mi. loop)
Water: OK
Access: Long dirt road
Season: June—October
Difficulty: Moderate
Elevation: 6050 to 7581
Use: Non-motorized only
Ownership: Mendocino NF
Phone: (707) 983-6118

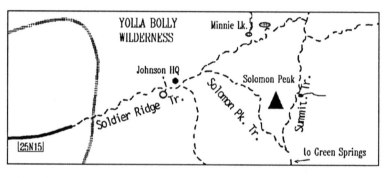

Directions: From Hwy 101 at Longvale, take Rt. 162 to Covelo. Turn right at the Ranger Station and continue on 162 to Indian Dick Road (M-1), just past the Eel River Bridge. Proceed 28 miles to the Indian Dick Guard Station. Turn right, just past the station, towards Soldier Ridge. It's 3 miles to the Soldier Ridge trailhead. Indian Dick Road is an excellent, gravel route. Soldier Ridge Road is wide and easily driveable but cut by numerous water bars to prevent erosion.

Of all the trails into the Yolla Bolly-Middle Eel Wilderness, this, to me, is the most scenic. In fact, Solomon Peak ranks among the loveliest mountains I've ever seen—and I've seen many. It's very different from the Trinity Alps, Cascades or Sierra Nevada, with a special Yolla Bolly charm all its own.

What's more, the hike into the area is remarkably easy, although it gets much more arduous if you elect to complete the loop around the mountain.

You have to really be a hard core scenery buff to seek out this place, however. It may be the most remote trailhead in this book—more so even than that of the King Crest or Caribou Lake Trail. From Hwy 101, north of Willits, it's 30 winding miles up the Eel River to the tiny village of Covelo, on the Round Valley Indian Reservation. From there, it's 10 miles to the Eel River bridge and 31 more, unpaved miles, to the trailhead, 6000 feet above sea level.

Solomon Peak is the highest summit draining into the Middle Eel River. It can be reached from both the Soldier Ridge and Green Springs trailheads. It can also be reached from any other trailhead in the Wilderness, since they all connect.

While the Green Springs trailhead is a slightly shorter drive, the walk to Solomon Peak from there is ¾ of a mile longer. To reach the Green Springs trailhead, leave Indian Dick Road at the Hammerhorn Campground turnoff. Follow that road (M-21) to road M-2 and turn left. There are plenty of signs. Hike the Summit Trail 4 miles from Green Springs to the Solomon Peak Trail junction.

Presuming you opt for the Soldier Ridge route, which I recommend, begin by following the trail 2¼ miles from the trailhead, climbing 700 feet at a steady, easy-to-moderate grade, with a long, level stetch in the middle.

The route winds along the top of a gorgeous ridge, decorated with outcropings, grassy balds and occassional meadows. Artistically placed, open forest stands occupy the sheltered pockets while gnarled, windswept patriarchs (or matriarchs), dot the crest. Look for white fir and sugar pine near the trailhead; red fir, Western white pine and Jeffrey pine at the higher elevations.

You'll find a spring and corn lily meadow at Johnson Headquarters, 2 miles up. There used to be a cabin at the site, named for an old time rancher. It's gone now.

The Soldier Ridge Trail ends at a fork, ¼ mile past Johnson HQ. There, the Minnie Lake Trail takes off left while the Solomon Peak Trail commences on the right. The Solomon Peak half of the sign was broken off when I visited. The latter path, most of which can be seen from the junction, reaches the high ridge just south of Solomon Peak in 1¾ miles. It contains some hefty grades over forested patches and bare rock, rising 800 feet in a mile at one point.

To climb Solomon Peak and/or make the loop around it, follow either the Solomon Peak or Minnie Lake Trail. Whichever you choose, first take the Solomon Peak Trail for ¼ mile (or less), to the high point on Soldier Ridge, just before it drops down to a small saddle, from which it charges up Solomon Peak's southwest flank.

The view of Solomon Peak from this vista point on Soldier Ridge is commanding. The peak is revealed as a massive block of beige sandstone, uplifted by faulting and carved by erosion and long departed glaciers. The sandstone, called graywacke, is the basic rock of the California Coast Range geological province. Solomon Peak is the second highest mountain (after Mt. Linn, highest in the Yolla Bollys), made of this rock type.

Speaking of glaciers, note as you climb to the vista point, that Soldier Ridge's north side is cut with steep cliffs while the south side is much more gradual. That's because the north side was gouged out during the last ice age by several small, hanging glaciers.

The area's largest glacial basin, above Minnie Lake, boasts dramatic cliffs, which can be seen from the vista point. The lake itself, however, is barely more than a large puddle.

The Minnie Lake Trail is similar to the Solomon Peak Trail, traversing open meadows, scattered forest clumps and exposed, rocky uplands. In two miles, it drops 600 feet to Minnie Creek, then ascends 650 feet to the high ridge.

Both the Minnie Lake and Solomon Peak Trails eventually meet the Summit Trail. If you came up via Minnie Lake, turn right on reaching the Summit Trail. If you came by the Solomon Peak Trail, turn left.

The Summit Trail, the Yolla Bolly's main north-south thoroughfare, follows the crest of the Middle Eel divide. This is a spectacular route over open, alpine country with long vistas in all directions. It skirts Solomon Peak to the east, missing the summit by a couple hundred feet. Early in the season, expect patches of snow on this and other area trails.

The best place to scale Solomon Peak is from the Solomon Peak Trail, at the saddle just before the path drops down to the Summit Trail. I haven't tried it, but the trail crest, at 7250 feet, is only 300 feet lower than the actual summit. The ridge above the trail crest appears fairly easily negotiated.

From the top, for reference, the peak immediately south is Hammerhorn Mountain, only about 30 feet lower than Solomon Peak. The line of gray outcroppings paralleling Soldier Ridge on the south is Hammerhorn Ridge, averaging about 6500 feet. Rattlesnake Creek separates Soldier and Hammerhorn Ridges.

The Middle Eel canyon lies two drainages north. Look also for the North and South Yolla Bollys, Lassen, Shasta, the Sacramento Valley, the King Range, Leech Lake Mountain—and so on into infinity.

89. FOSTER GLADES/ASA BEAN TRAIL
(Yolla Bolly Wilderness Area)

Length: 3 miles
Water: A little
Access: Excellent, long, gravel road
Season: May—Novovember
Difficulty: Moderate. Last ½ mile is very steep
Elevation: 3900 to 3250 feet
Use: Non-motorized only
Ownership: Mendocino NF
Phone: (707) 983-6118

*Directions: Follow Hwy 162, off US 101, from Longvale to Covelo.
Turn right at the Covelo Ranger Station and continue on 162 to the
Eel River Bridge. Just over the bridge, at the store, turn left onto
Indian Dick Road (M-1). Continue 27 miles to the trailhead, just
past Rattlesnake Creek, where the road rounds the point. Look for
a grassy area and a wooden drift fence. The only sign is a small
hiker emblem.*

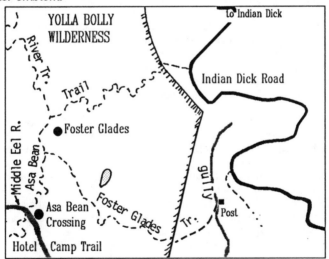

*An alternate trailhead, for the Asa Bean Trail, which intersects the
Foster Glades Trail, is located 1½ miles up the road. The sign is
presently down but there's a low post where it used to be. Parking
is plentiful at both trailheads. Note that on some maps, the Asa
Bean Trail is considered part of the Hotel Camp Trail.*

In all my explorations, over hundreds of trails, I've been irrevocably lost twice. This was one of them. Fortunately, while the trail vanished without a trace, my directional sense held up and I emerged at the trailhead. I hiked cross country from the Eel River to Indian Dick Road, climbing 800 feet in about a mile.

The Foster Glades Trail is also memorable for one of the loveliest, if most confusing, trailheads I've ever seen. Twenty-seven miles up Indian Dick Road, with it's stunning vistas of the Middle Eel and Leech Lake Mountain, the road dips into Rattlesnake Creek Canyon, then climbs a beautiful grassy knob. Indian Dick ranks among California's most remote and scenic drives.

A mile past Rattlesnake Creek, Road M-1 rounds a beautifully landscaped point. A large, bouldery mound, festooned by a charming white oak grove, juts from the rolling, grassy expanse. The trailhead is marked by a log drift fence with a hiker emblem in the middle.

From the trailhead, at a gap in the fence, a pathway goes behind the mound, then swings left. This is the route on which I became lost, following cow paths through open meadows, oak glades and brush choked gullies, down to the river. Or at least to the top of the gray bluffs above the river. The last 100 feet was a vertical drop.

The true trail is marked by a pole in front of a large white oak, straight downhill and across the grass from the path leaving the trailhead. Look for it just after the trailhead path cuts behind the mound.

From the pole, cross the gully, then bear slightly left around some bushes, before crossing a little grassy opening. A well defined trail begins at the edge of the trees on the far side of the opening.

After all my expended energy finding the trailhead, I'm sorry to report that the Forest Service suggests that hikers use the Asa Bean trailhead to reach Foster Glades and Asa Bean Crossing. The Foster Glades Trail is badly in need of maintenance (originally scheduled for 1990) and difficult to follow. It has been obliterated by slides and soil slumping in spots and is faint through grassy areas.

Which is unfortunate because this lovely path offers the easiest route to the Middle Eel inside the Wilderness Area. The Asa Bean trailhead is situated 600 feet higher in elevation, 1½ miles up Indian Dick Road. Its first mile is extremely steep as it tumbles towards the more level Foster Glades Trail.

If you have two vehicles, consider hiking in on Asa Bean and out via the Foster Glades Trail. It's impossible to get lost. Just remember that Road M-1 lies uphill and the river downhill. Remember, too, however you go, that the canyon can be excruciatingly hot in summer.

Once on the Foster Glades Trail, if you're brave enough to give it a shot (it can be done), the route contours to the right, through grassy openings, oak/pine forests and brushfields of manzanita, ceanothus and redbud.

Heron Lake is a one acre pond, 1000 feet above the trail, a mile down. A big landslide near Heron Lake has obliterated a section of the path.

Two miles down, Foster Glades presents a charming little opening, with a small pond in yet another grove of oak trees. The trail to Asa Bean Crossing takes off downhill at the Glades while the Foster Glades Trail continues ahead. A right turn onto the Asa Bean Hotel Camp Trail takes you to Asa Bean Crossing in ½ mile.

The ½ mile from Foster Glades to Asa Bean Crossing is quite steep but comprises the trail's highlight. Asa Bean is a wide, flat, easy crossing. Above Asa Bean, across the river, the Hotel Camp Trail climbs 3000 feet in 6 miles, connecting with the Leech Lake Mountain Trail. This west side pathway out of the canyon begins 200 yards downriver from Asa Bean Crossing.

After the effort negotiating the steep, dusty, brushy bluffs above the river, it's unfortunate that the beautiful Middle Eel is closed to fishing. Fish habitat was destroyed in the 1964 flood, which ripped out most streamside vegetation and swept away many pools and spawning gravels. The area is slowly recovering

90. ROCK CABIN TRAIL
(Yolla Bolly Wilderness)

Length: 4 miles
Water: Lots
Access: Long, good gravel and dirt roads
Season: May—November
Difficulty: Moderately difficult
Elevation: 4950 to 3750
Use: Non-motorized only
Ownership: Mendocino NF
Phone: (707) 983-6118

Directions: From Hwy 101, take Hwy 162 at Longvale, to Covelo. Turn right at the Covelo Ranger Station and proceed on 162 to the Eel River Bridge. Just over the bridge, at the store, turn right onto Indian Dick Road (M-1). Continue for 30 miles. The roomy trailhead is located past the Indian Dick Guard Station, down a short, well marked spur to the left, just before Lucky Lake.

This is probably the best trail into the Middle Eel portion of the Yolla Bolly-Middle Eel Wilderness Area. Longer than the Foster Glades Trail, its beginning elevation is 1000 feet higher and it follows a more forested route. The river crossing is 500 feet higher than Asa Bean Crossing, where the Foster Glades route bottoms out.

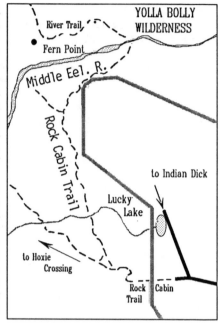

The path connects with a number of extremely long routes exploring the west (and east) half of the wilderness. Its beginning segment, from Rock Cabin Camp to the river, and up to Fern Point, makes a highly scenic, 4 mile day hike. The drive up Indian Dick Road to the trailhead, in itself, ranks among California's more surprisingly beautiful excursions.

From the trailhead area at Rock Cabin Camp, the path drops fairly steeply at first, then levels off for a mile before beginning its plunge to the river. Much of the route pushes through old growth Douglas-fir/ponderosa pine forests. As is typical of the area, however, there is no shortage of grass and brush openings, and hardwood glades—especially at lower elevations.

This is gorgeous country, highlighted by Fern Point and the Middle Eel crossing. The scenery differs from other northwest California regions in being drier and gentler than the Klamath Mountains and much drier than the coastal ranges. The juxtaposition of dense forest, park-like glades, spectacular canyons and grassy balds with long vistas, is breathtaking.

Fern Point, a mile beyond the crossing, is an outcropping 700 feet above the junction of the Middle Fork and the North Middle Fork. The trail up to it from the crossing, rises 400 feet in the first ½ mile, then levels off (the river drops). Beyond Fern Point, the path becomes considerably gentler.

There used to be a bridge at Fern Point but it is long since gone. Nor is the side trail to Hoxie Crossing, shown on Forest Service maps, recommended since that path is in extremely poor condition. The Rock Cabin Trail is better maintained and more scenic.

A word of caution to anglers, before they hike 4 miles for nothing: the Middle Eel is closed to fishing. After the 1964 flood washed away streamside vegetation, pools and spawning gravels, fish populations dropped frighteningly. They're slowly returning but as yet not enough to rescind the fishing ban.

In my 1991 visit, I spent the night at the lovely little campsite at the Rock Cabin trailhead. Driving there, I encountered only Forest Service vehicles on Indian Dick Road. All trailheads, including this one, were deserted—which wasn't surprising since it was a weekday and the canyon gets extremely hot in summer. Use is highest in autumn, during hunting season.

As I figured it, the nearest human was at least 15 miles away, at Hammerhorn Campground—and I don't know for sure that it wasn't also deserted.

Imagine my surprise when I heard a dog bark, not far from my tent, at 3 in the morning. The Hound of the Baskerville paying me a visit, perhaps? And no, it wasn't a coyote.

91. HELLHOLE CANYON TRAIL

Length: 3½ miles
Water: A little
Access: Excellent gravel road
Season: All
Difficulty: Moderately easy
Elevation: 2800 to 2100 feet
Use: Non-motorized only
Ownership: Mendocino NF
Phone: (707) 983-6118

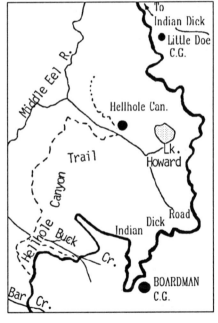

Directions: From US 101, take Hwy 162 from Longvale to Covelo. Just past Covelo, turn right at the Ranger Station and continue on 162 to the Eel River Bridge. Just over the bridge, at the store, turn left onto road M-1, Indian Dick Road. About 4 miles up,¾ mile past Bar Creek (just before mile post 27), you'll see a small trail marker on the left, at a wide spot on the shoulder. Note that the trailhead location is incorrect on the Forest Service map. There's parking for two or three cars.

This easy walk explores the spectacular Middle Eel Canyon just outside the Yolla Bolly Wilderness. The low elevation path makes a wonderful off-season destination but tends to be hot and buggy in summer. Indian Dick Road, off of which the trailhead is located, ranks among California's lesser known and more spectacular scenic routes. It merits a visit just for the drive.

At least one Middle Eel chapter should include a few words about Covelo. I found myself charmed by the 1800 population community. Among California's remotest towns, it's the "seat" of the Round Valley Indian Reservation.

I advise against approaching Covelo from any direction other than west, off Hwy 101. The Mendocino Pass Road, from I-5, Corning and Paskenta, is an experience but long, unpaved and excruciatingly slow. It isn't nearly as bad as the road from Weaverville, however. On that route, an attempted "shortcut" via Ruth Reservoir, took half a day. I drove 120 miles over winding, unpaved roads, rarely reaching 30 mph. Both the scenery and the white knuckle tedium will never be forgotten.

The Hellhole Canyon Trail resembles the Foster Glades Trail, a few miles upriver. Hellhole Canyon itself recalls Rattlesnake Creek Canyon, on M-1 near the Foster Glades trailhead.

Like other paths in the vicinity, the Hellhole Canyon Trail winds through open grasslands, Douglas-fir/ponderosa pine forests and oaken glades. The latter offers outstanding picnic spots. Views of the river are plentiful, as are cattle.

The canyon itself is a steep sided, gray rock gorge. It's larger than Rattlesnake Creek Canyon but with lower stream flow.

It takes the trail almost a mile, after rounding a point and entering the canyon, to finally meet the creek. The bulk of the path's 800 foot elevation drop is concentrated into this section. The trail here may appear a little precarious, with cliffs alongside.

Beyond Hellhole Canyon, the path is faint and unmaintained. It peters out after a couple miles. The Forest Service plans to extend it to Lake Howard, a beautiful, 30 acre pool in a pine grove. Until this new connection is built, the lake may be visited by driving a few miles farther up Indian Dick Road.

92. TRAVELERS HOME TRAIL

Length: 4½ miles
Water: A few side creeks
ccess: Wide, gravel roads
Season: All
Difficulty: Easy to moderate
Elevation: 2450 - 3700 ft.
Use: Non-motorized only

Ownership:Mendocino NF
Phone: (707) 983-6118

Directions: From Hwy 101, take route 162 from Longvale to Covelo. Continue on 162 past Covelo, turning right at the Ranger Station, to a mile before the Eel River Bridge. A sign uphill to the left there says "Bland's Cove and Ham's Pass." Follow this road two miles to the trailhead, which is down a very short side road on the right. Park on the road shoulder at the turnoff or at the wide trailhead area.

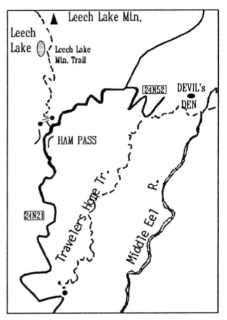

This National Recreational Trail can be divided into two day-hike segments, one 4½ miles long, the other 2½ miles.

The information at the chapter head describes only the first segment. The second segment is a shorter and more scenic but considerably steeper. The second segment trailhead can be difficult to find.

The first segment trailhead lies two miles up road 24N21, in the middle of a tight switchback. The lovely drive to it from 162 snakes through open grasslands with views of the Eel River canyon to the west. The ¼ mile side road to the trailhead is gated and a sign warns that the road is private. The gate is unlocked and I'm told it's permissible to drive to the trailhead as long you close the gate after going through. Since the road is rather poor, I'd recommend walking from 24N21.

The actual trail begins at a logging landing, uphill to the left. The first 3 miles are fairly uniform and level, contouring through a middle elevation forest of Douglas-fir, madrone, canyon live oak, black oak and ponderosa pine. Frequent grassy openings reveal views of the Middle Eel canyon but not the river. Equally frequent shaded draws are lined with stately bigleaf maples.

This is a good off-season hike which can be hot and buggy in summer. Spring is best for quiet walks, wildflowers and water in the creeks. The last 1½ miles descends to Travelers Home Creek and back out. The climb out is particularly steep and long.

Eventually, the path emerges on road 24N52. It's also possible to drive to this spot. Continue from the lower trailhead, up 24N21, past Ham's Pass and Leech Lake Mountain.

Just Past Bland's Cove, 24N52 takes off right. The trail crossing sits about 1½ miles down. This gravel side road is well constructed but full of deep, annoying water bars.

The middle trailhead lies at a small switchback on 24N52, with a landing on the right. The only marking visible from the road is a "National Recreation Trail" emblem tacked to a tree. The trail comes in on the far right and takes off for the Eel straight ahead.

This last 2½ miles drops 1500 feet. Circling the flank of Leech Lake Mountain, it crosses a high point and some extremely unstable sections. Because of land slides, the Forest Service has had problems keeping this upper section passable through Devil's Den.

Forests are a little denser in this section and the trail passes a couple of lovely springs. Devil's Den is interesting, with a huge landslide and a large oak opening. Below (and above) Devils Den, the trail crosses several logging clearcuts offering many views of the ubiquitous Eel River.

The trail is supposed to cross the river and connect to the Hellhole Canyon Trail but I wouldn't attempt this. The Middle Eel is closed to fishing at present.

93. LEECH LAKE MOUNTAIN

See map, chapter 92
Length: 3 miles
Water: A little
Access: Good gravel road
Season: May—November
Difficulty: Moderate to difficult
Elevation: 4750 to 6637
Use: Any
Ownership: Mendoncino NF
Phone: (707) 983-6118
See Map on Chapter 92

Directions: *Take Route 162 off Hwy 101, from Longvale to Covelo. Turn right at the Covelo Ranger Station and proceed almost to the Eel River Bridge. A mile before the bridge, turn up road 24N21 ("Bland's Cove/Ham Pass"). It's 9 miles to Ham Pass. Shortly after Ham Pass, a sign says "Leech Lake Trail-2 Miles."This is incorrect, as is the trailhead location on Forest Service maps. The path, which is actually a closed road, begins at the sign. Parking is plentiful.*

At 6637 feet, Leech Lake Mountain—and neighboring Red Rock Mountain—dominates the Middle Eel area in Mendocino National Forest, outside the Yolla Bolly Wilderness. It is particularly impressive from Road M-1, the Indian Dick Road, across the canyon.

Indian Dick Road, one of California's more surprisingly scenic drives, reveals Leech Lake Mountain as a sheer sandstone uplift. Massive purple and beige landslides decorate its steep east flanks above the river.

The approach to Ham Pass, just before the trailhead, offers the best view of the peak. The trailhead lies just beyond the pass, at a gated side road on the left. The Forest Service doesn't consider this a developed trail, just an old closed road. It's very steep, exposed, dusty and hot in summer but with a couple lengthy level sections.

Vistas of beautiful Round Valley, locale of the Round Valley Indian Reservation, are magnificent as the wide, eminently driveable path climbs the west side of the ridge, away from the Middle Eel canyon. The route switches steeply upward for a mile, then levels off for a mile, before charging upward again for a final mile.

En route, it passes rock outcroppings, brush fields and scattered forest stands. Near the trailhead, the forest consists of Douglas-fir, white fir, black oak and ponderosa pine. At the heights, you'll find Jeffrey pine, red fir and Western white pine. Some lovely springs dribble across the path. The ones near the lake form extensive glades of sedges and corn lily.

Leech Lake is a typical, if small, high mountain glacial cirque lake. The two acre, spring fed pond occupies a small terrace below a barren sandstone headwall—the typical rock of the California Coast Ranges. The actual summit is a jagged, ship-shaped outcropping poking from the ridgetop.

The trail's high point is about 300 feet lower than the mountain's. To reach the mountaintop, continue past the lake to the trail's crest—a saddle overlooking the Middle Eel Canyon. From there, scramble up the ridge to the right.

Not only can the canyon be seen from the top, most of the Yolla Bolly Wilderness can also, along with the rest of the main Mendocino crest. To the west, beyond Round Valley, the landscape recedes in series of lineal ridges and valleys. On the far western horizon, the King Range juts up from the Cape Mendocino peninsula. The King Range blocks the view of the ocean.

94. SUMMIT SPRINGS TRAIL
(Snow Mountain Wilderness Area)

Length: 4 miles
Water: No
Access: Very long, gravel and dirt road
Season: June thr. Oct.
Difficulty: Moderately difficult
Elevation: 5200 to 7056
Use: Non-motorized only
Ownership: Mendocino NF
Phone: (916) 963-3128

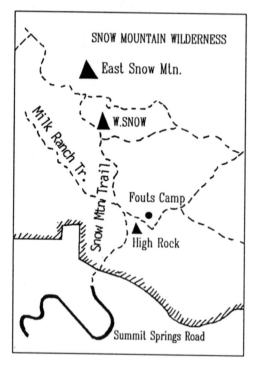

Directions: *Leave I-5 at Maxwell and follow the signs to Stonyford and East Park Reservoir. At Stonyford, turn west up road M-10. Follow the signs to the Summit Springs trailhead. M-10, though somewhat winding and steep, is wide and well maintained. It's paved at first, then gravel, then dirt. A well*

marked turnoff, 2 miles from the trailhead, leads up a narrow and steep, but driveable dirt road. The roomy trailhead lies 25 miles from Stonyford.

I did not expect, in researching this book, to discover a 7000 foot mountain and Wilderness Area in the brushy hills west of Maxwell. Maxwell, of course, along with the "W" towns (Willows, Williams, Woodland and Winters), strides I-5 amid the Sacramento Valley's flat expanse.

I'm amazed that this impressive peak is not better known or more written about. Especially since it's the second highest peak (after the heavily roaded Black Butte, 30 miles north) in the entire Mendoncino Range outside the Yolla Bolly Wilderness. The vast Mendocino Range extends from San Francisco Bay to Eureka and from the Sacramento Valley to the coast.

This may be the closest Forest Service Wilderness to San Francisco. Shooting up from sea level to 7000 feet in 25 miles, Snow Mountain offers scenery, hiking and a spectrum of other recreational opportunities.

A few miles beyond Stonyford, road M-10 enters Fouts Springs Valley, a low elevation basin surrounded by steep, brushy slopes riddled with dirt bike trails. Snow Mountain's sheer east face rises grimly to the west, 5000 feet overhead. At least four Forest Service Campgrounds compliment the Fouts Springs area.

Beyond Fouts Springs, the road begins its relentless climb to the high ridge. Like most climbs up from the valley, the vegetation transitions from grass and brush, to digger pines and oaks, to ponderosa pine, Douglas-fir, madrone and grand firs. Sugar pine, Jeffrey pine and Shasta red fir mark the highest elevations.

The ever ascending road eventually crosses the main crest of the range, then swings sharply north for a few miles. Look for a sign marking the turnoff to Summit Springs.

The last couple miles follows a narrow ridgetop, with views in both directions. The road here is a little precarious but not as bad as it looks. It soon ends at a roomy, open trailhead area with plenty of parking.

Virtually the entire south side of Snow Mountain burned in the fall of 1987. The aftermath can be seen all along the road and trail. This is a highly fire prone area, however, with plant species requiring an occasional burn to reproduce. The trail's first mile, for example, crosses fields of burned manzanita, black oak and scrub white oak. All thrive on intense sunshine and cannot live in shade. They indicate recent fires prior to 1987.

When I visited in 1988, the oaks and many shrubs showed vigorous basal resprouting. Manzanita is less able to resprout but fire stimulates seed germination. Higher up, the blaze killed many Jeffrey and sugar pines. Near the summit, sadly, some lovely red fir stands were scorched. But again, this is dry country with vast acreage of grass and bare rock. Its sparse forests are largely confined to sheltered, upper elevation clusters.

The trail is steep at first, as it traverses a narrow ridge of burnt manzanita. Snow Mountain's main summit, composed of gentle domes of grass and scattered forest patches, can be seen up a canyon in the distance, rising above a series of immense purple and gray rock slopes.

At the end of the first little ridge, the path climbs steeply towards High Rock, then levels off for a mile as it runs along the main front of the east facing crest. High Rock, a huge, barren dome, is easy to reach and worth a 15 minute side trip.

A few steps up to the ridge anywhere along this segment reveals outstanding views of the Sacramento Valley. Sutter Buttes, the world's smallest mountain range, rises out of the valley immediately opposite. The gray line of the Sierra Nevada marks the eastern horizon, with Shasta and Lassen dominating the northeast skyline.

At the peak's eastern base, the elongated, arrow straight valley containing Stony Gorge, East Park and Indian Valley Reservoirs, can be seen. The valley is shaped by the huge Stony Creek Fault, forming the boundary between the Coast Range and Central Valley geological provinces. The low foothills just east of the fault are unrelated to the Coast Ranges.

Most of Snow Mountain is composed of graywacke sandstone, typical of the California Coast Ranges. Look also for outcroppings of chert, a crumbly, brownish red quartz which makes excellent arrowheads. You'll also find areas of serpentine, marked by the presence of Jeffrey pine and scrub white oak.

Beyond High Rock, the trail enters the woods and cuts to the west, into Cedar Basin, passing several side trails. Cedar Basin is a lovely little sheltered bowl and an excellent campsite. There's nary a cedar to be found there, however.

Past Cedar Basin, the trail winds steeply upward for another 3 miles, through woods, sheltered draws and grassy prairies. The trail then crosses the top of West Snow Mountain, 18 feet lower than East Snow Mountain. It's almost a mile from West Snow to East Snow.

The main summit (East Snow) lies slightly off the trail but is easily attained. At the path's highest point, near a switchback and side trail intersection, you'll find yourself in a small saddle amid several rounded hills. Hike uphill, to the right (east), up easy, open slopes, for the top of mountain. The steep side trail is under construction from Fouts Springs.

The summit view is similar to that from High Rock, except with vistas to the north and west. Much of the trail looks west, on row after row of steep, rather low mountains covered with grass and pines. Goat Mountain (6100 feet) dominates to the south. The northward view reveals the full extent of the immense north/south ridge comprising the backbone of the Mendocino Range, culminating with the South Yolla Bollys.

A request from the publisher.

It is our intention to periodically up-date all hiking guides we publish.

If you have first hand knowledge of trails that you would like to suggest to be included in the next issue of this book, please give us a call, or write to let us know about it.

Art Bernstein will gladly check all trails, and consider it to be included on his next revision.

Notes:

Location:

Lenght:

Access:

Season:

Difficulty:

Elevation:

Use:

Ownership:

Phone:

Direction of how to find th e trail head:

Notes:

Notes:

Notes

Notes:

Notes: